MALAYSIAN SON: A PROGRESSIVE STORY — A JOURNEY IN THE HEART OF SOUTHEAST ASIA

Nik Nazmi Nik Ahmad is the Member of Parliament for Setiawangsa, Kuala Lumpur and Vice President of Malaysia's most successful multi-racial party, the People's Justice Party (KEADILAN).

He was elected as a state legislator in the neighbouring Selangor at 26, the youngest candidate to win in the 2008 elections.

Born in 1982, Nik Nazmi grew up in the suburb of Petaling Jaya. He attended the prestigious Malay College Kuala Kangsar before receiving a scholarship to read law in King's College London, where he became active in student organisations during the Reformasi and anti-Iraq War movements.

He returned in 2005 to serve his scholarship sponsors but resigned less than a year later to work for Opposition Leader Anwar Ibrahim.

As a state legislator, Nik Nazmi was appointed to various positions in the Selangor Government and KEADILAN. He was re-elected to the State Assembly in 2013 and was appointed to Selangor's EXCO (i.e., the state cabinet), overseeing the education, human capital and science portfolios.

In 2014, he was elected as the Leader of KEADILAN's Youth Wing and later became the opposition coalition PH's Youth Leader.

In the 2018 election, Nik Nazmi contested in Setiawangsa, a stronghold of the dominant UMNO party. That election not only saw Nazmi's victory but UMNO's first-ever defeat at the federal level.

Nik Nazmi has authored multiple books. He also founded the Mentari Project, an urban educational access program as well as a community football club, Setiawangsa Rangers FC. He lives in Petaling Jaya with his wife, Farah and their children.

ADVANCE PRAISE FOR *MALAYSIAN SON*

'A famous painter once lamented that he spent a lifetime trying to learn to paint like a child. Citizens the world over, too, can only hope that our legislators would stay just as true, if not quite as innocent, in the hurly burly cynical world of realpolitik.

Elected at 26, Nazmi's journey to date has been anchored on an admirable ethos of *'khidmat ku berikan'*—both a line from the MCKK anthem and a deep value inherited from his parents. This book is but a prologue, and at this critical juncture in our nation's history, all fair-minded Malaysians will cheer Nazmi and others on all and every side, to remain true to serve the cause of social justice, for all.'

—Azman Mokhtar, Chairman of Tabung Haji,
former GM of Khazanah Nasional Berhad

'A thoroughly engaging personal account of the latest political scenario in Malaysia. Nik Nazmi's reflections and experiences give us a glimpse into his life as an inspiring activist and public figure. *Malaysian Son* is also a challenge to anyone who dares to dream for long-lasting democracy and social justice in multi-racial Malaysia.'

—Jannie Lasimbang, Kepayan State
Assemblywoman and Sabah indigenous activist

'I have known Nik Nazmi since 2009, and this book provides an important record of events and thoughts of one of the most prominent next generation of leaders that Malaysia needs and deserves.'

—Wong Chen, Subang MP

'A young Malay idealist strives to reform his country and learns much along the way. Nik Nazmi reminds us nothing worthwhile

comes easily and in politics the battle never ends. A must-read account for anyone seeking to understand Malaysia's present perils.'
—Claire Rewcastle Brown, journalist and founder of
Sarawak Report and *Radio Free Sarawak*

'Nik Nazmi's experience as a Malaysian politician is a fascinating insight into a possible future of Malaysia. A Malaysia which at its core, is democratic not just in name, but endowed with strong institutions in a multi-racial setting. This is a highly readable book which I would strongly recommend to anyone with a deep interest in Malaysian politics and society.'
—Pritam Singh, Singapore Opposition Leader and
Workers Party Singapore Opposition Leader

'The last time I spoke to Nik, was probably in 2005, when I worked for *Malaysiakini* and interviewed him for my now defunct column, *I Am Muslim.*

Now I remember when my piece was published, there were a few tut-tuts at my quoting Nik in my op-ed. 'He doesn't speak for the rakyat. He comes from a wealthy family, and he went to MCKK. He's an elite.'

Today, Nik is an MP and has experienced politics as a student activist, young politician and as a Malaysian wanting a better Malaysia. I used to think he and his friends were idealistic, but they're still in politics, still wanting reforms and change. Other people would have just quit—Malaysian politics can be heavy on the mind and soul—but he and his peers soldier on.

Nik's book reflects who he is: tenacious.'
—Dina Zaman, writer and co-founder, IMAN Research

'". . . the what ifs that we can only ask so often because it is all in the past" is a line you will find midway through this memoir. The author's experiences as captured here are at once different and similar to mine. Reading them I wondered if our paths would have merged more meaningfully had he or I made different choices to the similar questions we were asked.

No matter, as this memoir is a guide to rediscovering the same dilemmas that continue to plague our political discourse—in hope that we can better resolve them in the future.'

—Shahril Hamdan, UMNO Information Chief
and Deputy Youth Leader

'Nik Nazmi's memoir perfectly represents the generation that came of age in the 1990s and early 2000s, sparked by political consciousness and the desire for reform. It reminds us that young people can and will carry the torch for change. Writing about PH's governing experiences, Nik is critical and reflective. A crucial read for anyone in the often confusing and complex business of policy and politics in Malaysia—to inspire, allow us to learn from history, and do better.'

—Tricia Yeoh, CEO Institute for Democracy
and Economic Affairs

'Nik Nazmi is no stranger to choices and consequences. At 10, he chose to support the Kelantan state football team after a heart-breaking Malaysia Cup final. And 14 years later, his crossroads was between a promising corporate career and an uncertain plunge into the deep end of politics.

Malaysian Son is not Nik Nazmi's first book, but it is his first memoir. In its pages, he takes us on a colourful journey from his childhood growing up through concurrent political developments then. His storytelling lays bare his passion for public service and the path that led to his decision to be a career politician—a story that included being paid to watch football in London to mortgaging his mother's property and eventually becoming the youngest candidate to contest the 2008 Malaysia elections.

I highly recommend aficionados of Malaysian politics to read this memoir for a reminiscent journey of how a regular Malaysian childhood was in the 1990s and what contemporary politics was like back then. Nik Nazmi also shares a personal perspective on key political events in the last decade, including the historic 2018 general election results, and key lessons forward for a better Malaysia.'

—Tony Fernandes, Group CEO of AirAsia

'Nik Nazmi is the kind of politician Malaysia needs right now: decent, principled and smart. His message of how the country must regain the centre ground cannot be ignored.'

—Karim Raslan, regional commentator and columnist. Founder and CEO of the KRA Group

'Reading *Malaysian Son* by Nik Nazmi is like walking through a time tunnel of political events from the 80's until today. The twists and turns are explained from his lens, a young aspiring politician with his own ideals who decided to be in the ring at a very early stage of his life.

This book is also a useful reference to young Malaysians who are considering to have a go into politics. You have to be prepared to deal with realpolitik as what Nik Nazmi had gone through and endure. The expectations on the ground and how the political game is really played will test your conviction and commitment to your ideals and principles.

As a relatively young nation, we need more enlightened and principled young Malaysians to be involved to shaping our future, including driving change through their involvements in politics. While this book provides an honest and realistic picture of the hurdles young politicians would have to endure in making Malaysia a better place for everyone, the progress of Nik Nazmi to where he is today should motivate people to stand up and be counted.'

—Nik Mohd Hasyudeen Yusoff, former CEO of Tabung Haji

'This book is an assertation of patriotism based on an understanding of how this country must move forward from the eyes of a legislator . . . Nik Nazmi simply wishes to state that, having come to the crossroads of his life, he remains a son of Malaysia whose love for his country is undiminished and which remains his main inspiration for being in politics.'

—Mujahid Yusof Rawa, former Religious Affairs Minister and Parit Buntar MP

'*Malaysian Son* is a story of change and hope. As we get intimate with the life of Nik Nazmi, including his upbringing and personal battles; we also dive deep into the story of Parti Keadilan Rakyat, including the struggles, the glory and the behind-the-scenes drama. Detailed and compelling writing.'

—Tharma Pillai, co-founder of Undi18, the movement that successfully campaigned for lowering Malaysia's voting age

'I enjoyed reading this book, and I am sure others will too. Nik Nazmi has much to tell not only about his personal life and the travails of being a political activist, but his narration of the events that had taken place in the country in the last 20 years is most enlightening.'

—Zaid Ibrahim, former Law Minister and Kota Bharu MP

'*Malaysian Son* brought back so many memories as I read through Nik Nazmi's account of our early days in politics. Long before the Keluarga Malaysia slogan was conceptualised, Nik Nazmi was already living out the true spirit and ideals of this concept through his writings. *Malaysian Son* encapsulates what it means to be truly Malaysian.'

—Hannah Yeoh, MP for Segambut and former Speaker of Selangor State Assembly

MALAYSIAN SON:
A Progressive's Political Journey in the Heart of Southeast Asia

Nik Nazmi Nik Ahmad

PENGUIN BOOKS

An imprint of Penguin Random House

PENGUIN BOOKS

USA | Canada | UK | Ireland | Australia
New Zealand | India | South Africa | China | Southeast Asia

Penguin Books is part of the Penguin Random House group of companies
whose addresses can be found at global.penguinrandomhouse.com

Published by Penguin Random House SEA Pvt. Ltd
9, Changi South Street 3, Level 08-01,
Singapore 486361

First published in Penguin Books by Penguin Random House SEA 2022
Copyright © Nik Nazmi Nik Ahmad 2022

ISBN 9789815017724

Typeset in Adobe Caslon Pro by MAP Systems, Bengaluru, India
Printed at Markono Print Media Pte Ltd, Singapore

www.penguin.sg

Contents

List of Abbreviations

ABIM   Angkatan Belia Islam Malaysia (Malaysia Islamic Youth Movement)
AH   After Hijrah (the beginning of the Muslim Calendar)
AMANAH   Parti Amanah Negara (National Trust Party)
AMCJA   All-Malayan Council for Joint Action
API   Angkatan Pemuda Insaf (Awakened Youth Organization)
AWAS   Angkatan Wanita Sedar (Conscious Women's Movement)
BA   Barisan Alternatif (Alternative Front Coalition)
Bersih   Gabungan Pilihanraya Bersih dan Adil (Coalition for Clean and Fair Elections)
BMF   Bumiputra Malaysia Finance
BN   Barisan Nasional (National Front Coalition)
BRU   Badan Revolusi Ugama (Islamic Society in MCKK)
BTN   Biro Tatanegara (National Civics Bureau)
CE   Common Era (beginning of the Gregorian Calendar)
CPA   Commonwealth Parliamentary Association
DAP   Democratic Action Party
DLP   Dual Language Program
EC   Election Commission
EMCO   Enhanced Movement Control Order

FMS	Federated Malay States
FOSIS	Federation of Students Islamic Societies
Gerakan	Parti Gerakan Rakyat Malaysia (Malaysian People's Movement Party)
GLIC	Government-linked investment company
GPS	Gabungan Parti Sarawak (Sarawak Parties Alliance)
GRS	Gabungan Rakyat Sabah (Sabah People's Alliance)
GST	Goods and Services Tax
HINDRAF	Hindu Rights Action Force
HKL	Kuala Lumpur Hospital
ICERD	International Convention on the Elimination of All Forms of Racial Discrimination
IDEAS	Institute for Democracy and Economic Affairs
IPF	Indian Progressive Front
IPU	Inter-Parliamentary Union
ISA	Internal Security Act
ISMA	Ikatan Muslimin Malaysia (Malaysian Muslim Solidarity Organization)
JIM	Jamaah Islah Malaysia (Malaysian Reform Group, an Islamic civil society organization)
KEADILAN	Parti Keadilan Rakyat (People's Justice Party)
KLCC	Kuala Lumpur City Centre
KLIA	Kuala Lumpur International Airport
KLSE	Kuala Lumpur Stock Exchange
KYUEM	Kolej Yayasan UEM
LSE	London School of Economics
MACC	Malaysian Anti-Corruption Commission
MARA	Majlis Amanah Rakyat (People's Trust Council)
MCA	Malaysian Chinese Association
MCKK	Malay College Kuala Kangsar
MCO	Movement Control Order
MCOBA	MCKK Old Boys Association
MCS	Malayan Civil Service
MIC	Malaysian Indian Congress

MNP	Malay Nationalist Party
MSC	Multimedia Super Corridor
NEP	New Economic Policy
NOC	National Operations Council
NUS	National Union of Students
OBS	Outward Bound School
PAS	Pan Malaysian Islamic Party
PH	Pakatan Harapan (Coalition of Hope)
PKN	Parti Keadilan Nasional (National Justice Party)
PKNS	Perbadanan Kemajuan Negeri Selangor (Selangor State Economic Development Corporation)
PN	Perikatan Nasional (National Alliance)
PNB	Permodalan Nasional Berhad
PPBM	Parti Pribumi Bersatu Malaysia (Malaysian United Indigenous Party)
PPM	Piala Perdana Menteri (Prime Minister's Trophy)
PPR	Projek Perumahan Rakyat (People's Housing Project)
PPSMI	Teaching and learning of science and mathematics in English
PR	Pakatan Rakyat (People's Pact)
PRM	Parti Rakyat Malaysia (Malaysian People's Party)
PSM	Parti Sosialis Malaysia (Malaysian Socialist Party)
PTPTN	Perbadanan Tabung Pendidikan Tinggi Negara (National Higher Education Fund Corporation)
PUTERA	Pusat Tenaga Rakyat (Centre for People's Force)
RMC	Royal Military College
RTM	Radio Televisyen Malaysia (Malaysian Radio and Television)
SELCAT	Select Committee on Competency, Accountability and Transparency
SIC	Sultan Ismail College
SOAS	School of African and Asian Studies
SPM	Malaysian Certificate of Education

TNB	Tenaga Nasional Berhad (National Electricity Corporation)
UCL	University College London
UEC	Unified Examination Certificate
UKEC	UK and Eire Council for Malaysian Students
UM	University of Malaya
UMNO	United Malays National Organisation
UN	United Nations
UNISEL	University of Selangor
UPSR	Primary School Achievement Test
UTM	Universiti Teknologi Malaysia (Malaysian University of Technology)
WARISAN	Parti Warisan Sabah (Sabah Heritage Party)

Introduction

My name is Nik Nazmi Nik Ahmad. I am an MP for Setiawangsa, a constituency in Kuala Lumpur, Malaysia.

I decided to write this book in April 2021. On 9 May 2018, the coalition that I was a member of, the Pakatan Harapan (PH), won Malaysia's 14th General Elections. That was the first time the ruling Barisan Nasional (BN) coalition, which had governed the country in one form or another since we gained independence six decades before, had been voted out of office.

Malaysians were euphoric and hopeful. Muslim-majority and multi-racial, our country is blessed with natural resources, and most importantly, a talented population. The World Bank had declared the country to be an upper middle-income economy. Indeed, we had a 'Vision 2020'—announced three decades before—that we would emerge as a united people and a high-income industrialized economy by 2020.

Nevertheless, decades of BN rule had infected the country with divisive racial politics and massive corruption. PH largely consisted of multi-racial and progressive parties, at the heart of which was the historic alliance between mentor-protégé turned adversaries, Dr Mahathir Mohamad and Anwar Ibrahim.

Despite all the hope that carried the PH government to victory, there were tensions beneath the surface. I felt that the 2018–2020 PH government did not meet the legitimate aspirations of the Malaysian youth, the engine of our historic victory. I had led the PH Youth into the election and was proud of what we achieved—not just in getting young candidates elected but in getting our issues and policies at the forefront of PH's manifesto. But Mahathir's second administration failed to keep its promises to young Malaysians. It did not put forward bold economic policies to uplift ordinary Malaysians and pursued harmful, divisive austerity instead. PH also neglected institutional reform. It can seem not only boring and abstract, but temptingly counterproductive, now that we are on the other side of the aisle.

The impressive success also disguised how divided the electorate was. It was, after all, largely a three-cornered contest in the Peninsula. There were stark differences between the Malays in the Peninsula West Coast—especially from Selangor to Johor (who were pro-PH)—and the East Coast (who were pro-PAS) and between the East Coast Muslim Bumiputeras and Christian Kadazans in Sabah (both pro-WARISAN). The Christian Dusuns mostly rejected the new party.

The racial and religious discourse did not subside, and, in fact, worsened during the PH administration. UMNO and PAS cooperated openly and succeeded in attacking our fervour for ratifying international treaties and cutting the budget for the rural folk as attempts to marginalize the Malays. Our communications strategy was virtually non-existent. It seemed that we did not learn from the rise of Donald Trump in the US and Brexit in the UK.

Again, the problem of trust kept cropping up. PH had told the public that Dr Mahathir would be PM when we won the election, and after the release and pardon of Anwar, there would be a timeline for him to take over the baton eventually. Mahathir had initially said that this period would be up to two years.[1] Eventually, the PM refused to specify a date. Instead, he encouraged UMNO MPs to

---

[1] Alastair Gale, James Hookway and Bradley Hope, 'Malaysia's Mahathir expects to stay in power for a year of two', *the Wall Street Journal*, 15 May 2018, https://www.wsj.com/articles/malaysias-mahathir-expects-to-stay-in-power-for-a-year-or-two-1526363537, Accessed 14 March 2022.

crossover to his new party—PPBM—and allowed elements in PH, UMNO, and PAS to push for him to stay for a full term, by which time he would be ninety-eight years old![2, 3] These were the factors that led to the PH government collapsing after twenty-two months.

The political crisis also took place during the emergence of the COVID-19 pandemic. Malaysia went into its first lockdown on 18 March 2020, just over two weeks after Muhyiddin took office and we have been grappling with the coronavirus ever since. PH—now consisting of Parti Keadilan Rakyat (KEADILAN), Democratic Action Party (DAP), and Parti Amanah Negara (AMANAH)—took time to recover from the fall. Some opined that we needed to get back with Dr Mahathir's camp. But for many others—including myself—it was time to move on.

Initially, the country handled the pandemic reasonably well and the number of cases were brought under control. Then, an attempt was made by forces linked to Muhyiddin to topple the Parti Warisan Sabah (WARISAN)/PH state government in Sabah, which resulted in the Sabah State Elections. While WARISAN obtained a plurality of the seats, Muhyiddin's PN and BN combined again to form the new state government.

The election also led to a new wave of COVID-19 cases that has continued to wreak havoc in the country at the time of writing.[4] Today, many have lost their jobs, or had to take pay cuts. Businesses closed down.

---

[2] 'Dr M: Ex-UMNO members can bring in more Malay votes for PPBM' *New Straits Times*, 19 December 2019, https://www.nst.com.my/news/politics/2018/12/441953/dr-m-ex-umno-members-can-bring-more-malay-votes-ppbm, Accessed 14 March 2022

[3] 'Six UMNO MPs, all 18 PAS MPs want Dr Mahathir as PM for full term' *Borneo Post*, 25 October 2019, https://www.theborneopost.com/2019/10/25/six-umno-mps-all-18-pas-mps-want-dr-mahathir-as-pmfor-full-term/, Accessed 14 March 2022

[4] Lim, Jue Tao et al, 'Estimating direct and spill-over impacts of political elections on Covid-19 transmission using synthetic control methods', PLoS

As I fretted over the difficulty of seeing my son, who lives in Penang, I saw the massive impact it had on everyone. The middle-class, too, felt the squeeze, while the poor were left living from hand to mouth. Previously, most of our requests for aid were from low-cost and public housing estates. Now, I had calls for help from tenants and retirees living in condominiums. Interruptions in schooling and the botched roll-out of online learning meant the urban poor and rural communities were left further behind, obliterating education as the great equalizer. From an abstract disease, not only did more of everyone's family and friends were infected with Covid, we had someone we knew die due to the disease as well.

On my 39th birthday in January 2021, the government proclaimed a State of Emergency, and parliament was suspended as Muhyiddin's razor-thin majority started to dwindle. I was reduced to trying to hold the government accountable through Facebook and TikTok as well as scrambling to source funds and resources to maintain my parliamentary service centre and providing assistance to my constituents. But the number of cases kept growing: a total lockdown was declared in a public housing estate in my constituency, the second biggest community to be subjected to the measure.

In August 2021, Muhyiddin resigned as PM, replaced by UMNO vice president Ismail Sabri, while the political instability persisted.

As I worked day and night to get aid to that community, my old itch to write came back. I had spent a third of my life as an elected legislator. When I first contested my state seat in Selangor in 2008 for a unique multi-racial party with a single elected legislator nationwide, it was seen as crazy and certain to end in failure. I was the youngest candidate at that time. People

---

computational biology vol. 17,5 e1008959, 27 May 2021, doi:10.1371/journal.pcbi.1008959.

thought that having left university just three years earlier, I was just trying to get politics out of my system. Then, I could move to other things that were more stable and financially fulfilling.

However, things took a different turn. It's 2021 as I write these words and I am still seeking a progressive path forward for Malaysia. I have been blessed with the opportunity to serve, especially when I consider the other great patriots in the past who failed to win seats in their quest to challenge the establishment.

After my first electoral victory in 2008, a friend told me to keep a diary. I did not. I did, however, write articles and books on politics and current affairs. But a memoir feels different, daunting even. Nevertheless, I believe this is an opportunity for me to reflect and take stock of what is, God-willing, a mid-point of my career. If anything, this exercise will help my readers hold me accountable in the future.

In 1999, I made it to the national press when I was part of the team that won both the prestigious national level debate tournaments. In one of the tournaments, there was a program book prepared for the final round where the finalist debaters were profiled, including our ambition. Typically, debaters said they wanted to be politicians or lawyers. The more confident (or pretentious) wrote that they planned to be the PM! I was dabbling in web design and programing at the time, so I wrote: 'programming engineer'.

I eventually *did* read law for my undergraduate degree and, then, went into frontline politics. Twice, I contested BN fortresses that were never penetrated by the opposition and won. In the beginning, I had to mortgage my mother's property, then landed in court for organizing a rally that attracted 120,000 people protesting the 2013 election results and spent time in police lockup. I always felt that I had a responsibility to stand up for the people. I believe God had given me so many privileges: being born inro a middle-class family with a strong religious tradition and provided with educational opportunities others could only dream of.

Public service is my way of paying back.

I am doing something close to my heart. When I was younger, I taught at low-cost flats, just a few kilometres away from my comfortable family home, that I never encountered prior to politics. This morphed into struggling to break through hostile BN-strongholds in land schemes in rural Malaysia to listening to the plight of the indigenous Dayaks in a longhouse in Sarawak. These confirmed what I had long suspected: that Malaysia must be more just and inclusive for all its people. It has been a road less travelled, but as Robert Frost noted, it is one that has made all the difference.

At a time when politics is regarded with contempt, and the Malaysian political scene is riddled with party-hoppers, I hope this book can be an opportunity to share not only my journey but also the story of Malaysia through my own eyes. I sincerely believe that our struggle for democratization, social cohesion, and equitable development resonates with all moderate, progressive movements in Southeast Asia and the Muslim world seeking to overcome divisions in their countries, of learning from the lessons of the past in order to move forward.

One of Anwar Ibrahim's many speeches that captured the imagination of the public was, 'A Malay child is my child. A Chinese child is my child. An Indian child is my child. An Indian child, or an Iban child or a Kadazan child: they are all mine.' He also liked to say in Mandarin, '马来人、华人、印度人，我们都是一家人 (We are all one family).'

Therefore, I decided to name my book *Malaysian Son*. I hope to show that while I am proud of my Malay Muslim heritage, at the end of the day, I am a Malaysian, doing my best to serve my fellow citizens. One could argue that I was born 'into' Malaysia's political, economic, and ethnic 'system'. I share the story of the roots of my family in Kelantan. Migration is common for many Malaysians of my generation as the country goes through socio-economic change. As the son of a civil servant, in many ways I benefitted from it and I believe that some of its policies were good for the country. But I feel that Malaysia can only survive by becoming more inclusive, including in terms of race. I believe history will vindicate me.

Thank you, Keith Leong and Idlan Zakaria, for your valuable inputs. Nora Nazerene Abu Bakar, from Penguin Random House, was open to the idea of this book when I pitched it to her and I would like to express my appreciation for her taking a chance on this. I would like to express my appreciation to my editor Thatchaayanie Renganathan for going through my work in detail and providing edits and suggestions. Any mistakes made are entirely my own. Ultimately, this is a memoir and the views expressed are mine.

To KEADILAN leaders Anwar Ibrahim and Dr Wan Azizah Wan Ismail, your leadership and inspiration have touched many. I have been fortunate to work as a part of your team in building a new, progressive, and multi-racial movement that, in a space of two decades, has become one of the biggest political parties in the country. Your incorrigible optimism and never-say-die attitude gave hope to Malaysia in its most difficult days, even as you made the ultimate sacrifice.

I like to blame my MCKK senior and KEADILAN mentor Rafizi Ramli for dragging me into politics. Your faith in developing talents has paid off not just in the party but beyond. You put everything in building PH going into the 2018 General Election, only to be cast aside because you spoke truth to the power.

I have been blessed with a wonderful team in my Setiawangsa parliamentary constituency service centre: Raja Mazlan, Kah Yong, Ahmad Nadzrin, Farid Iqmal, and Mohammad Hisyam. Some had joined me when we were challenging a seat UMNO had never lost, others came as we expanded the office as part of the federal government and stayed on when we were relegated to the opposition. Your sacrifices have enabled us to serve Setiawangsa.

My parents have not only inculcated in me a deep interest in public service but has also provided unconditional support for my unconventional career choices. Most importantly, they imparted to me the values of integrity and being true to myself.

To Ilhan, Aisyah, Maryam, and Sarah—I am not sure when you will be able to read and appreciate this book, but when you do, I hope you understand that I did what I did for the sake of your generation.

Farah had to put up with endless late nights with a husband, who was already busy with his work as an MP, as I attempted to finish this book. I dedicate this book to you. Your love has enabled me to continue pursuing the two other great passions of my life: writing and politics. One day, I hope to become not only a better writer and leader, but, most importantly, a better man.

Nik Nazmi Nik Ahmad
Kuala Lumpur, 2021

Part One

1. Kota Bharu

Kelantan is located on the east coast of the Malay Peninsula and has a small coastline with the South China Sea. For centuries, its population has been centred around the large Kelantan River delta (that flows from the Titiwangsa Range), which experiences massive floods on an annual basis. The annual flooding, however, keeps it fertile for farming. Separated from much of the Malay Peninsula by steep mountains and thick jungle, the state has a unique identity. Here, the influence of Siam and the extinct kingdoms of Champa and Pattani are clearly felt. Compared to the other states, there were not many Chinese and Indian indentured labourers brought by the British or the migrants from the rest of the Malay Archipelago. The minorities that do stay in the state speak fluent Kelantanese Malay and are adept in the local culture.

Kota Bharu was established in 1844 as the capital of the state of Kelantan. My parents are related and hail from Kubang Pasu in Kota Bharu. Kubang Pasu is situated near the historic centre of the city, the Istana Balai Besar, which remains the official palace of the sultan. It houses the royal family, aristocracy, and the royal servants, including the Nik and Wan clans. There is also an old market that attracts people from across the city.

I was shaped by the strong and unique Kelantanese culture, in spite of my parents moving to the Klang Valley for almost two decades when I was born. We spoke an eclectic mix of the Kelantanese Malay dialect and English at home. The thickness of the dialect—which makes many consider it to be a separate language and largely incomprehensible to other Malays—was also diluted as the family stayed in the Klang Valley. I speak it casually to my parents and siblings, and even to my Kelantanese friends. But my Kelantanese friends call it 'bunyi Siae', which means sounding like a Siamese (or rather Pattani, which speaks a variant of the dialect)—in short, not authentically Kelantan.

The identity is a powerful one, beyond just family ties, one that transcends statehood, more similar to some atavistic tribalism or Ibn Khaldun's 'asabiyyah'. It binds people who were not only born in the state (regardless of race) but also those who speak the dialect. In some ways, how this distinct identity was shaped by the marginalization and can even supersede the national identity is similar to the Scouse identity in England or the Catalonian identity in Spain.

As far back as 1365, Kelantan was mentioned as one the vassal states of the Majapahit Empire in the Nagarakretagama manuscript while in 1413, the Chinese imperial records speak of a 'Raja Kumar of Kelantan'. By the end of that century, the kingdom was conquered by Melaka. However, unlike most of the kingdoms on the peninsula, Kelantan was once ruled by Queens—Cik Siti Wan Kembang and Puteri Saadong. At one point, it fractured into smaller kingdoms till when Long Yunus reunited Kelantan and founded the present-day dynasty in 1764. Until 1909, the Kingdom of Siam ruled over not just Kelantan but Perlis, Kedah, Terengganu, and Northern Perak. After that, all the states, together with Johor, formed the Unfederated Malay States, which fell under British influence.

Father

My father, Nik Ahmad, came from a family of religious scholars. His father, Nik Hassan Nik Mat, was originally from Langgar, though he eventually settled in Pasir Hor. Both are now part of

Kota Bharu. Nik Mat planted rice and betel leaves. His wife, Saadiah, was said to be the daughter of a cloth-seller from inner Mongolia, who travelled first to Singapore, and then Kelantan, selling his wares.

At the age of thirteen, Nik Hassan was sent to study with Wan Musa Abdul Samad in Kubang Pasu. Wan Musa was the third mufti of Kelantan (1909–1916). His father was Abdul Samad Muhammad Salleh al Kelantani—also known as Tuan Tabal—who married Wan Kalthum Wan Abdul Rahman. Wan Abdul Rahman Lebai Muda was a palace scribe for Sultan Muhammad II, known by his Thai title, 'Tok Semian'.

Wan Musa's daughter, Nik Khatijah, was married off to Nik Hassan when she was seventeen and he was twenty. Seventeen was considered a relatively advanced age for girls to get married at that time, but she had suffered earlier from a leprosy-related illness.

Nik Ahmad was their eldest child, born in Safar 1349 AH, which was June/July 1930 CE.

Five years later, Wan Musa sent Nik Hassan to study in Mecca. The former mufti provided a monthly stipend to his son-in-law in the Holy City, but Nik Hassan sold a piece of inherited land to pay for his sea voyage.

In June 1940, Nik Hassan returned to Kelantan. There was an offer to work as a qadi or a judge in the sharia courts which had limited powers in matters of family law and religious observances, but Nik Khatijah was against it as those who held the position had a reputation of being polygamous! He ended up obtaining the job of a religious teacher at the State Religious Council. During the day, he would teach at a private school at Wan Musa's *surau*, while in the evening, he would teach at the police station. The family grew steadily: five boys and one girl.

My father started his education like most Muslims, by learning the Quran. He finished the Quran at the age of ten years. He also enrolled in the Malay School before transitioning to the private Islah School where his father taught. He completed standard seven there (where, normally, students would be around thirteen years old), qualifying him to be a teacher. The idea was for him to continue the tradition of furthering his studies by going to the Middle East in 1948 and becoming a religious scholar.

Unfortunately, his father did not have the means to send Nik Ahmad to Egypt. But his uncle Nik Mohd Mohyideen, who was at the prestigious Al-Azhar University, suggested he switch to English education. This was a contentious idea: English was deemed an infidel language. There was widespread fear of Christian proselytization. But ironically, many progressive religious Muslim families were among the first to take up English education.

After facing some initial resistance, Nik Ahmad managed to get into the second form class in the only English secondary school in Kelantan at that time, SIC. However, he was eighteen and technically too old for that school. That notwithstanding, he filled out a statutory declaration stating that he was fifteen, and so he got in. This was a common practice then as the British wanted to encourage more locals to attend English schools.

Three years later, he was among nine students who were selected to further their studies. There were no sixth form classes in Kelantan. My father was not selected to sit for the MCKK entrance examination and Victoria Institution, Anderson School, and Penang Free School were all full. However, he managed to get a place in Victoria School, Singapore.

In 1954, Nik Ahmad was admitted to UM Singapore for the Bachelor of Arts program, majoring in history. The Kuala Lumpur branch would only open five years later, while the Singapore campus would eventually become the National University of Singapore. Among his roommates were Ramon Navaratnam. Navaratnam would later join the Malayan Civil Service and retire as a senior civil servant, before joining the corporate sector and frequently commenting on current affairs. Every time my father prayed, his roommate felt uncomfortable and would leave the room, but my father insisted Navaratnam stay.

In his memoirs, Navaratnam wrote:

'My roommate was Dato' (sic) Nik Ahmad. He was a good Muslim from conservative Kelantan but we enjoyed each other's company as brothers. It's difficult to have that warm relationship today! Today, it's odd to find Muslim and non-Muslim students sharing rooms.'[5]

Student life was a hub of activism then. There was the Socialist Club, the Malay Language Society, and the Association of Peninsula Malay Students. Many of his friends in the latter organization travelled across Malaya and Indonesia. But Nik Ahmad could not afford that.

When he went back to holiday in Kelantan, he would teach to earn pocket money. My father would identify and assist students with potential. One student could not get into a good school as the headmaster was asking for a bribe. My father wrote to the school and the student was admitted. This became a pattern throughout his career in the civil service: he would use his authority and influence not to benefit himself, but to provide opportunities to others. It helped that he still had his family's income from their rubber estate. Prices were good due to the Korean War.

My father graduated with an Honours degree in 1958, and like many graduates then, joined the MCS as a cadet.

Mother

My mother was born to Nik Mahmood Nik Mohammad and Nik Jah Nik Mat. The latter was the only grandparent I met as she survived until 2012, when she passed away at the age of 96! She lived to meet my son, who was born the year before.

---

[5] Navaratnam, Ramon V *My Life and Times: A Memoir*, Kuala Lumpur: Malaysia Institute of Management, 2010, p.48.

Nik Jah was also second cousin to Nik Ahmad's mother, Nik Khatijah, which makes my parents third cousins.

It was typical at that time to keep things in the family. Those with 'Niks' and 'Wans' in their names were prized. Some—the so-called 'inner Niks', like both of my grandmothers— can trace their lineage to Fakeh Ali al Malbari, a 17th century Bugis scholar who studied in Malabar, India and resided in Pattani. This was also the family of Long Yunus and thus, the current Kelantanese royal family. One version has it that he was also known as Syed Ali Murtadha and Raden Santri, with a line stretching through the Prophet Muhammad through Persia and the kingdom of Champa in Vietnam. His brother was Raden Rahmat, also known as Sunan Ampel, one of the mystical 'Wali Songo' or 'nine saints' who brought Islam to Java. Whether this is true, or an exaggeration, no one really knows.

Nik Mahmood, my maternal grandfather, was orphaned at a young age. He was raised by his sister and brother-in-law. Through sheer determination, he took English classes at night. He joined the Kelantan Civil Service, and rose all the way to become the State Treasurer.

He was strict, and had a love for both reading and smoking. I managed to keep a copy of the Children's Encyclopaedias from the 1920s that he bought. While having a broad, liberal outlook, the articles still had imperialistic undertones and a Christian-centric worldview! He and Nik Jah had twelve children together, but only eight of them survived till adulthood. My mother, Nik Rahimah, was born in December 1940 and was the third child. She went to the Majlis Malay School in Kota Bharu, and then the Kuala Krai Malay and English Schools when Nik Mahmood was posted there.

She then joined the Zainab School. She was the Head Prefect and represented her school in English debate, even going to Terengganu for a competition. My mother wanted to be a lawyer. She completed form five before marriage came into the picture.

Her elder sister had finished primary school as was the norm during that time, while my mother completed secondary school as was the norm during *her* time. Her younger sisters, however, all managed to go to university.

Marriage

My parents married in December 1959. My mother joined her husband in Seremban, returning to Kota Bharu only to deliver her eldest child, Nariman, in 1961. A few months later, my father succeeded in getting a transfer to Kelantan. This was followed by Nazli and Najihah.

In 1963, Nik Mahmood succumbed to cancer. He passed away at the age of 53. His widow Nik Jah was left without a pension as, at that time, the widows were not entitled to them. Instead, she and her sister earned by writing love letters or 'kuih kapits' which would be collected by a Chinese distributor. Her working children helped out as well. The law changed only in 1980 and so, Nik Jah was, finally, able to get a pension.

2. Kuala Lumpur and Petaling Jaya

In 1964, Nik Ahmad was posted to the Treasury in Kuala Lumpur. He brought his family along. Like many Kelantanese who have come to the Klang Valley since, the move would prove to be permanent.

Initially, my family rented a few places in the upcoming satellite town of Petaling Jaya, before moving to a spacious colonial-era government house in Jalan Pegawai, Ampang towards the end of the decade.

At that time, Kuala Lumpur was about a hundred years old. It was the centre of tin mining. Three icons—Yap Ah Loy, the Kapitan Cina of Kuala Lumpur; Raja Abdullah, a member of the Selangor royal family; and Sutan Puasa, a Mandailing entrepreneur from Sumatra—played key roles in the rapid growth of the town. It was the epicentre of the Selangor Civil War from 1867–1874. The conflict involved various figures of the royal family, supported by Chinese clans. Eventually, the British intervened and Selangor became a British protectorate.

In 1880, Kuala Lumpur was made the capital of Selangor. But it was frequently plagued by fires and flooding. Soon, the city was rebuilt with mostly brick and tile buildings, with sanitation and cleanliness improving as well.

While Kuala Lumpur's establishment in the 19th century was due to tin mines, it was the rapid growth of automobiles and demand for rubber tires that drove its expansion in the

20th century. Plantations circled the town while industries were set up. During the Emergency, when the authorities were fighting the Communists, the British interred Chinese residents across Malaya (who were seen as Communist sympathizers) into the 'New Villages'. Many of these new villages were established in Kuala Lumpur, significantly increasing the population.

13 May 1969

As my family got settled in Kuala Lumpur, the 13 May 1969 racial riots erupted. At that time, my aunt, Nik Esah Nik Mahmood, was studying in an overwhelmingly Chinese college. With rumours gripping the city, Nik Ahmad brought Nik Esah home to Ampang.

There had long been festering tensions due to the socio-economic disparities between the Malays and the non-Malays, particularly the Chinese. The British had built Malaya's colonial economy through a divide-and-rule policy: the Malays were mostly farmers and petty-bureaucrats, the Chinese were allowed to own small and medium-sized businesses or work in the mines, and the Indians were mostly consigned to the estates. The elites became comfortable with English. Ordinary folk spoke colloquial Malay across the communities, but retreated to their own languages internally. This was sustained through vernacular schools and newspapers. They worshipped different gods.

When Malaya became independent, and then formed Malaysia with Singapore, North Borneo (Sabah), and Sarawak, these tensions continued to simmer beneath the surface. Not to forget, this was during the Cold War, and the Emergency was in full swing, where the predominantly Chinese communists were fighting a guerrilla war against the government.

Malaysia's constitution was underpinned by a consensus. The Malays were to have a 'Special Position' (later extended to the Bumiputeras of Sabah and Sarawak), while the non-Malays were granted citizenship on generous grounds. But the constitution defines a Malay as 'a person who professes Islam, habitually speaks the Malay language, [and] conforms to Malay custom ...'

In effect, it does not require one to be of Malay *ethnicity*. The second and the third provisions of 'habitually' speaking Malay and conforming to Malay custom is difficult to prove. I know of rabid Malay nationalists whose children and grandchildren can hardly speak a word of Malay, as they are educated either abroad or in international schools. This leaves us with the first definition, which is being a Muslim, as the easiest way to define what a 'Malay' in Malaysia is or isn't. My father would argue with me that this was inserted in the constitution to include Malaysia's Arab and Indian-Muslim communities. This would allow Malays to emerge as the majority community when Malaya became independent. Otherwise, 'the Malays' would not have been the majority.

The formation of the Federation of Malaysia in 1963 with Sabah, Sarawak, and Singapore changed our demographics, as did the departure of Singapore in 1965. The Bumiputeras of Sabah and Sarawak consists of many ethnic groups. Unlike the Malays in Malaya, many of these ethnicities in Borneo are Christian.

Malay was proclaimed the national language (although, in practice, English continued to be used widely in business and for formal purposes), yet primary vernacular schools and newspapers were allowed to operate.

The 'Special Position' of the Bumiputera meant that the government could reserve places in the public service, scholarships, and business licences for the 'natives'. But the newly independent government, led by the Anglophile Tunku Abdul Rahman, our first PM, pursued laissez-faire economic policies that meant the existing tensions in the country's economic structure, not just between locals and their former colonial masters but also between the races, remained unresolved.

Many younger Malay leaders were unhappy with this and pushed for far-reaching measures to uplift the Malays.

The community's insecurity was real. On the other hand, the non-Malay opposition was vocal in resisting what they saw as attempts to erode their rights. There was an equally lucid fear of a suppression of minority cultural and language rights that neighbouring Thailand and Indonesia were indulging in at that time.

When the ruling Alliance Party lost its two-thirds majority in the 1969 elections, certain opposition parties celebrated and a racial riot erupted, largely involving the Malays and the Chinese. Officially, 196 people were killed, but estimates point at a much higher figure. As my father would tell me, the British had given us ten years to survive. We proved them wrong by just two years. Ethnic relations, the national language, and the 'Special Position' of the Malays had been highly-divisive, emotive issues during the campaign.

NEP

After the riots, PM Tunku Abdul Rahman was sidelined, following a declaration of a State of Emergency by the king. Parliament was suspended and while Tunku remained as premier on paper, his deputy Abdul Razak Hussein took charge through the creation of NOC. In 1970, Razak replaced Tunku as PM.

Razak introduced the NEP to address the economic grievances that led to the 1969 racial riots. The NEP had two objectives—eradicating poverty regardless of race, and removing the identification of economic function with race. It was only supposed to last for twenty years. The NEP basically supercharged government intervention into our economy; not surprising, as Razak was involved with the Labour Party and the Fabian Society as a student in the UK. Many progressive thinkers were roped in to act as the government's brains in framing the NEP. They challenged the orthodox, conservative economic approach that had prevailed since independence.

Young Malays like my father welcomed the NEP. He knew all too well the vicious cycle of poverty, which meant that Malays like him were minorities in universities back then, preventing the community from enjoying the fruits of independence and development compared to other races. There were also intangibles: young Malays like him seethed at how their betters seemed happy to be more British than the British! There was a feeling that Malaysia, as a young country, was lacking a sense of identity. Furthermore, the core of the NEP was always about human capital and development: to provide educational opportunities for the Malays.

As a civil servant, my father was part of the generation that implemented the NEP. By 1972, he was the Deputy Director General of the Public Services Department. Its budget was RM11 million (RM61 million today). Realizing that this was insufficient for the objective of improving education—particularly at secondary and tertiary levels, for the Malays and Bumiputera—that the NEP had, he more than doubled it to RM25 million for the following year (RM134 million). That still wasn't enough for him. In 1974, he got the budget whacked up to RM50 million (RM242 million). My father travelled across the world for two-and-a-half months, not on fun-filled junket trips, but to seek university places for Malaysian students, primarily the Malays.

The NEP took place mostly when Malaysia's economy was growing. While the media and the academia often focus on how the NEP impacted Chinese businesses in favour of the Malays, much of the initial gains made by the Bumiputeras actually came at the expense of foreign interests.

However, the NEP eventually morphed into race-based affirmative action, in favour of the Bumiputeras, specifically the Malays. While, in a way, it made sense when the Malays were predominantly poor, eventually, as a Malay middle-class came to being—*thanks* to the NEP—it became difficult to pursue a race-based, instead of a needs-based affirmative action. The policy became conflated with the constitutional consensus, which was far more limited in nature, and became somewhat of a sacred cow. It also created a sense of entitlement among the elites, while the gap between them and the working class or rural Malays continued to widen. Furthermore, the policy was intended to last for two decades, and yet, it has mostly survived till date.

Razak's Deputy PM, Dr Ismail Abdul Rahman, went even further. He regarded the constitutional 'Special Position' for the Bumiputeras as similar to a golfing handicap. 'This handicap will enable them to be good players, as in golf, and in time the handicap will be removed. The Malays must not think of these privileges as permanent: for then, they will not put their efforts to the tasks. In fact, it is an insult for Malays to be getting these privileges.'[6]

The NEP in its mutant form has led to deep resentment among the non-Malays. Both non-Malays and Malays have emigrated to seek opportunities abroad. It has also hindered integration in the sense that it perpetuates private sector discrimination against the Malays in 'retaliation' to their dominance of the civil service. Some non-Malays believe Malays only succeed because of the colour of their skin, through connections and quotas, a belief that persists even now.[7] And so, Malaysia is stuck in a vicious cycle.

Tunku's Alliance Party expanded to become the BN. The BN absorbed most of the major opposition parties, except DAP. Eventually, UMNO became more dominant. Separately, the 'Rukunegara' as a national ideology was introduced to foster unity, similar to Indonesia's 'Pancasila'. The NEP and Malaysia's industrialization meant the Klang Valley experienced massive immigration. In the 1970s, only 15.5 per cent of urban dwellers in peninsular Malaysia were Malays. By 2016, the number was

---

[6] Kuok, Hock Khee, Phillip (1991) Philip Kuok Hock Khee (privately published and circulated autobiography), Landmark Books Pte Ltd, p.217.

[7] Hwok Aun Lee and Muhammad Abdul Khalid, 'Discrimination of high degrees: Race and graduate hiring in Malaysia', *Journal of the Asia Pacific Economy*, vol. 21, no. 1, 2016, pp.53–76.

56 per cent. Squatter settlements sprouted up. The government encouraged this, believing that better jobs and schools in the cities were good for the Malays coming from the kampungs.

When Hari Raya Aidilfitri came, there would be a 'Balik Kampung' exodus, where people would go back to their homes and villages to celebrate with their families. Klang Valley would be quiet when I was younger. Nowadays, it has been less so as more and more Malaysians make Klang Valley their home, like my parents.

My father said that, early in his career, he had plans to retire and go back to Kelantan, like many of his peers. The cost of living was cheaper in Kota Bharu, allowing government retirees to stretch their pension further. But with all his children marrying non-Kelantanese (or 'marrying outsiders', as we described it) and settling in the Klang Valley, it made sense for him to remain in Petaling Jaya to see the children, the grandchildren, and now the great grandchildren.

Childhood

I was born on 12 January 1982 in HKL. I was the only boy, and by far, the youngest of the five children. I was the second to be born in Kuala Lumpur, after Nik Nazifah in 1970.

Since 1971, my family resided in Section 14 Petaling Jaya. My parents still live there. My father had bought the plot in 1970. It was a former mining tract that had been subdivided into bungalow lots. Our house was located on the main road and overlooked the Sri Aman Girls Secondary School. It had a nice compound for me to play in. I had a happy and fulfilling childhood there. As the youngest (Nariman, my eldest sister, was twenty-one, and Nazifah was twelve when I was born) and only son, my parents and sisters doted on me. Except for Nazifah, the rest were already furthering their studies when I was born.

My father was a no-nonsense man. But he had his own sense of humour and would test me with riddles. Other times, he would play chequers with me and allow me to win when I complained of losing to him.

As my siblings were much older, I frequently had my cousins come to sleepover at my house or go to their house. It was with them or my sisters that I would watch a movie and do things kids my age would do. While he travelled extensively for work (and sometimes brought us along to sneak a holiday in), my father spent most of his free time at home and was careful with his money. He would read in English, Malay and even managed to brush up the Arabic he learned before transferring to English school. Otherwise, we spent time watching the one television set we had in the house in the warm and humid room upstairs.

I enjoyed the serious conversations we had. We spent time with me asking one question after another and my father sportingly answering it. As I grew up reading the old family Grolier encyclopaedia from the 1960s (that's life before the Internet, kids!) and other books, I started to share what I read with my dad, too. And he acted as if it was all new to him.

I had a doting mother. Except for a brief period early in her marriage, my mother did not work and focused on raising the family. Food was mostly home-cooked meals. Weekends meant fish curry and roasted Indian mackerels dipped in 'budu', the fish sauce popular in Kelantan and Terengganu. A treat meant going to the Lake Club, the haunt of many senior civil servants. At six years of age, I started swimming classes there, and having completed that, moved to taekwondo. In between, I would go to the children's library at the club and read, as well as borrow, books.

My mother entered me in a few fancy-dress competitions. I remember once dressing in just my underwear and some vines, carrying a soft-toy monkey to be Tarzan. Another year, I was an office worker, wearing a suit that my mother bought for me and carrying my father's old briefcase. I am not sure whether I won! I was very attached to her and tried to stop her from going out to her social functions or meeting her friends. If I wanted money for anything—books mostly, and sometimes toys—I would tend to ask her, rather than my father, although she probably claimed it back from him!

I grew up with a lot of books. Everyone in the family read. I picked up a lot of my dad's and sisters' books even as a kid, and before long, read at an advanced stage for my age. My father insisted we master both English and Malay. I enjoyed the comics such as *Gila-Gila*, *Topper* and *Tintin*. But I also read Enid Blyton's books and general knowledge books on science, history and geography. While my father would read the news and the opinion pages of the *New Straits Times*, I would ask for the funnies and the sports pages. I also drew a lot. When my cousins came over, we played in the garden. Yes, we had the television, but we were able to nourish our imagination without the distraction of video games!

So, when 'Balik Kampung' came, we would go back to Kota Bharu and stay in my maternal grandmother, Tok Wan Jah's home. We celebrated most of our Hari Rayas in Kuala Lumpur, but I remember looking forward to the ones we spent in Kota Bharu, as I could spend time with my cousins and eat delicious Kelantanese dishes. Mostly it was cooked by my grandmother, but breakfast would be the various delicacies from the Kubang Pasu market.

Kubang Pasu is pretty much at the centre of Kota Bharu, and being a dense, old city, houses were built close to each other. Nevertheless, my grandmother's place was still a traditional Malay wooden house, raised from the ground to enable it to survive the annual floods. The severity of every year's flood was measured by how many steps the waters rose to. A mild year meant water on the street or just into the compound. A bad year meant going almost all the way up to the top of the staircase.

There was a small 'sampan' kept beneath the house. I believe one of my cousins still has it. My mother would tell me that during her childhood, they would explore the neighbourhood on the 'sampan' during the floods, enjoying tapioca and tea. While adults had to crouch to go under the house, as kids, we could happily run there, playing hide and seek amidst the damp and dark spaces. There was still an outhouse and a 'kolah' or water reservoir that we bathed in, but my grandmother had built proper bathrooms inside the house as well. Somewhere in the compound used to be a bomb shelter that the family used during World War II.

Mahathir 1.0

I was born less than a year after Dr Mahathir Mohamad became the PM of Malaysia. The first Malaysian premier from a commoner's family, and the first to not be educated in Britain, he left an indelible mark—for better or for worse—on Malaysian politics.

After graduating and working as a doctor, he was elected as an UMNO MP in 1964. In the fiercely contested 1969 elections, he lost his seat. Mahathir, then, made a name among young Malays for attacking Tunku by writing a scathing letter. The letter underlined why the Malays rejected UMNO: he accused the poker-playing prince of being too chummy with the Chinese.

Mahathir was eventually sacked from UMNO. In 1970, he published his infamous book, the *Malay Dilemma*. While repeating the need to adhere to the constitutional consensus, it also claims to dissect why the Malays were supposedly so tolerant and whether they should accept government assistance. Filled with sweeping generalizations and non-empirical observations that implied Malays were genetically inferior to other races, the book was nevertheless popular with many who were disillusioned with the lack of progress after independence.

Mahathir's thesis was thoroughly refuted by the intellectual-politician Syed Hussein Alatas in *the Myth of the Lazy Native*, which was first published a few years after the *Malay Dilemma*. Syed Hussein's book was described by renowned Palestinian-American scholar Edward Said in his book *Culture and Imperialism* as 'startlingly original'.

While describing the basic thesis of Mahathir's book as being in the same pattern as the typical elite Malay capitalist outlook that blamed the problems of the Malays on their own individual attitudes, Syed Hussein contended that the *Malay Dilemma* was more extreme in degrading the Malays themselves. The physician attempted the difficult task of a study of national character, without any academic training in the social sciences. Fundamentally, Mahathir's belief in the racial inferiority of his people was not grounded in facts and figures, but vague generalizations.

Pointedly, Syed Hussein wrote that the easy, indolent lifestyle that the colonialists and figures like Mahathir tried to pin on the Malays may, at best, represent the lifestyle of the feudal elite, but not the common farmer in the kampung who works hard to eke a living!

However, Mahathir returned to UMNO, and in 1976, he became Deputy PM. In 1981, he was elected as UMNO President, and then became PM. Following clashes with the UK, Mahathir launched a 'Buy British Last' campaign. In early 1982, he also launched the 'Look East Policy' to learn not just from Japan's economic success, but the discipline and ethics that shaped it—something uniquely Asian in Mahathir's eyes.

Ironically, Mahathir and his long-time rival, Singapore's Lee Kuan Yew, agreed that the region could only succeed by holding on to 'Asian values'. This argued for a distinct form of Asian exceptionalism—a focus on social harmony, deference to political authority, and a sense of collectivism. Another long serving strongman, Suharto of Indonesia, joined them in subscribing to this ideal as the recipe for prosperity and development.

Mahathir confronted the Malay rulers in order to limit their constitutional powers in terms of royal assent, mobilizing public fervour against the royals. In 1987, UMNO faced a fractious party election as Mahathir was challenged by Tengku Razaleigh Hamzah for the presidency. Mahathir triumphed narrowly and sacked his opponents, who initiated a legal challenge.

In February 1988, the High Court ruled that UMNO was an illegal organization.

Mahathir succeeded in registering a new party, 'UMNO Baru', or New UMNO, while attempts by Tengku Razaleigh (who was backed by both the country's first and third PMs) to register 'UMNO Malaysia' was blocked. They decided to start another Malay party, 'Semangat 46', claiming to represent the spirit of UMNO at the time of its inception in 1946. The Lord President of the Supreme Court was then sacked by the king on the advice of a tribunal set up by Mahathir. At the same time, a vicious crackdown was launched in October 1987, called 'Operasi Lalang', ostensibly to control rising racial tensions. Four newspapers had their licences revoked, while countless opposition politicians were detained under the ISA. However, most of the government politicians who took part in the racially charged events were untouched.

The country also experienced massive financial scandals after Mahathir took over. These included botched attempts to control the price of tin; a failed steel production joint venture between the Malaysian government and a Japanese company; as well as the BMF-Carrian scandal.

BMF was a subsidiary of Bank Bumiputra, which was established in the 1960s to promote Bumiputera participation in the economy. It operated in Hong Kong in the 1970s. By 1982, Bank Bumiputra suspected something was wrong with BMF and sent their senior auditor, Jalil Ibrahim, to investigate. It turned out that loans amounting to RM2.5 billion at that time (RM6.3 billion today) had mostly been offered to just three companies, with the bulk of it going to the Carrian Group, a dubious real estate company in Hong Kong. When talks of the return of Hong Kong from Britain to China accelerated, the real estate market collapsed. Jalil was found dead in a banana plantation in New Territory. One of Carrian's solicitors committed suicide as the police began investigations.

Malaysia was an imperfect democracy since its birth; but never had the various institutions been challenged like this. As a child,

I was oblivious to all of this. But later, I read magazines and books bought by my family members. My parents visited Musa as well, after he resigned as the DPM. He was a classmate of my father in UM. An old-school civil servant, my father was unhappy at the deterioration of the independence of the civil service and the judiciary, while the PM became ever stronger.

La Salle Petaling Jaya

In 1989, I continued the family tradition of attending Christian mission schools like my sisters (Nariman, Nazli, and Najihah attended Bukit Bintang Girls School, while Nazifah attended the Assunta Girls School) by enrolling in La Salle Petaling Jaya. These were all schools that were teaching the national curriculum, but were established by churches. When I asked my father, a religious Kelantanese hailing from a family of scholars, about the reason behind this, he said he valued the multi-racial nature and the quality of English at these schools.

Racially, La Salle was truly diverse at that time. We had middle- and upper-class children from the bungalows in Bukit Gasing, but we also had working-class kids from the squatter areas in Kampung Baiduri, Kampung Medan, and Kampung Lindungan (the latter of which was part of the Seri Setia state constituency that I represented). I remember when I took the school bus. One of my friends was from Kampung Baiduri and once, when the connecting bus to school did not come, we took the Srijaya bus on our own. It felt like quite an adventure! The well-off students were usually Chinese and Indians (with some Malays), while the poorer students were generally Malays or Indians, with one or two Chinese in each batch.

Often, we were placed in different classes, based on academic performance. This basically ended up reflecting the class divide among the students, but even so, we would always get more than a handful of those from humbler backgrounds being able to make it to the so-called 'top' classes. One of my classmates was Abdul Jalil Rasheed, who then went on to the La Salle Secondary School and became the CEO of PNB and later the Berjaya Corporation.

In national schools back then, we learned all the subjects in Malay.

One of the first songs I remembered listening to was Richard Marx's 'Right Here Waiting' before moving to local rap band KRU. Their *Awas* album was the first cassette I owned. I managed to persuade my mother to buy it for me, but she had a hard time trying to appreciate the songs when I put it on! I also listened to a few 'rock-kapak' songs on KL Hits that were played on Radio 3 KL, complete with the annoying local DJs, who would interrupt the songs with their comments. We would record the songs to play back again and again. 'Rock kapak' had a big following among the Malay students. The singer Zainal Abidin was popular across the races. In standard six, an up-to-date classmate of ours was among the first to latch onto the alternative and grunge scene and listened to Nirvana. But for a twelve-year old, that kind of music seemed too dark and dangerous.

I was quite playful in school, but always ended up ranking high enough in class. When I bothered with lessons, I would be the teacher's pet, raising my hands again and again to hog all the questions, while annoying my classmates. In standard six, I put in more effort as we had to sit for UPSR. I managed to emerge first in my year and score straight As. My father memorized the SPM and degree results of his family members—my cousins included—and I remember how many of them were nervous every time they came over to our house after a big exam, as they would be subjected to my father's grilling. In hindsight, seeing how big a difference academic achievement made in the fortunes of his generation, where university education was a luxury—especially to the Malays—it made complete sense.

At school, I was also a debater and storyteller—in Malay—but did not top in either. I also enjoyed writing. Other than drawing imaginary worlds in empty exercise books, I would write a lot, too. I got my first essay, about the TV3 documentary *Majalah 3*, published in my school yearbook in 1991, if I am not mistaken.

I would also pull off pranks and play games like 'galah panjang' on the badminton courts. The game is played between two teams with the objective to go past obstructed lines. It is said to have originated from a game played in Kerala, India.

It was in standard four, I think, when I started being sent to tuition class at Puan Sharifah's house in Kampung Tunku. Being in an all-boys school, it was quite a thrill, because I got to meet girls there! Sometimes, I would tell my mother that the class was scheduled for earlier than it actually was, but would use the extra time to walk down about half a kilometre from Puan Sharifah's house to the Indian grocer to buy Panini World Cup stickers.

I played football on the tar-paved hockey field. Being an only son, and in many ways like an only child (recall that my sisters were far older and most were already away in university when I grew up), I craved to belong. Our football field was barely adequate in size and was barren during the dry season, and covered in mud during the rainy season. But sports were not my thing.

Nevertheless, like most Malaysian boys, I started following local football, and like my schoolmates, supported Selangor. But I was heartbroken watching the 1991 Malaysia Cup Final, when Selangor lost to Johor.

I decided to switch my allegiances to my parents' state of Kelantan the following year. Unlike Selangor, which had a glorious footballing history, the east coast state was not as illustrious. But the change came at the right time. In 1993, Kelantan went all the way to the semi-finals of the Malaysia Cup. During a trip to Jalan Tunku Abdul Rahman, I managed to persuade my mother to buy me my first football shirt, a proper Le Coq Sportif Kelantan jersey. Kelantan was led by the prolific striker Hashim Mustapha. In the following year, he scored 29 goals in 30 games, earning the Golden Boot.

World Cup 1994 was also the first World Cup that I followed. Most of my friends supported the obvious favourite with a strong history—Brazil. Being a contrarian, I decided to support Italy. The star was undoubtedly the Divine Ponytail, Roberto Baggio. As it was played in the US, some of the games aired around 7.00 a.m. in Malaysia. Unfortunately, Italy lost to Brazil on penalties in the final, with Baggio missing the decisive kick.

The Roaring 90s

Malaysia had tried to follow the example of the other, so-called 'Asian Tigers'—South Korea, Taiwan, and Singapore—by pursing an export-led industrialization policy since the 1970s. Under Mahathir, the government shifted from focusing merely on massive educational and rural development during the introduction of the NEP to heavy industries and manufacturing.

One of the major projects was the Proton Saga, Malaysia's first national car (using Mitsubishi technology) that was launched in 1985. I remember the launch of Proton Wira (one of the Saga's sequels) in 1993. We felt proud and optimistic about the future of the country at that time. I remember, when I visited my sisters in the UK in 1990 and 1993, I was more eager to get photos with any Protons that I saw rather than any of the other sights!

Mahathir also embarked on a policy of privatization. This was also a global trend as Margaret Thatcher in Britain and Ronald Reagan in the US implemented similar policies.

Privatization was seen as advantageous as it allowed for more investment in the relevant sectors, while making it more efficient. The idea, then, was that the government would be streamlined to focus its resources in other sectors that cannot be privatized. As it turned out, there was little that was not out of the reach for the private sector.

As the Secretary General of the Ministry of Energy, Telecommunications, and Post, my father was at the frontlines of privatizing the big, state-owned utilities. Nik Ahmad was privy to some of the discussions that was going on in Cabinet, and he remarked how his friend from the UM and the then Deputy PM Musa Hitam would always ask a lot of questions about the impact of the government's actions, while Mahathir would listen quietly.[8] My father was involved in a lot of efforts in negotiating with the unions concerned about their jobs and benefits.

By the 1990s, the economy began to grow at unprecedented rates of eight to nine per cent per annum. In 1991, Mahathir launched Vision 2020 for a developed, high-income Malaysia in the year 2020, when a truly united 'Bangsa Malaysia' would be created. This required quadrupling the per capita income and embarking on massive industrialization. In 1996, Anwar Ibrahim's book *Asian Renaissance* was released. It discussed the intangible implications of the East Asian Economic Miracle. Anwar argued that by revitalizing the heritage of Asia and Islam, the region could achieve a prosperity and equity that was relevant for the times. Besides Islam, he drew heavily from Chinese and Indian philosophy.

The rapid economic growth, racial unity and moderate values promoted by Mahathir and Anwar (who had joined UMNO after being an anti-establishment, Islamist youth activist, and risen to become the former's Deputy PM) captured the optimistic mood of Malaysia's Roaring 90s era. Malaysians were urged to adopt an attitude of 'Malaysia Boleh'. We were told we could do anything: from economic development to winning international sporting tournaments.

The market capitalization for KLSE increased from RM132 billion in 1990 to RM807 billion six years later, making it one of the largest in Asia. Once known to most of the world as the country 'between Thailand and Singapore', Malaysia was building a new administrative centre, the world's tallest buildings and a brand-new airport at one of the world's largest sites.

---

[8] Nik Nazmi Nik Ahmad, *In the Public Service: The Life of My Father, Nik Ahmad.* Kuala Lumpur: Pusat Sepakat, 2018, p. 115.

3. Kuala Kangsar

Malay College Kuala Kangsar (MCKK) was established as the first fully residential school in the country in 1905. Located in Kuala Kangsar, the royal town of Perak, it caters to Malay boys. The British wanted to prepare elite Malays to play a bigger role in the colonial administration and MCKK was created for this. The four Rulers of the Federated Malay States (FMS) officially founded MCKK. Most of the early students were from the royal or aristocratic families. It was only after World War II that it was opened to all Malay boys, based on merit. Seven of the kings of Malaysia came from MCKK. Both the founder of UMNO—Onn Jaafar—and the second PM—Abdul Razak Hussein—were old boys. The term itself comes from Britain, where the upper class tends to attend a small number of elite schools, and this becomes a powerful network in the corridors of power.

Anthony Burgess, the English writer and composer, (of *A Clockwork Orange* fame) was a teacher there in the mid-1950s. He arrived in crumpled clothes and without a tie. He spoke Malay, wrote in Jawi, and encouraged students to write about communism (yes, this was a British teacher during the colonial era, when the communist insurgency was in full swing). He did not blend well with the British headmaster and the other teachers. Burgess' reflections on his time in Malaya—including Kuala Kangsar— is preserved in the *Malayan Trilogy* novels. Every Malaysian should read this book, in which he playfully comes up with names such as Kuala Hantu, Jalan Gila, Sungai Kencing, and the state of Lanchap![9]

The Joy of Admission

In one of the 'balik kampung' trips to my grandmother's place in 1994, my mother received a call from my father, informing me that I had received a letter of admission to MCKK! This was a dream come true for me. Then, we had to go shopping for new uniforms and the other items needed for my new school. Unlike most secondary schools, MCKK boys wore white pants. In fact, mine was the first batch not to wear the combination of white short trousers (similar in style to the dress of colonial sepoys and policemen) and knee-length white socks.

Every student in MCKK wore black leather shoes. A funny thing happened. According to our rulebook, the cost of our leather shoes must not exceed RM50! My father, who was quite earnest and straightforward in terms of rules, said we need to get a shoe that fell within the price. We looked high and low, and finally bought a synthetic leather shoe that cost RM49.90. Within a few weeks, the shoes were torn. I realized no one audited my shoes! My father, then, bought a new pair of leather shoes (about RM70, if I am not mistaken) which lasted much longer.

The rule book also mentioned various arcane rules and regulations. There were designated areas where the students were allowed to go in the quaint royal town of Kuala Kangsar. Lembah—the area next to the Perak River where the locals take the boat to cross to Sayong—known today for its Perak Laksa and cendol, was out of bounds, as were the upper floors of shops and cafes.

Anyway, as much as it was a hassle to prepare for boarding school, I was excited and looking forward to it. More importantly, I was from a comfortably well-off middle class family who

---

[9] Translations: hantu–ghost, gila–crazy, kencing–urine, lanchap/lancap–masturbation.

could afford it. I know of relatives and friends—and today my constituents—who were presented with these life-changing opportunities at renowned educational institutions, but couldn't take it up because just the cost of preparing to attend is prohibitive. This includes government boarding schools which are heavily subsidized.

On 4 December 1994, my father drove my mother and me up to Kuala Kangsar. We were able to use the North South Expressway. The construction of the highway began in 1981 and from 1982 onwards, it opened in stages.

Four years later, due to the economic crisis, the project was privatized and given to UEM (formerly known as United Engineers Malaysia), which was helmed by Halim Saad, an MCKK old boy. The Ipoh-Changkat Jering section, which included the Kuala Kangsar exit, was opened in 1987. It was fully completed in 1994. It used to take over five hours by car using the old trunk road or the old diesel train. Now, it would take less than three hours to complete the 240-kilometre journey.

Kuala Kangsar lies between the capital city of Ipoh and the old retirement town of Taiping. The Iskandariah Palace is the official palace of the Perak Sultan. Nearby is the Ubudiah Mosque that adorns many postcards. The centrepiece of the sprawling MCKK grounds is the Big School, designed by Arthur Benison Hubback and completed in 1909. Hubback had designed many other heritage buildings in Malaya. It was built along the lines of Greco-Roman style and sandwiched between the newer East and West Wings. A huge raintree—called the Big Tree—sits in front of the East Wing. The football and rugby field in front of the Big Tree is said to be the site of executions when MCKK was used by the Japanese military during World War II. Behind the Big School is one of the few Eton Fives courts outside of the UK, where former UK Cabinet Minister Michael Portillo played fives with the students for a BBC series in 2019.

MCKK is located smack in the middle of the town, or rather, the town grew around it. The hospital, bus and train stations, the

town centre—all were within walking distance from MCKK.
Prior to my registration day, my parents and I stayed at Double
Lion, a small Chinese hotel on top of a coffee shop in the middle
of the town, for RM30 a night. The Federal Government Rest
House, which was the popular choice, was already fully booked.

The next day, we registered at the prep school in MCKK.
The building was completed in 1913. The L-shaped building
housed the dorms, the prefects' cubicles as well the common room.
A newer building housed the dining hall and the bathrooms.
In the UK, the prep school, or preparatory school, prepares students
for admission to boarding school. In MCKK, form one students
would be housed in the prep school, while form two students
would be housed in the new hostel. Only in form three, we would
stay with the seniors in the Big School.

Being the disciplined person that he was, my father ensured
that we were at the school gates by 7.30 a.m. The letter had stated
registration was from 8.00 a.m. to 10.00 a.m., and no one was
there! Soon, however, my cousin, Tengku Ihsan Sani Tengku
Hamzah came over to help with registration. He was a form five
student and a prefect.

He brought along a fellow prefect, Mohd Nizar Najib. Also
in form five, he was the son of the then defence minister, Najib
Razak. When Najib first entered politics in the late 1970s, he was
the Deputy Minister of Energy, Telecommunications, and Posts,
while my father was the Secretary General. They got along well
with one another, as my father was a big admirer of Najib's father,
PM Abdul Razak Hussein.

Both Ihsan and Nizar helped carry my luggage to my dorm.
We had double-decker beds and I was assigned the top bunk.
We were given double-decker beds in the first two years and I was
lucky to get the top bunk in both years. It was cooler and brighter.

I could see my mother's face fall upon catching sight of the
small and rundown locker assigned to us. She wondered aloud,
'Can this fit all your clothes?'

While my parents unpacked, Ihsan and I went to the school shop to get the various things we had to buy. It turned out that I was part of the Mohd Shah House. Remember the four FMS Rulers who founded MCKK? Well, my house—the yellow house—was named after Muhammad Shah of Negeri Sembilan. Ihsan told me, 'That's Anwar Ibrahim's sports house!'

The prefects proceeded to teach us how to put on the impossibly stretched bedsheets and fold the mosquito nets (which were compulsory then). I could do it decently but it was not great, and I can't say the skill stayed with me.

Later, the new students and their parents had a briefing at Hargreaves Hall. The headmaster kept emphasizing on how we were the crème de la crème—each year 100 best Malay boys from schools across Malaysia, plus about 20 from the MCKK Old Boys Association (MCOBA) quota that met the minimum requirements, would be admitted to the school. I remember my father stating that information repeatedly when he met family and friends, to my embarrassment (but I guess I was proud deep inside).

Some students found the transition hard. One student would hog the public phone to call his family. He would cry and switch to Urdu in his conversations, which attracted much teasing from the other boys. Some wet the bed. Some of these boys would quit the school within the next few weeks and months. My mother would later tell me that she was sure her youngest child—and only son—would be homesick and quit MCKK within months of registering. But she was wrong. By the second day, I bought some MCKK postcards and was happily writing to my family and friends. I could hear some boys sobbing at that time.

The worst was when Hari Raya Aidil Adha came. It fell on 10 May 1995, a Wednesday. I remember some kids from Kelantan, where Aidil Adha is a bigger celebration than Aidil Fitri, who took a five-hour bus-trip on the evening of 9 May (and then travelled further to their homes) just to spend one day with their families. I, on the other hand, was so happy to celebrate it at school that

I told my family I would not go back, although Petaling Jaya was not that far away. After the morning prayers, everyone gathered at the dining hall in Big School to enjoy the Raya meal (consisting of rubbery chicken satay and some other dishes). My mother decided to come visit me anyway with my fourth sister, Nazifah, with some food.

In the first month or so, I was actually part of a Kelantan clique. We all spoke in Kelantanese to one another, and spent most of the time together. This is a typical thing in many Malaysian schools and universities, where the Kelantanese like to stick together. I was the only 'fake' Kelantanese as I was born and bred in the Klang Valley.

But before long, we were summoned by the fierce Kelantanese disciplinary teacher, Cikgu Baharuddin Hassan, who told us we were not in Kelantan and should disband our little clique! He was also called 'Gedebe' (the Kelantanese word for gangster). He was known to be generous with his rattan cane and slaps! We immediately obeyed. However, one thing stuck with me— my nickname. I ended up with the nickname 'Budu'—yes, the Kelantanese fish sauce!

Boarding School Life

At that time, all I could think of was getting to form five. Hierarchy was big in the boarding school. We were taught that beyond all else, our batchmates were everything. They were our *brothers*. Then, we had ragging sessions called fire drills and common rooms. Fire drills were conducted like a real fire drill, when the prefects and/or seniors would ring the fire alarm at some ungodly hour at night. We were, then, expected to gather at the assembly point within a certain period. Otherwise, we would be considered 'rentung' or burned bodies!

Afterwards, we were subjected to long lectures and punishments by the prefects, irrespective of whether we made it to the assembly point in time. At the end, we would huddle up and sing patriotic songs in a mass of sweaty, teenaged bodies. After assembling, the whole batch was then 'tortured' by running across the school field. We were also asked to do 'half-way downs', where we had to squat half-way down and be in that position for as long as the prefects deemed it appropriate.

Getting used to boarding-school food took time. Every day, we were provided with breakfast, morning snack, lunch, tea, dinner, and supper. Lunch was usually fried fish with some gravy, while dinner was either chicken or beef. We looked forward to the chicken as the beef was actually frozen Indian buffalo meat. It was packed frozen for so long that it was hard to see which part of the buffalo it was when it arrived on our trays.

We looked forward to Friday dinners—we had to wear the 'full Malay'—all-white 'baju Melayu' and MCKK 'samping' along with the 'songkok' and black leather shoes. Dinner was either chicken rice or biryani rice, with ice cream for dessert. In true British public school/Oxbridge tradition, the wardens and the prefects dined on the high table while the regular students took turns for the privilege. At that time, we still kept the old tradition of dining at the same time and opening with a prayer, just as grace is recited prior to dinner at the high table in the Oxbridge colleges. This meant we did not have to queue for food like most residential schools. The downside, however, was that the food was quite cold by the time it was ready for everyone to eat.

During Saturday outings, we would buy food from the town. The highlight was KFC. McDonald's was a luxury then, only available in Ipoh or Taiping. Late at night, there was an illicit supply of nasi gorengs from a stall near the train station. Whenever we were hungry, especially during Ramadan when our appetites were not satiated by the fare at the Dining Hall, we resorted to ordering this nasi goreng.

In form two, in order to decorate the class noticeboard, I started writing a series of short stories on a whim. This was a time when Chinese comic series translated into Malay were the craze in the school.

So, I started with 'Catatan Seorang Gila', a story about a teenage sociopath. He started by killing his parents, his maid, and then strangers, as he sought refuge in Kuala Kangsar. He fell in love with a local girl and was confused about whether to like her or kill her. In 'Kanibal Karnivor', a boy started by eating his cat before developing an appetite for human flesh. Every night, I would put up one episode. Slowly, in this pre-blogging era, I developed a following, where even my batchmates from other classes would stop by to read the latest episode. My classmates started pestering me to write an extra episode or so each night, or at least to get some spoilers for the upcoming episodes. I loved writing, but this was getting bothersome. I eventually stopped.

It was in form two that I started to 'graduate' in my music taste. I started listening to the burgeoning alternative rock music. My first local alternative rock band was Carburetor Dung. Another local band that caught our eyes was OAG and then, Butterfingers. Butterfingers held a special place for us as three of the members were old boys from the Class of 1994. As for international bands, many were into Nirvana, Pearl Jam, and Oasis. I also grew to like Weezer.

Kurt Cobain, Nirvana's iconoclast, had just killed himself in 1994. In addition, alternative rock captured the angst of the youth disillusioned by the dominant free-market system that seemed to be accepted by all mainstream politicians at that time. It was a shift from the rock music of the 1980s that had gone mainstream and commercial.

I also graduated to reading Jeffrey Archer and John Grisham at this time. There was still some stash of my sisters' books at my parents' house, and my mother continued to be generous when I asked for books. When I took the bus from Puduraya station to Kuala Kangsar, there were book rental shops there. You pay to get the book and get a smaller amount back when you return it. I kept most of the books. Some of my friends were into Stephen King's novels, but the only one I enjoyed was his non-horror collection of novellas, *Different Seasons,* that were adapted into the movies *Shawshank Redemption, Apt Pupil* and *Stand by Me.*

Sports

We also memorized the prefects' sports. Some of them listed 'Kapal layar', or sailing, as their sport. It turned out to be code for someone who does not play any sports for the school. We were all asked to pick a sport in MCKK. Evenings from 5.30 p.m. to 7.00 p.m. was games hours and everyone had to go to the field. We had to wear proper games attire—t-shirt, track bottoms, socks, and sports shoes. Only in this attire we could step on any grass surface in the school. I guess this helped in maintaining how beautiful our school fields were.

As mentioned from my time in La Salle, athleticism was not, and is not, my strong suit. I tried basketball. MCKK had a strong tradition in the sport under the guidance of Liew Yong Choon, who was a policeman by day, but volunteered to coach basketball in MCKK. Mr Liew hailed from Kuala Kangsar, but kept training the team even when he was posted elsewhere. As for the Hamdan Sheikh Tahir Trophy for boys' basketball, introduced in 1974, MCKK won it a record nineteen times as of 2020. MCKK also had a record of defeating several Chinese schools in the northern states. It was significant as basketball in Malaysia was traditionally dominated by the Chinese.

I wasn't that great, but being the only lefthander in my batch it gave me some advantage. And my shots were not bad. Even today, I can shoot a basket decently. We were told to do push-ups to build up our physique. I remember doing 100 rounds of push-ups at 5.00 a.m. for a few weeks, in an effort to bulk-up. Most of us were scrawny teenagers and gaining weight seemed like a challenge. In fact, I was unhappy at being slightly underweight then. Boy, how I wish to trade places with myself today!

There was one time when we were finishing our basketball training. We got back slightly later than usual, nearing the Maghrib azan. We were all expected to be bathed and ready in the *surau* for prayers. This time, a warden came over and whipped many of us with a rattan cane—one boy even bled and cried. The warden was soon transferred out of school for transgressing his powers.

While in MCKK, I finally chose a side in the English Premier League. Many of my peers supported Alex Ferguson's Manchester United, which started to dominate the league at that time.

Somehow, I wanted something different, and started with an 'Anything but MU' approach. My room at home was covered from floor to ceiling with posters of players from various big, non-MU clubs. Eventually, I came to settle on Liverpool.

Around this time, the Reds players were dubbed the 'Spice Boys'. They were known more for their modelling than filling the boots of their illustrious predecessors, although many of them were really good: Jamie Redknapp, David James, Steve McManaman, and Robbie Fowler. Nevertheless, Liverpool carries with it a long history not just of glory but of suffering. They dominated English and European Football in the 1970s and 1980s. Yet, the fans also suffered from the deaths of ninety-six fans at Hillsborough and were demonized by the right-wing press. The city also has a long working class history and their legendary manager, Bill Shankly, once declared, 'The socialism I believe in is everybody working for the same goal and everybody having a share in the rewards. That's how I see football, that's how I see life.'

Teachers

MCKK had a tradition of dedicated, non-Malay teachers, just like Mr Liew. I found this incredible, as the school was entirely Malay, and many of the old boys ended up leading Malay nationalist parties that fed on resentment against the non-Malays. My physics teacher was Ms Grace Margaret, an Indian-Malaysian. She had a shrill voice that she put on to nag us repeatedly. But she had a good heart. She would get postcards from old boys in the UK and I remember her reading out the ones sent from the top overseas universities.

Another was the late Mr Tan Gim Hoe. He started teaching mathematics and additional mathematics at MCKK immediately upon finishing his training at the teachers' training college in 1972. I never attended his formal classes, but he organized free extra classes for us for additional mathematics. He would repeat that mathematics is 'kacang' (or simple) and we were provided free notes of the calculations to his exercises; cyclostyled and made smaller to allow for more to be copied at a cheaper price. He left the college in 2005.

MCKK had many female teachers, too. My English teacher in form five was Mrs Noor Hayati Uteh. Her husband, Anand Baharuddin, was twenty years my senior in MCKK and was also teaching English. Anand would later become the headmaster of the school from 2010 until 2020. In one of the classes, she introduced us to chapters on MCKK in *Malaysian Journey* by old boy Rehman Rashid.

The Internet

The Internet was introduced to Malaysia in 1995 and, within a year, our computer laboratory was online. I remember registering for my first e-mail account—on Hotmail. I was clueless about it in the beginning. My cousin, Harith, said he wanted to e-mail me via his Jaring account.

'I have Hotmail. Can I get e-mail there?'

One of my friends, Firdaus, created his own website, and I started envying him. My father had just bought me an NEC computer, and soon, I managed to convince him about how important the Internet was and we got a TMNet subscription. It used the noisy dial-up modem. This was definitely a privilege— only 2.3 per cent of Malaysians were using the Internet in 1997. While the number has increased to 84.2 per cent today, many are still struggling to afford access to data even in the urban areas, while those in the rural areas struggle for coverage.

I started studying HTML coding on my own, and then moved on to Flash animation and some JavaScript coding. Before long, I had my first website. A year or two after MCKK received its Internet connection, the school's official website became dormant. So, we decided to make an official website. We had an 'About' page, where we listed our bios and e-mails.

Soon, I received an e-mail from Rafizi Ramli, Class of 1994. While I came to MCKK after he had left, he was still remembered as the Best Student Award Winner (which he received from Anwar), President of the Students Union, President of Badan Revolusi Ugama (BRU), and twice champion Piala Perdana Menteri (PPM) Malay debater. His e-mail basically went along the lines of, 'I read your bio. You remind me of myself.'

That was a lesson in recruiting impressionable young minds! Rafizi was, at that time, pursuing his engineering degree from Leeds University as a Petronas scholar.

In the meantime, we began using a program called mIRC. Previously, we communicated with students from outside (read 'girls') using letters and had pen pals. I remember waiting to receive letters for days—checking the school office daily, in case one had arrived. A few students were featured in magazines. They advertised the fact that they were MCKK students and were instant hits with the girls, receiving letters from many admirers. The more popular ones could even be selective and offer those they were not interested in to the rest of us.

In 1996, as Malaysia's impressive economic growth continued, the PM launched the Multimedia Super Corridor (MSC). It would stretch from Kuala Lumpur City Centre (KLCC) to Cyberjaya. Cyberjaya was planned to be Malaysia's Silicon Valley, while MSC was supposed to be a special business district focused on information technology. In order to attract multinationals to set up shops in the MSC, the PM promised that the Internet would not be censored—unlike the mainstream media. This was to differentiate us from Singapore, where Internet service providers were controlled by the government. Ironically, Mahathir made this promise to investors while the government ignored the right to freedom of speech and expression spelled out in the Federal Constitution; but looking at his views and track record, maybe it was not much a surprise after all.

The 1997 Asian Financial Crisis

Malaysia's 'miracle' came tumbling down in 1997. It began in Thailand (known as 'the Tom Yum Goong Crisis', after the kingdom's sour and spicy soup) after it had to abandon its currency peg to the US dollar. This, in turn, caused a domino effect across the region. Malaysia, too, suffered, as the unregulated capital that had flown into the country abandoned it in droves. The ringgit, which at one point traded at 2.40 to the US dollar, lost 50 per cent of its value. The stock market lost 60 per cent of its value. Corporations that had debts in foreign currencies suffered considerably. The economy shrank 6.7 per cent in 1998, compared to a growth of 7.7 per cent the year before.

For a teenager from a senior government pensioner's family, the crisis seemed abstract. But I did see family members who were involved in business bearing the brunt of the crisis. I remembered hearing about severe cuts in overseas university scholarships, which were widely available only a few years before that. The confident 'Malaysia Boleh' swagger disappeared. For us, born in the early days of the Mahathir premiership, this was the first economic crisis (or any crisis) that we were conscious of. The economic and political upheavals of the mid-1980s happened too long back to register in our minds.

Debate

MCKK was famed as a debating powerhouse. At that time, the school had won the PPM Malay language debating competition (open to only fully residential schools) three times—in 1980, when it was led by popular newscaster Suhaimi Sulaiman and politician Saifuddin Abdullah; and in 1992, and 1993, when the captain was Rafizi Ramli. The finals were telecast live on television once.

As mentioned earlier, my foray in Malay debate in primary school was not successful. But in Kuala Kangsar, my batch had Ahmad Azizi Kamil—who not only defeated my team in the Petaling district competition when we were in primary school, but also impressed us with his debating ability. Soon, he made his mark in MCKK and became a school debater in form two, when the team went all the way to the final.

I recognized that I did not have a future in sports and quit basketball to focus on debate. I officially became part of the five-member team in 1997 (three in the first team and two as reserves). We lost early in the tournament in Penang and I remained a reserve debater that year, not debating even once. In the following year, the number of debaters in a team was reduced to only four. I lost my place to Imran Idris, who, later, followed my footsteps to Kolej Yayasan UEM (KYUEM). He went on to get his medical undergraduate degree from Cambridge and a PhD from Oxford. So, losing my place to him does not seem too bad, I guess, in retrospect. We went all the way to the finals, but lost.

While we did use the Internet to conduct our research whenever we could use the school facilities or go to the cyber cafes in town, we still relied heavily on books and magazines. We spent time in the Language Room at MCKK. One of the reasons why I did not make the first team was that I was bad at memorizing texts and was not a great speaker either. But I was good at churning out arguments to help the team and could think on my feet reasonably well.

I was back in the official team in my final year in MCKK. I managed to debate a few times as we did well in both the PPM and the Dato' Shukor Abdullah Trophy, a national-level Malay debating championship which was open to all schools. We cruised through by winning at the district level. We met the Teluk Intan

Secondary Science School in the state final. They had defeated us in the PPM final the year before, but we emerged victorious this time. The national final was held in Perlis, where we defeated the Labu Federal Religious Secondary School.

Getting success in debate in my final year was not easy. We sacrificed week-long school holidays by staying in MCKK, preparing for the Malaysian Certificate of Education (SPM) trials that was coming the following week, when time permitted. PPM was held in Malacca and I debated a handful of times as the team progressed all the way to the final. In the PPM final, we fought off Teluk Intan Science Secondary School again, in a rematch of the 1998 final. This time we won. It was one of my happiest moments in MCKK.

To recognize the achievements of our debating team, the old boys organized a bilingual Old Boy-Present Boy debate in MCKK. The two teams were mixed, including both old boys and present students. We were also allowed to choose Malay or English. Among the old boys who took part was Azman Manaf, who led MCKK to its only English PPM trophy at that time, back in 1975. Rehman Rashid, the author of *A Malaysian Journey* was on my team. We debated about MCKK being overrated, and Rehman and I argued that yes, we are overrated.

Rehman's *A Malaysian Journey* is part personal memoir, part reflection on Malaysia's journey through the years. Popular even decades after it was first published, he recalled his time in our alma mater fondly, but he was not uncritical. Later on, he reflected on the parallel growth and challenges that Malaysia faced. I enjoyed all his writings that were filled with wit and insight, as he made his subjects come to life.

Life as a Senior

Other than debate and preparing for SPM, I was active in BRU and edited their newsletter. I also assisted in editing the Students Union newsletter and was on the editorial board of the MCKK magazine. The two fiction pieces in the magazine—one Malay and one English—were both written by me.

At that time, the BRU—myself included—took quite a religious hardline regarding issues such as playing musical instruments and the wearing of shorts. Inspired by the Pan Malaysian Islamic Party (PAS), we also took 'Tajdid Hadhari' as our rallying cry—rather than *Reformasi*. Thinking back, we were young and impressionable, and I guess we tried to be different by taking this line. We had sympathies for PAS. Now I probably would not be able to bear my younger self, but I guess it is a learning process, a process of political maturity.

Inspired by *Reformasi*, I also wrote an English play titled *The Red October*. I can't remember much of it, but as I could not refer to much of the Malaysian political scene, I used parts of the Russian Revolution in my play. I had good fun writing it.

In terms of academics, we had no choice then in Upper Secondary. Everyone in fully residential schools had to take the Science Stream to make up for the alleged shortage (particularly among the Bumiputera) of students taking up science subjects. But we had to take a tenth subject, and could choose from accounts, commerce, Islamic worldview, and art. I decided to take art. Our classes depended on our tenth subject. Art was by far the noisiest class and students were more prone to sleep than study. But I thoroughly enjoyed it. Accounts was seen as the 'smart' class, as opposed to art, which was seen as the 'fun' class.

Like many other students, I struggled with additional mathematics. I found biology and chemistry difficult too. Physics was okay as I found it straightforward, like basic mathematics. After diligently doing additional mathematics exercises late into night, my grades in the subject gradually improved.

Other than my own Malay debating team, the 1999 football and rugby teams did well too. We all came down to support and cheer our teams, complete with designated chants and fight songs, just like fanatical football ultras.

I once went with two friends to a computer fair, all the way in Penang, by train. I also attended a *pondok* opposite the Internal

Security Act (ISA) detention centre in Kamunting, Taiping, a few times. The *pondok* was established by Muhammad Saman Muhammad, who was known as Mat Saman Kati and was close to the Perak Palace. He was an expert in Sufism. There was a long tradition of MCKK students attending the *pondok*. By then, Mat Saman Kati had passed away, but I attended classes by Sabran Asmawi, who, in the 1999 General Election, became a PAS state assemblyman. As they taught in the style of the '*kitab kuning*' or traditional texts, it was difficult for us to follow, but getting out of school was fun, especially as going to Taiping meant being able to go to the McDonald's, which was not available in Kuala Kangsar at that time!

Interestingly, I was never a prefect, whether at La Salle or at MCKK.

Politics

I was already into politics from a very young age, thanks to my father. Starting from when I was young, our constant talks about history, religion, and politics never ceased. People recall the first book they bought, or the first music album they obsessively listened to, or the first World Cup they watched. For a political junkie like me, I recall the first elections where I took sides—the 1990 General Election (yes, I was eight). I remembered my cousins, who were all excited about Barisan Nasional (BN). It was no surprise as you could only read, watch, and listen to their propaganda at that time. Whether it came from my preference to root for the underdog (just like how I came to settle on Liverpool) or being shaped by father's views, I rooted for PAS.

My father admired an eclectic mix of politicians: Dr Burhanuddin Helmy, Abdul Razak Hussein, Asri Muda, Nik Aziz Nik Mat, and Anwar Ibrahim. I suppose, in a way, these men influenced me as well.

Dr Burhanuddin (1911–1969) led the leftist Malay Nationalist Party (MNP) and, then, PAS. His outlook was rooted in a progressive view of race and religion. In 1937, my great-grandfather, Wan Musa Abdul Samad, joined with Burhanuddin in the famous Dog Saliva debate in Kelantan, pushing for a reformist approach with regards to Islamic law. In 1963, my father drove Burhanuddin from his constituency in Besut to Kota Bharu to treat my cancer-stricken maternal grandfather. Burhanuddin, among many other things, was a homeopathy practitioner. Two years later, he was detained under the ISA for protesting against the formation of Malaysia. While Burhanuddin was PAS President from 1956 to 1969, the PAS establishment today hardly celebrates his legacy.

Abdul Razak (1922-1976) was an aristocrat from Pahang. He furthered his studies in London after World War II. At the age of 35, he was appointed as the Deputy PM of Malaya. But he made his real mark holding the portfolio of Minister of Rural Development. Later, as elaborated earlier, Razak brought about the NEP. He started to groom young Malay leaders, bypassing protocol and seniority. Dr Mahathir Mohamad, Musa Hitam, and Tengku Razaleigh Hamzah were all 'Razak boys'.

But he did not apply this approach to politics alone. As Deputy PM, in the early 1960s, Razak invited my father, then a junior civil servant, to join him in a car ride from Kota Bharu to rural Kelantan. The state, then, was in the hands of PAS. Razak wanted a non-partisan observer—who was also a local and a civil servant—to give his views on who would be the best person to lead United Malays National Organisation's (UMNO) challenge in the state. From that encounter, Nik Ahmad would be invited by Razak to join him for functions at his residence several times, even after the latter was appointed as PM from 1970 until his untimely death six years later.

Asri Muda (1923–1992) took over the presidency of PAS from Burhanuddin and led it until 1982. Without a tertiary education, and yet renowned for his quick mind and eloquent rhetoric, he led the nationalist youth group Angkatan Pemuda Insaf (API) in Kelantan before joining PAS. From 1964 to 1974, he was also the Chief Minister of Kelantan and the opposition leader from 1971–1973. A believer in Malay unity, he brought PAS into the BN and was given the position of Minister of Land and Rural Development. However, PAS was kicked out of BN in 1978 and, eventually, Asri's Malay nationalist outlook was rejected by the religious Young Turks of the party, resulting in his own ouster.

Nik Aziz (1931–2015) was the spiritual leader of PAS and another Chief Minister of Kelantan. His father was a student of my great-grandfather, Wan Musa, and would arrive at the latter's house on a horse or on a cart pulled by a horse, a step above the other students at that time. Nik Aziz also studied philosophy with Wan Musa's son, Nik Salleh.

Just before my father's retirement from the civil service in 1988, Nik Aziz visited our house in Petaling Jaya. Nik Aziz was part of the Young Turks of PAS (including another cleric, Abdul Hadi Awang), whose rise to party leadership had been inspired by the traumas of the party losing control of Kelantan, being ousted from the BN, and Asri Muda's booting. In 1986, PAS was left with a single seat. But Nik Aziz had slowly built the party from the ground up.

UMNO was caught in a major crisis as Tengku Razaleigh, who led UMNO's takeover of Kelantan in 1978, split from Mahathir. Nik Aziz was forming a coalition with Razaleigh and was confident of taking back the state in the next election.

Nik Aziz knew of Nik Ahmad's family background and political sympathies. He wanted someone with experience in the civil service to run and be appointed as the State Executive Council (State EXCO). Thus, he offered my father the safe seat of Lundang. My father consulted with my mother and decided against it. At that time, my mother said that she did not want her family to be involved in politics! True enough, PAS did win and Nik Aziz served as the Chief Minister from 1990 until his death in 2015. While certainly making the state more conservative in its policies, the erudite politician was also steadfast in rejecting

UMNO and racial politics. Known as the 'Tok Guru', he was seen as the gentle face of the Islamic party, impressing Muslims and non-Muslims alike. PAS grew closer to UMNO not long after his death.

Against this backdrop of diverse but broadly anti-establishment politicians (even Razak was an iconoclast in his own way), I found my friend's copy of the *Autobiography of Malcolm X* in 1996. This was the edition published along with Spike Lee's film that was released four years earlier.

Malcolm X (who died as el Hajj Malik el Shabazz) was an African-American nationalist and icon. He stood against not only racism but oppression and colonialism. To this day, I still recall his powerful letter from Mecca when he rejected a racial approach to fight White Supremacy.

> During the past eleven days here in the Muslim world, I have eaten from the same plate, drunk from the same glass, and slept on the same rug—while praying to the same God—with fellow Muslims, whose eyes were the bluest of blue, whose hair was the blondest of blond, and whose skin was the whitest of white . . .
>
> I could see from this, that perhaps if white Americans could accept the Oneness of God, then perhaps, too, they could accept in reality the Oneness of Man . . .
>
> Perhaps it could be in time to save America from imminent disaster—the same destruction brought upon Germany by racism . . .
>
> Each hour here in the Holy Land enables me to have greater spiritual insights into what is happening in America between black and white. The American Negro never can be blamed for his racial animosities—he is only reacting to four hundred years of the conscious racism of the American whites. But as racism leads America up the suicide path, I do believe, from the experiences that I have had with them, that the whites of the younger generation, in the colleges and universities, will

see the handwriting on the walls and many of them will turn to
the spiritual path of truth . . .

What struck me was that while Malays are Muslims, one does
not see enough of the universalism of Islam as a key pillar in
upholding justice and mercy. Instead, religion and race become
divisive identities that drive a wedge between the different
communities. Too many politicians had been inculcating a
sense of insecurity to make themselves relevant, even though,
as pointed out by Syed Hussein Alatas, they rely on colonial
stereotypes to support their argument. Like a drug, racial and
religious fanaticism provides short term benefits but damages the
community in the long run.

Reformasi

While the country was still reeling from the Financial Crisis, in
September 1998, Anwar Ibrahim was unceremoniously sacked by
Dr Mahathir Mohamad.

Anwar was an active debater representing MCKK and was the
third president of the BRU. For the first five years, his headmaster
was N.J. Ryan, the last British headmaster of the school. Until
today, Anwar shares the English traditions that were deep-rooted
in MCKK at that time. In his outings from MCKK, Anwar
would go to the *pondoks* to teach the students there English and,
in exchange, they would teach him religious subjects and Arabic.
He also provided classes to the poor in the small town.

He furthered his studies from the University of Malaya (UM).
There, he built his name as a nationalist and Islamic student activist.
At the same time, the Socialist Club was also powerful. These
different groups were all critical of the Tunku Abdul Rahman
administration. Following the 13 May 1969 riots, Anwar played
a role in duplicating Mahathir's scathing letter and spreading it
across the campus and beyond.

After graduating, Anwar formed the Angkatan Belia Islam Malaysia (ABIM). It became a pioneer of the Islamic revival in Malaysia and also took on many progressive causes: national unity, economic inequality, and the plight of the Muslims in southern Thailand and Palestine. In contrast, PAS adopted a more Malay-centric outlook under Asri, and consequently joined the government (we all know how that went). This allowed ABIM to fill the role of the de-facto opposition in a country where democracy was curtailed and dominated by a big-tent coalition. This culminated in the Baling demonstrations, which were against the hunger and economic difficulties facing the peasants in the state of Kedah. The rubber tappers had endured severe hardship due to falling rubber prices. Anwar was imprisoned under the ISA for twenty months for his role in the protests.

In 1982, Anwar shocked everyone by joining UMNO at the invitation of Mahathir. Many had expected him to join PAS. He rapidly rose in the government—eventually becoming the finance minister in 1991 and the Deputy PM in 1993.

As Finance Minister, he presided over the unprecedented economic growth that the country enjoyed. He was the last to preside over a budget surplus (reaching a peak of 5.45 per cent in 1994). Anwar also introduced the Projek Perumahan Rakyat (PPR) public housing scheme initiative in 1995. That year alone 58,200 houses were approved across Kuala Lumpur, including in my present constituency.[10] *Euromoney* rated him as one of the top four finance ministers, while *Asiamoney* named him as the Finance Minister of the Year.

As mentioned earlier, during the Roaring 90s, Anwar wrote the *Asian Renaissance*, focusing on the cultural strengths of the region and rallying against blind imitation of the West—just as Mahathir did through his idea of Asian values. Anwar, however, also argued

---

[10] DR Deb, 28 Oct 1994, Bil. 37, 6253, https://www.parlimen.gov.my/files/hindex/pdf/DR-28101994.pdf

that the wisdom embedded within our traditions—whether from Muslim, Chinese, or Indian civilizations—also mandated the need for transparency, accountability, and justice. These are, hence, not merely Western constructs.

The Asian Financial Crisis emphasized the differences between the guru and the protégé. Mahathir essentially wanted to protect Malaysia's state-led capitalism and the crony beneficiaries of privatization. Anwar was more open to the ideas from the international financial institutions that focused on transparency and good governance. In a two-month period as the acting PM, Anwar had focused on fighting corruption. Later, some experts credited Mahathir's unorthodox policies for mitigating the worst effects of the crisis; yet, other countries that took the conventional approach recovered just as well and managed to overcome the structural problems that continue to bedevil Malaysia.

Anwar's rise was abruptly halted with his sacking on 2 September 1998. He was accused of engaging in sodomy. We were all astounded. I had a friend, Helmy, who was my regular sparring partner in politics (while most were uninterested at that age) and we were talking about what this all meant.

Anwar began to tour the country to address Malaysians in massive 'ceramahs' for eighteen days between his sacking and his subsequent arrest. Every event attracted tens of thousands of people. In his constituency of Permatang Pauh in Penang, he proclaimed what underpinned his struggle: a reform movement focused on upholding the dignity of all Malaysians, an equitable economic system, and fighting corruption and injustice. Eventually, Anwar was arrested under the ISA by the police. Donning balaclavas and wielding M16 rifles, they stormed his home.

On 28 September 1998, he was brought to court with a black eye, after being beaten up by the Inspector General of Police, Abdul Rahim Noor. Mahathir claimed that Anwar had inflicted the black eye on himself. In front of the Royal Commission of Inquiry, Rahim admitted to attacking Anwar. That image captured the imagination of Malaysians: if this could happen to a former

Deputy PM, what could ordinary folk expect? The *Reformasi* movement was born.

Another *Reformasi* had first taken place in Indonesia. In spite of the common bonds between Malaysia and Indonesia that were only broken when the British and the Dutch divided the two polities, Indonesia fought a bloody war of independence against their imperial masters. Many Malaysians followed the upheavals with great interest. Mahathir's ally, Suharto, started to lose his grip on the republic not only due to the financial crisis, but because of decades of mismanagement and corruption in favour of his family and cronies. Many saw parallels between Malaysia and Indonesia. Student protests broke out, but so did violent pogroms against the Chinese-Indonesians and other minorities. Suharto, finally, handed over power to vice president B.J. Habibie in May 1988. Democratic elections were held in Indonesia a year later and political reforms were enacted by Habibie as well as his successors.

Calling the Malaysian protest movement *Reformasi* as well was a contentious decision. Many were hopeful that Malaysia could embark on its own process of democratization. But others were fearful that the violence that had erupted in Indonesia—especially against its minorities—would likewise occur in Malaysia. Perhaps the latter argument prevailed in the end, given the time it took for the minorities to support the cause—a decade for *Reformasi* to gain a sizeable electoral impact and two decades for a change in our government.

But one also cannot help but wonder if—despite all the turmoil, and even violence, that Indonesia had to suffer—its gamble of breaking away from the comforts and certainties of autocratic rule ultimately paid off. Certainly, for all its lingering imperfections, Indonesia is an exemplar to Southeast Asia when it comes to democracy, including a fiercely independent media and civil society that will rarely do the bidding of the rich and powerful.

Initially, I was still unsure of what to make of Anwar and *Reformasi*. In a sense, I still felt that he was an UMNO leader.

But witnessing how the people had rallied to Anwar as a way to challenge the government was inspiring. Not long after that, I was part of the BRU delegation from MCKK attending a Muslim student gathering in Negeri Sembilan. One of the Muslim student groups close to Anwar had traditionally conducted the event. In hushed whispers, our facilitator told us that the government was victimizing Anwar. One of the speakers at the event was afterwards arrested under the ISA. After the event, probably at the behest of the authorities, one of our teachers called the MCKK delegation and told us, 'I know we are all sad about what has happened to our old boy, Anwar. But I have seen the proof (of the alleged homosexual act). It's all true.'

I went back home immediately for school holidays. Most of my family members had rallied to Anwar's cause. As I listened to them—some of whom had gone to the 'ceramahs' and attended the demonstrations—I was persuaded to support *Reformasi*. The 1998 Commonwealth Games was taking place in Kuala Lumpur, and we attended some of the events—but the conversation was all about the *Reformasi* demonstrations. Soon my father—who, like most old school, senior Malay civil servants, read *the New Straits Times* on a daily basis—decided to change to *the Sun* tabloid instead. He would also reserve *Harakah* (PAS newspaper) from the Indian Muslim newsagent, which started to cater to their burgeoning middle-class readership by starting an English section.

Back in MCKK, I started buying *Harakah*. There was a shop near the banks of the Perak River that sold books and magazines related to the opposition. It also sold audio cassettes and CDs of 'ceramahs'. I would buy many of the items. One aspect of life in MCKK was the Saturday inspections. At 8.00 a.m., we had to be in our full uniform. The wardens and the prefects would perform inspections, checking our locker, ensuring that we had a clean set of towels, toiletries, and polished shoes. There was a warden who would stop by my locker and read my stash of political newspapers and magazines, while the prefects conducted the inspection.

I was in form five, so the inspections did not worry me much. The more rebellious students would get the juniors to go and hide their stash of cigarettes and jeans (which were illegal in MCKK).

The *Reformasi* activists took over a small dormant party and launched the multi-racial Parti Keadilan Nasional (PKN) on 4 April 1999, in the packed Renaissance Hotel in Kuala Lumpur, draped in the colours of the party: sky blue and white. The message from Anwar Ibrahim's wife, Dr Wan Azizah Wan Ismail, about the launch of the party was shared across Internet discussion lists a week before that. Wan Azizah would be the president of PKN, and then Parti Keadilan Rakyat (KEADILAN) for almost two decades. She made history as the first female leader of a major Malaysian political party, the first female Malaysian opposition leader, and then, the first female Deputy PM of the country. Many saw the soft-spoken ophthalmologist as an accidental politician, who jumped into the fray to free her husband, but she managed to not only hold the fledgling multi-racial party together when her husband was imprisoned, but to turn it into a winning national party.

The founding committee of the party included former UMNO leaders; human rights activists; leaders of the Islamic movements; Church activists, and many others. My uncle, Nik Aziz Nik Hassan, who was active in UMNO Kelantan, joined as part of the founding committee.

The Barisan Alternatif (BA) coalition was formed consisting of PKN, PAS, Democratic Action Party (DAP), and Parti Rakyat Malaysia (PRM). Traditionally, the Alliance Party—and subsequently BN—did well in elections due to their multi-racial coalition. However, the Alliance was not the first to come up with this formula. The first multi-racial coalition was actually between the All-Malayan Council for Joint Action and Pusat Tenaga Rakyat (AMCJA–PUTERA), which was driven underground by the colonial administration. Then, there was the multi-racial Socialist Front consisting of the PRM and the Labour Party in the 1950s and 1960s. PAS joined the BN briefly after the coalition's founding. In the 1990 election, Tengku Razaleigh

Hamzah had to have two-coalitions to accommodate DAP (Gagasan Rakyat) and PAS (Angkatan Perpaduan Ummah)— the biggest non-Malay and Malay parties respectively in the opposition. Thus, BA was historic in that these two parties came together.

In fact, when my SPM exams came around, it overlapped with the 1999 General Election. More of my peers were politicized than before. Our headmaster, Alimuddin Mohd Dom, came storming through the dorms and asked us to remove all political paraphernalia. We all crowded in the common room to watch the results come in live via television. My physics teacher, Ms Grace, dropped by, dressed in a light blue sari. We excitedly asked her which party she had voted for. She was quiet at first, then whispered, 'Look at the colour of my sari.' PKN's colour was light blue.

UMNO suffered a bloody nose as more than half of the Malays voted for the opposition (largely for PAS, and some for PKN). But the non-Malays as well as the Sabahans and Sarawakians remained largely loyal to BN, as they were sceptical of the Islamic PAS, in light of the anti-Chinese and anti-Christian riots during *Reformasi* in Indonesia.

Even the seats won by PKN were largely on the coattails of the PAS. In the parliament, other than Anwar's old seat of Permatang Pauh—which was won by Dr Wan Azizah—the new party won one seat in Terengganu and three seats in Kelantan. PAS defended Kelantan and took over Terengganu. PAS and PKN's partner in BA, the predominantly non-Malay DAP suffered in the election as well. They did increase their parliamentary seat tally by one to 10 seats, but party Secretary General Lim Kit Siang and Deputy Chairman Karpal Singh lost their seats.

Realizing that PKN's core was in the urban areas, the party had fielded heavyweights such as Deputy President Dr Chandra Muzaffar, Central Committee member and former Bar Council President Zainur Zakaria, and Vice President Marina Yusof in seats in Kuala Lumpur (Marina in Wangsa Maju which was split into Wangsa Maju and Setiawangsa in 2004). But they all lost.

4. Lembah Beringin

I took my driving lessons after SPM. I remember the man who was teaching us traffic laws telling us, 'Do not blow your horns near hospitals, but if you pass through a *Reformasi* demonstration, you should honk your horns in support!'

Immediately after SPM, my father enrolled me in the A-Level program in Kolej Damansara Utama (KDU). He was planning for me to do the Australian law twinning program. I took economics, English literature, and law. My father thought I should take mathematics rather than all these subjects, but I stood my ground.

Life in a private college in the Klang Valley was like a cultural shock to me. Most of my classmates (and indeed my closest circle of friends at KDU) were all Chinese students. Sometimes, I would borrow my father's old Honda Accord and drive some of the outstation students who did not have a car. They were respectful and, often, we would spend time in the mamak stall near the Hindu graveyard next to KDU. I joined them at the Chinese coffee shops too, where I would just have coffee or 'teh tarik'.

My SPM results were decent. I got distinctions in all the subjects except for chemistry, biology (both expected), and Islamic studies. I applied for a few scholarships. My father was not keen on me following his footsteps as a civil servant, but I still applied for the Public Services Department scholarship to do international studies. The idea of being a diplomat appealed to me. I did not receive a call back. However, I attended a few rounds of scholarship interviews for Permodalan Nasional Berhad (PNB) and the Securities Commission. The Securities Commission interview process was, by far, the most rigorous. I had to write an essay on capital markets as part of my initial application, and then I was called to two rounds of interviews, including doing a role-playing game with other applicants.

I was awarded both the scholarships to study law. But, as I received PNB's offer first, I decided to accept PNB. Mine was the fifth batch to receive the all-Malay overseas scholarships.

KYUEM

We were sent to KYUEM in Lembah Beringin. It was only around 20 kilometres from the border with Perak, and the nearest town was Tanjong Malim, 15 minutes away. This was a township built during the Roaring 90s. The financial crisis meant that the town was largely uninhabited. Nevertheless, the college—then called Kolej Matrikulasi Yayasan Saad—opened its doors in 1998, while the financial crisis was still wreaking havoc.

Just like MCKK, it was modelled after British public schools. It was established by old boy Halim Saad, who had been behind the North–South Expressway. The difference was that it was a private institution that opened more than nine decades after my alma mater and functioned specifically as a sixth form college. It had modern and comfortable facilities and better food. We stayed in chalets that had four cubicles each, and shared a common room with a common computer. Some students who came from day schools complained about the food and the facilities, but for us MCKK old boys (five from my batch), it was a stark improvement.

There was also a British headmaster and British teachers. My sponsors told me to take four subjects—and I was finally persuaded to take mathematics along with history, economics, and English literature. I still struggled in mathematics—in class I would frequently disturb Ikmal and Fikriah, the two girls in front of me, trying to understand the subject. After a few months, I dropped English literature, and just focused on the minimum three A-Level subjects.

Most of the other students struggled in economics. I however did well as I had already started A-Level economics in KDU. However, a boy from Perlis named Loh Siang Ling emerged as a rival and we dominated the economics class. We found Mrs Rahazana Rahmat, our economics teacher, strict at first, but eventually we warmed up to her teaching and personality.

For history, I had Mr John Wilkinson, an eccentric Scouser. It took time for us to understand his accent but he was a determined teacher. I was so confident in my writing skills and knowledge of history that I was sure I would get an A or at least a B in my first assignment, but he failed me. Eventually, we got to grips not just with the topics—the French Revolution, the rise of European Nationalism and the Cold War—but also writing academic essays. I was awarded a prize as the best student in history at the end of my time in KYUEM.

Unsurprisingly, Wilkinson was also a massive Liverpool fan. I would visit his teachers' apartment sometimes to watch Liverpool games—including the famous FA Cup final against Arsenal when Liverpool came from behind with two Michael Owen goals to clinch the trophy.

I also decided to be more active in student life at KYUEM. In MCKK, I had kept myself to mainly secondary roles. So, I ran for Chair of the Cultural Performance (a tradition for new students in the college). I remember having to adjust myself to my new surroundings, dealing with girls and non-Muslims, all novelties compared to MCKK. So, it was no longer the issue of the permissibility of playing the guitar or the need to cover the knees, but dealing with boys and girls, Muslims and non-Muslims, with different viewpoints. It does put things in perspective.

When the Student Council election was held, I decided to run for the position of president. We had hustings where all the candidates had to present the manifesto to the students. I won, but only narrowly. I had two deputies—one male and one female. My male deputy was Azmil Khalili, a capable orator who was naturally funny. The female deputy, Tengku Amatullah Madeehah, was a smart, hardworking student with strong opinions. Along with the rest of the EXCOs, we made a wonderful team.

Dealing with the British headmaster, Mr Peter Morris, was a challenge, however. He was strict and no-nonsense, with a dose of his own eccentricity. Many of the students were not fond of him. While I was exposed to a multi-racial environment in primary school, the challenge of co-ed and multi-racial late-teen students with expat teachers was a different kettle of fish altogether. Many of the Malay students like myself came from all-Malay—or predominantly Malay—boarding schools. There were also students—Malay and non-Malay—from multi-racial national schools in the cities. The British teachers had a certain worldview as the college's founders wanted KYUEM to be a British public school. Sometimes, conflict would emerge from these different worldviews.

I was also close to Mr Noor Zaidi Mohd Noor, the Deputy Headmaster, who happened to be an MCKK old boy and former teacher (he spent his final few years in MCKK during my early days there) and Mrs Rogayah Ibrahim, the student services manager. They helped to smooth over the different viewpoints in college.

When it came to university applications, I really wanted to try out for Cambridge University. As mentioned, my MCKK senior Adlan Benan Omar was one of the top students at Cambridge. Similarly, I had KYUEM seniors from the university coming back and extolling the merits of applying to the university. I was taken in by the fantasy of being able to stay in one of the medieval colleges, dining in the Hogwarts-style dining halls, and engaging with the distinguished teaching faculty—not to forget the distinction of attending one of the top universities in the world. I submitted my application, took the test, and attended an interview to read law there. However, I was either too political in the interview, or, well, just not good enough!

I also applied to London School of Economics (LSE) and King's College, London. Eventually, I received offers from both universities. However, I decided on King's as I felt that too many of my accounting friends were going to LSE.

While we were waiting for our A-Level results in 2002, the PNB scholars were sent off to Outward Bound School (OBS) in Lumut. We took the maximum length of twenty-five days, but it was altered slightly from the famous standard course that were taken by the Royal Military College (RMC) students. All of us PNB students were placed in one group We did join the standard course participants in kayaking to and around Pangkor Island, off Lumut. It was while we were at OBS that we received our A-Level results. I received two As in economics and history, while a B in mathematics.

Political Involvement

I wrote prolifically on my personal website. One of the articles that attracted a lot of attention on the website's guestbook was 'The Informal Apartheid'. It was about how the students in KYUEM ended up in Malay and non-Malay tables, in spite of there being no prohibitions on sitting with one another; a subconscious racial divide. Rafizi Ramli read my articles and persuaded me to start writing for *Reformasi* websites. I also tried to send some pieces to the recently set-up *Malaysiakini* website and some ended up being published.

I also started a web magazine named *Suara Anum* and harnessed my web design skills to put the website up. I updated it twice a month and managed to get young writers to contribute to the website. *SuaraAnum* had a loyal, niche following. Eventually, I was interviewed by Sharaad Kuttan for *RadiQRadio*, an online radio portal at that time, as well as by writer and filmmaker Amir Muhammad for *The Edge*.

I had conversations about politics with my Perlis friend, Siang Ling. He said that I would be able to get Chinese support if I represented PKN, but not with PAS. 'The Chinese would have a hard time of supporting the Islamic party,' he told me.

I was still inspired by progressive politics, reading about Che Guevara (like many teenagers), but I was gradually getting fascinated by the Third Way politics of US President Bill Clinton and British PM Tony Blair. Unable to come out of the appeal of privatization and the free-market economies from the era of Ronald Reagan and Margaret Thatcher, Clinton and Blair sought a middle path that embraced globalization and did not challenge market fundamentalism. At the end of 2001, my piece 'KEADILAN's future lies in the political centre' was published in *Malaysiakini*.

It was the radical appeal of KEADILAN's multi-racial politics and how it essentially pursued a Malaysian Third Way— between racial and religious politics—that attracted me to, finally, choose the party. Even in those early days, when most saw this merely as Anwar Ibrahim's party with no future, I found that it has enormous potential as a Malay-led, multi-racial party. For a Malaysian multi-racial party to succeed, it must be credible among the Malay-Muslim majority—and KEADILAN possessed that credibility.

At the end of 2000, Adlan Benan Omar came to visit me at home. Soon he brought me along to meet young professionals who were helping out *Reformasi* at Anwar's house in Bukit Damansara—the house that was raided by the police and where Anwar was arrested. There, I met his eldest daughter, Nurul Izzah—future Balik Pulau MP, Senator Yusmadi Yusoff, and many more. I was asked to help party president Dr Wan Azizah to prepare her Parliamentary speeches and assisted PKN Youth Leader Ezam Mohd Nor. I also started writing opinion pieces for the party's official newspaper *Berita Keadilan*.

Anwar's residence functioned like a salon for *Reformasi* activists. The house still bore marks from his dramatic arrest in 1998. We had passionate discussions about human rights, political philosophy, and economics. On a more practical level, we discussed the direction of the movement and the party. Every Thursday night, the Muslim activists would gather for prayers to ask for Anwar's release, while the non-Muslim comrades would join in solidarity and listen to the talk afterwards.

In April 2001, prior to the 'Black 14' demonstration, the government detained six *Reformasi* leaders, including Ezam, under the ISA. This caused a major setback for the movement. There was a lighthearted personal moment when Ezam's wife, Bahirah Tajul Aris, called me to help her prepare her speech for the 58th session of the UN Commission on Human Rights in Geneva. Bahirah called the fixed-line at my house, and my mother picked up the phone. The moment she heard a female voice, my mother started grilling Bahirah until she had to explain to my mother that she was married with three children and was not interested in her 19-year-old son!

On 12 January 2002, on my twentieth birthday, Benan came over with a few friends to fetch me from KYUEM. We drove all the way to Perlis for a by-election. It was a Chinese seat. A year after the prior General Election, PKN had won the state seat of Lunas in Kedah after the opposition made inroads among the Chinese voters. PKN had yet to have a non-Malay representative, in spite of its multi-racial ideals. I remember helping Saifuddin Nasution, the Lunas State Assemblyman and Vice Youth Leader for PKN at that time with talking points. Unfortunately, BN not only retained the state seat of Indera Kayangan, but won with a bigger majority. For whatever reason, I was able to write critical articles under my name and campaign for the opposition while on a GLIC scholarship without any trouble during my time in Lembah Beringin.

11 September 2001

I was at my parent's house when the terrorist attacks on the World Trade Center in New York and Pentagon in Washington DC took place. Immediately, the incident received a rolling coverage on cable news stations. I switched on CNN and was trying to make sense of it all. Eventually, blame was placed on the terrorist group Al-Qaeda, led by Osama bin Laden. After the demands made on the Taliban, who were in control of much of Afghanistan, to expel bin Laden went unheeded, the US invaded the country.

The attack seemed to have punctured the self-confidence of the US, which had not ebbed since the fall of the Berlin Wall. The threat was no longer communism, but Islamic terrorism driven by non-state actors. As young Muslims, many did not share the hardline literalist and violent views of the terrorists; but we also witnessed rising Islamophobia while civil liberties and human rights took a backseat in the name of national security.

Locally, the government had already been facing terror threats, even prior to the US attacks. In 2000, an Islamist militant group called Al-Ma'unah, which described itself as a martial arts and Islamic medicine organization, raided an army reserve camp not far from Kuala Kangsar and took weapons and ammunition. This eventually led to a standoff with the armed forces and the police. One commando, one special branch officer, and one member of Al-Ma'unah died prior to the resolution of the conflict. The group was found guilty for waging war against the king.

The relationship between DAP and PAS had come under enormous strains after the 1999 election, as the latter became emboldened in its Islamic state agenda, while the leadership of DAP had to pay the price of losing their seats. The tipping point was the 11 September terrorist attacks. Ten days later, DAP left BA.

5. London

I flew to Heathrow in mid-September of 2002. Rafizi and a few of his MCKK friends received me. It was his birthday; so, after my arrival, we went to Chinatown to celebrate. Rafizi had already graduated with an undergraduate degree in electrical and electronics engineering from Leeds University and was in his final months of pursuing his chartered accountancy training in London.

Being in London meant I was at the centre of action. Most of my friends during my stay passed through London. It is one of the great overseas Malaysian outposts—you can always find Malaysians there. I had easy access to entertainment. Movie premieres took place in Leicester Square. There was also an abundance of musicals on the West End. Halal food—including halal fast food (mostly kebabs and fried chicken)—was everywhere. The trade-off was largely the cost, which we coped with by living in Zone Two or Three. We navigated around the city using London A-Z, as this was before the advent of Google Maps and smartphones.

My parents were used to getting aerogrammes from me. I remember reading my sister Nazifah's aerogrammes when she was in the UK and now it would be my turn. Since my time in MCKK, they expected our correspondences to be in English. Calls had become cheaper by then due to calling cards, but my father was always very brief on the phone—his questions tend to focus on my studies and sometimes he would put the phone down before the conversation ended, as he feared it was too expensive!

My mother, on the other hand, managed to teach herself to e-mail me and eventually have her own social media accounts!

King's College London

King's College London was established in 1829 as a response to the establishment of UCL as a secular establishment (which earned the latter the nickname of 'the Godless institution in Gower Street'). King's College was, therefore, established firmly within the Anglican tradition, but was open to all students. This was, initially, challenged by some who wanted King's to be like Oxbridge, where there were barriers to non-Anglicans, and resulted in a duel between the PM, the Duke of Wellington (who stood for an open admissions policy), and the Earl of Winchilsea.

Eventually, King's and UCL formed the University of London. The university would encompass LSE, SOAS, Imperial College (until 2007), and Queen Mary University of London, among others.

The main campus and the Law School are located along the Strand at the heart of London. Slightly more than a kilometre away from Trafalgar Square, it is within walking distance to the LSE. 700 meters away, across the Thames, is the Waterloo Campus. My classes were held at one of the two locations. I remember missing my first lecture as I thought that all the classes were held at the Strand.

London Residences

I first stayed at the Hampstead Residence, part of the students' residences for King's College. Located in Zone Two along Finchley Road, this was a relatively posh neighbourhood. It was part of the estate of a famous East Indian trader in the 19th century. My block was built in 1927. I had a relatively large single room to myself. We shared showers, bathrooms, and used a common kitchen for every floor. Also, there was no Internet connection in the rooms and, instead, we had to use a common computer room with ancient, slow computers. To ensure fair access, there was a two-hour limit per student.

So, Benan and Rafizi convinced me to move out of my student residences for the sake of my political work for *Reformasi*. I lost my deposit as my stay was too short. I found a place even farther and in a tougher neighbourhood—Walthamstow in Zone Three at the end of the Victoria line. It was not far from Leytonstone, where David Beckham grew up. The house was pretty run down. The other tenants were final year Malaysian students—including two from MCKK. They happened to have a spare room.

While I had started cooking in Hampstead, moving to Walthamstow meant I had to join the daily roster where we took turns to make dinner. I remember being embarrassed of my (lack of) cooking skills. Every time my turn came, after cooking dinner, I would call everyone down and then, take my plate and finish the food in my room to avoid seeing my housemates react to my cooking.

For my second and third years, I decided to move in with three King's medical students: two from KYUEM—Khairul Shahdan and Franscois Robert Runau, a Sino-Iban—and British-Tamil Bala Karunakaran. Bala was born to two Malaysia-born Sri Lankan Tamils, who returned to Sri Lanka. Later, as the conflict in the country worsened, his parents migrated to the UK. Khairul and Franscois were both government scholars, with very low allowances (less than mine), so we decided to stay in a house on Flaxman Road near the Loughborough Junction train station. This was near Brixton, at the other end of the Victoria line, in Zone Two.

After World War II, Brixton was the destination for many immigrants from the West Indies. The first wave came on the ship *Empire Windrush*. After this, all immigrants from West Indies came to be known as the 'Windrush Generation'. Brixton was also the setting of the infamous 1981 Brixton riots, fuelled by severe economic hardship and oppressive police tactics. The police had arrested a huge number of people from the predominantly black community, prior to the riots.

However, a Brixton man by the name of John Major replaced Margaret Thatcher as the UK PM, and the Conservative Party made full use of that in the 1992 General Election. Another riot took place in 1995, and four years later, Brixton market became the first site of the London rail bombings. Thus, whenever, I told friends that I stayed in Brixton, I would attract raised eyebrows.

To go to class, I would normally take the train from Loughborough Junction, which was less efficient than the underground, but was less than five minutes' walk from our house. I would, then, change to the district/circle underground line to go to Temple. My housemates took the bus on a different route as the King's medical school was in an entirely different part of London.

We continued the cooking roster. Here, we would take turns cooking halal dinners for the entire house for four nights from Monday to Thursday, and we had to deal with our own meals from Friday to Sunday. I, finally, took the plunge to learn how to cook proper Malay meals with Khairul, who was meticulous in all his endeavours. It was a good mix—Khairul and I would prepare mostly Malay dishes, Bala would prepare Tamil dishes, and Franscois would do a mix of Chinese and Sarawak dishes. Bala eventually became a vegetarian, but that was, fortunately, after I graduated! During Christmas, Franscois would get a halal turkey to roast. We also had passionate discussions on politics and religion.

In my room, I proudly displayed a *Jalur Gemilang* and the PKN flag that Nurul Izzah handed to me prior to my departure, with a Liverpool scarf below.

Sports and Games

During my first Boxing Day, my old history teacher at KYUEM, Mr Wilkinson, managed to obtain Premier League tickets to watch Liverpool at Anfield against Blackburn. The deal was that he would pay for lunch (fish and chips) if we paid for the tickets. The experience of being at Anfield for the first time was priceless. Unfortunately, it ended in a draw—Liverpool scoring first through Jon Arne Riise and Blackburn equalizing through Andy Cole.

I also worked as a match steward at Stamford Bridge, the home ground for Chelsea. We worked for five hours, arriving two-and-a-half hours before kick-off. We were then asked to examine tickets and assist the police with match security, although I doubt that with my 167 cm height and 55 kilogram weight (at that time), I could do much against the English fans. We were also asked to spot those smuggling alcohol. While booze was sold on the grounds, it was not supposed to be brought to the stands. But I could not complain: being able to watch football matches *and* get paid for it was good fun. This was the final season Gianfranco Zola played for Chelsea and he was in amazing form.

Otherwise, I would get my football updates through BBC's *Match of the Day*. Many of my friends subscribed to Sky Sports which broadcasted live telecasts, but that was a luxury to me. But Champions League games were shown on terrestrial television. Two months before my graduation and return to Malaysia, the Champions League final between AC Milan and Liverpool took place. AC Milan was one of the glamour clubs when I was growing up in the 1990s and I used to follow them intently, but following the Serie A in Malaysia was a bit more challenging than the Premier League.

Most of the Milan line-up were the best players in the world. By the end of the first half, Milan was easily 3-0 up and I knew it would take a miracle to win. Not only was the Italian club superior in talent, Liverpool was playing badly as well. In the second half, Steven Gerrard led a spirited comeback. The match went to extra time and, then, penalties. Liverpool edged out Milan on penalties. It was the biggest moment for me as someone who started supporting Liverpool after the golden years.

Sony PlayStation (and the FIFA series) were also popular among boys, but we did not have either at Flaxman Road. I did, however, play games on my computer—mostly strategy games like *Rise of Nations* or the football management game *Championship Manager*. I played *Rise of Nations* online with my housemate Khairul as well as future writer and commentator Tunku Zain al 'Abidin Tuanku Mukhriz, who was then at LSE.

I joined the boys kicking the ball around Hyde Park, and even represented King's in some of the Malaysian Games. The Malaysian Games are a sporting tournament hosted by a few universities around the UK with big Malaysian populations. Along with the cultural event 'Malaysian Night', it became a regular event for Malaysian students to catch up with friends as well as get Malaysian food.

Student Bodies

Into my second year, in 2003, I contested for the position of the Vice Chair of the King's College London Malaysian and Singaporean Society. The number of Malaysian students at King's was rather limited, which made forming a standalone Malaysian society difficult previously. It was traditionally dominated by Singaporeans. In my first year, I did look for ways to form a Malaysian Society but found that the Student Union at that time was not friendly to the effort, saying that the existing Malaysian and Singaporean Society was sufficient. Plotting with the other Malaysians, we managed to win all the positions in the Society in 2003, with the exception of the Vice Chair, which existed to represent Singaporeans. I was voted in as the Malaysian Vice Chair.

Within a week after that, however, I had to step down as I was voted in to be one of the Vice Chairpersons of UK and Eire Council for Malaysian Students (UKEC). The founding chairman was Adlan Benan Omar. Rafizi Ramli was one of the chairpersons. It was formed to bring together Malaysian societies in UK universities together. As my university's Malaysian and Singaporean Society was an affiliate society, I could not hold a position in an affiliate as well as in UKEC's executive committee. I roped in Ong Cheng Boon, whom I knew as a contributor to *SuaraAnum*, to assist me and, in the following year, she went to the executive committee. She has made a career of working in humanitarian agencies globally.

Since its establishment, UKEC was supposed to be above Malaysian political rivalries. During my time, there was a strong rivalry between the UMNO Club and al Hizbul Islami UK and Eire, popularly known as Hizbi (which was an underground PAS group). Rafizi had established KEADILAN International Europe, which sounded grand but consisted of a smattering of students mostly in the UK! I replaced Rafizi in coordinating the organization. We operated underground with Hizbi, as sponsors would discipline the students who were involved with the opposition, including cancelling scholarships. In one meeting, where the Malaysian High Commissioner to the UK, Abdul Aziz Mohammed, summoned the UKEC leadership, he brought up getting the UMNO Club affiliated to the UKEC. But I fought back hard, reminding him about the ethos of UKEC's establishment.

In spite of my mischief against the Singaporeans in King's, we got along well. I joined a debating competition among Singaporean societies in the UK and played football with them. One of them who joined our games was Pritam Singh. He was, then, doing his masters. In 2011, he was elected as an MP for the Workers' Party, became the party's Secretary General in 2018, and in 2020, became the first officially recognized opposition leader in the Singaporean Parliament.

A decade after I graduated, the Malaysian and Singaporean Society did split, with the formation of the Malaysian Society, an event that was cheekily described as independence by the Malaysians!

I also volunteered with Projek Kalsom. The project was started in 1994 by Malaysian students in the UK who read about the plight of Kelthom Abdullah, who was living in Kelantan and unable to support her children's education. The project involved motivational and English classes for secondary school students. It was first held in Pahang. During my time, the project was held in Besut, Terengganu. We spent almost a week there. One of the girls that I noticed there spoke English with a British accent and some grammatical errors here and there. It turned out that she watched *Harry Potter* movies avidly and picked up the accent. As most of us were from the UK, many of them were excited to hear our stories about the opportunities a good education can bring.

Malaysian Politics

Within a month of my arrival in London, Rafizi and I arranged for Nurul Izzah to come over and give a talk in London and Dublin. I joined Izzah and her friend, Yolanda Augustin, in the trip to Dublin. In London, we held a forum at LSE, with Kamarul Rashdan Salleh from the UMNO Club, which was moderated by Tunku 'Abidin. However, the UMNO Club students distributed leaflets attacking Adlan Benan, Rafizi, and me. Later, Rafizi decided to expose the UMNO Club members for intimidating the Malaysian students in attendance.

In a halal restaurant at Edgware Road, Rafizi also introduced me to future Parti Pribumi Bersatu Malaysia (PPBM) leader Wan Saiful Wan Jan, who was then heading Hizbi. I remembered an incident around the same time when my father, as a trustee of the Tenaga Nasional Berhad (TNB) Foundation, had to persuade the TNB Chairman and UMNO politician Jamaluddin Jarjis against making a last-minute decision to cancel sending students to the UK. Jamaluddin claimed that the students there were becoming anti-government!

A few days after the LSE forum, I received an angry call from my mother in Malaysia. She said as the guarantor to my scholarship, my father had received a warning letter from PNB over my political involvement. She reminded me that they could not afford to pay for my education in London if the scholarship was withdrawn and asked me to cease my political activities immediately. I said yes, though I was already thinking of ways to get around the restrictions. I found it hypocritical that while the scholarship contract prohibited us from being involved in anti-government political activism, it allowed scholars to be involved with UMNO. It was as if PKN was an illegal party, when, in fact, it was a legally registered political party. I also felt it was weird that while I could get away with political activism in Malaysia, I faced more hurdles in the UK.

I got involved the Abolish ISA Movement in the UK. Along with Yolanda, we worked with a British campaigner, Liz Fekete, and a few Malaysians who had settled in the UK. A lot of coordination was done with the Abolish ISA Movement in Malaysia which was a coalition of over eighty NGOs. I took part in a protest against the ISA in front of the Malaysian Tourism Office in Trafalgar Square. Many protests were held there instead of the Malaysian High Commission because of the former's visible location. Nevertheless, spooked by the trouble I got for bringing Izzah to London earlier, I put on a snow cap, dark glasses as well as a scarf wrapped around my neck to avoid being identified!

Towards the end of my stay in the UK, I was able to host Saari Sungib, one of the founders of Jamaah Islah Malaysia (JIM). One of the ISA detainees arrested in 2001, he and his wife came to thank the Abolish ISA campaigners in London. I would work closely with him as we would both wind up as state assemblypersons in Selangor.

After my first year, PNB made it compulsory for all its scholars to attend Biro Tatanegara (BTN). Established in 1974 to counter the vibrant and vocal student movement, it was rebranded in 1981. Officially, it was supposed to inculcate patriotism among youths and civil servants.

By the time I attended it in 2003, it had degenerated into a political tool promoting UMNO's interests and the doctrine of

Malay supremacy. Anwar was branded either as a sodomite or a CIA agent, PAS were religious deviationists, and DAP were Chinese chauvinists. Some students were given the chance to give the morning religious talks after prayers—and I was one of them. But we were not allowed to speak freely as there were set topics and texts. I settled on 'Malaysia is an Islamic State', which I found more palatable than 'the ISA is halal according to Islam'. I skipped some of the most partisan parts. Fortunately for me, I saw that the facilitator was dozing off in the corner of the surau. We even had to answer questions in a test which was blatantly partisan.

During that same summer holiday, PKN sealed its merger with PRM. The merged entity was named KEADILAN. This was to commemorate the progressive heritage of PRM which followed the footsteps of the early Malay nationalist organizations—the Malay Nationalist Party (MNP), Angkatan Wanita Sedar (AWAS) and Angkatan Pemuda Insaf (API) that were active after World War II. It was the progressive movements that had the courage to push for independence earlier than the conservative and feudal UMNO. At the same time, they pioneered the first multi-racial coalition through AMCJA-PUTERA. In 1947, the coalition presented the People's Constitution. The following year, however, the colonial administration declared an Emergency and AMCJA-PUTERA was banned, with many of its leaders arrested.

PRM was launched in 1955 by Ahmad Boestamam, the former API leader. Dr Burhanuddin Helmy, who was in PAS, was in attendance. PRM later joined the Labour Party under the Socialist Front. PRM won two seats in the 1959 Election—Ahmad Boestaman in Setapak (from where my future Parliamentary constituency was carved out) and Karam Singh in Damansara. I would be acquainted with Keshminder, his son, in my first foray into grassroots KEADILAN politics. But with the end of local elections and the rise in religious consciousness, PRM became isolated and had no parliamentary presence from the 1960s onwards.

In 1965, the party officially adopted scientific socialism as its ideology and incorporated 'socialism' into its name. It continued to drift with little support from the masses. Former academician and an ISA detainee for six years in the 1970s, Dr Syed Husin Ali, took over in 1989 and removed the socialist references from the party. In the following year, it allied itself with the Semangat 46-led coalition. In 1998, it was an early supporter of *Reformasi* and became a part of BA.

While still unable to win seats, its long tradition in progressive politics and multi-racial leadership made it appealing to the founders of PKN to strengthen their fledgling party. The merger was not a straightforward process: there were Islamic activists in PKN who were suspicious of the socialist heritage of PRM. On the other hand, there were PRM members who did not trust the big tent structure of PKN that did not seem to be rooted in any progressive ideology. Eventually, the process was approved by the respective parties and on 3 August 2003, KEADILAN was launched.

I was also contacted by Dr Syed Husin, then the Deputy President of KEADILAN, when he became a visiting fellow at Cambridge in 2005. The first time we met, he treated me to dinner at Mawar, a Malaysian restaurant on Edgware Road, popular among students then. I also organized an event with a small group of students in the University of Surrey. We went to Surrey on train from Waterloo. Syed had assumed I had bought both of our tickets; I, on the other hand, had only bought mine and was too shy to tell him to buy the tickets. So, it was at the last minute—as we were about to walk to the platform—that I had to whisper to him that he did not have a ticket yet!

Blogging

In 2004, I bought my own domain *niknazmi.com* and started having a full-blown WordPress blog. Moving to Web 2.0, this meant that readers could comment on my articles without having to go through a guestbook like they had to do in my website designed with raw HTML previously.

Globally, blogging had started along with the advent of the Internet. But it was only in 2002 that the public started to take notice of blogs as they began breaking stories on their own, beating the mainstream media. In Malaysia, there was another reason: the stifling environment of the mainstream media. Various laws—from the colonial era Sedition Act and the ISA that was originally introduced to fight the communist insurgency—curtailed media freedom. Newspapers and magazines needed an annual licence due to the Printing Presses and Publications Act introduced in the mid-1980s.

Utusan was founded in 1939 by Yusof Ishak, the future President of Singapore, and Abdul Rahim Kajai as the voice of Malay nationalism. After the independence of Malaya, it became broadly supportive of UMNO but it looked critically into social issues. Said Zahari took over from Yusof Ishak as the editor-in-chief. Eventually, UMNO took over *Utusan* in 1961 and Said became active in left-wing politics in Singapore against the Alliance and People's Action Party (PAP). In 1963, Said was detained without trial in Operation Coldstore.[11] Said was held for sixteen years. UMNO maintained a substantial stake in *Utusan* until 2019.

Other than state-broadcaster *RTM*, the major terrestrial television channels were owned by Media Prima—which was linked to UMNO. Astro, that had a monopoly for satellite television services in Malaysia from 1996 to 2017, is majority-owned by Mahathir-confidant Ananda Krishnan. Media Prima also owns English and Malay newspapers—including my father's traditional newspaper of choice, *New Straits Times*. *The Star* is owned by Malaysian Chinese Association (MCA). It was common for changes in the country's leadership to lead to changes in editing

---

[11] This was a clandestine operation where 113 individuals were detained without trial in Singapore in 1963 in a move approved by the British, Singaporean, and Malayan authorities. (https://www.malaysiakini.com/news/337515)

rooms as well, as Malaysian premiers often want to be able to dictate to the press. As a result, especially since the 1980s, the government promoted so-called 'responsible', developmentalist journalism.

2004 Malaysian Election and Anwar's Freedom

In October 2003, after 22 years, Mahathir handed the Premiership over to Deputy PM Abdullah Ahmad Badawi. Mahathir had seen off one way or another three previous deputies, and it turned out that it was the calm, quiet son of a religious scholar that succeeded. Certainly, Abdullah was an outsider. In fact, after Anwar's abrupt sacking, it was assumed that the younger Najib Razak, would be appointed Deputy. Abdullah worked under my father in the Public Service Department. He left the civil service to run for office in 1978.

True to form, Mahathir's retirement was filled with drama. During the UMNO General Assembly in June 2002 he had focused on his failures to change what he saw as the 'weaknesses' of his people that he had diagnosed in *the Malay Dilemma*. In his winding up speech, he tearfully and abruptly declared at the end that he would resign from all party positions. It caught everyone by surprise, with key leaders tearfully shouting, surrounding and persuading Mahathir to stay on. Abdullah took the microphone and asked Mahathir to change his mind. Afterwards, Abdullah announced that the Supreme Council proposed an emergency resolution rejecting the resignation, which was refused by Mahathir. Eventually the shouts of 'Long live Mahathir' were heard in the hall. However, after the session was adjourned for an hour, Abdullah announced that the PM had retracted his resignation, overwhelmed by the party's support. It was reminiscent of dictators and authoritarian parties.

I was in a cinema with a friend, watching Tom Cruise in *Minority Report*, when the news of the resignation came in our phones. My knee-jerk reaction to my UMNO-supporting friend was that this was all a ruse, a tactic to gauge the support for him from the party grassroots and extend his time in power.

'The Old Man would not resign,' I said dismissively. I did not realize how many twists-and-turns the story of Mahathir's 'resignation' would take for another two decades!

When Mahathir passed the baton to Abdullah a year later, there was a sigh of relief. I was born a year into the era of Mahathir 1.0, and it was twenty-one years later that I would finally witness a new premier. Mahathir was a maverick; Abdullah was a diplomat. Mahathir was critical of the religious establishment that he argued contributed to the laziness of the Malays; Abdullah was the son of a respected religious scholar. Mahathir was seen as the progenitor of money politics, Abdullah was known as 'Mr Clean'. Immediately on becoming PM, he emphasized on fighting corruption and the concept of 'Islam Hadhari' or Civilizational Islam. In short, he was stealing the platform of PAS through Islam Hadhari and Anwar Ibrahim's by pushing for reforms.

In early 2004, Malaysia went to the polls. I was watching from afar in the UK, but I did volunteer to do a simple website for the party. Reading *Harakah, Berita Keadilan* and *Malaysiakini*, I thought that it would be another close election. There were predictions that in addition to the PAS-controlled Kelantan and Terengganu, Kedah might also fall. In addition, my uncle, Nik Mahmood Nik Hassan, was running for the Kota Bharu Parliamentary seat. In 1999, PKN had won the seat with Ramli Ibrahim. Another uncle, Nik Aziz Nik Hassan, unsuccessfully contested a state seat in Kelantan in 1999. In 2004, the original plan was to offer KEADILAN's new deputy president and veteran activist, Dr Syed Husin Ali, as the candidate from Kota Bharu. Syed Husin had contested twice previously in the Klang Valley, but did not succeed.

The other Nik Aziz, the Kelantan Chief Minister, publicly protested against this, saying that as the former leader of PRM, Syed Husin was a socialist, which in his eyes, was the 'little brother' to communism. Syed Husin had met Nik Aziz earlier and was informed that allowing him to contest would cost PAS a few seats in the state. And so, the idea was scrapped.

Nik Mahmood was a corporate figure and businessman who had joined PKN in 1999. He was roped in to replace Syed Husin Ali as the candidate in our hometown, Kota Bharu, against lawyer Zaid Ibrahim. I was regularly updated by my family about the election campaign.

Abdullah led BN to the biggest win in the country's history, winning 90 per cent of the parliamentary seats. The popular vote for his coalition was 63.9 per cent, but gerrymandering and malapportionment had amplified it to an almost total victory.[12] PAS lost twenty MPs and the state of Terengganu, leaving a rump of seven MPs. The Kelantan State Assembly was won by PAS by a slim three-seat majority. Firebrand PAS President Abdul Hadi Awang, who made the Islamic State as a cornerstone of his party's campaign, lost his seat. DAP made a gain of two seats and both party stalwarts Lim Kit Siang and Karpal Singh returned to the parliament.

KEADILAN was nearly wiped out, down from five parliamentary seats to a single seat. Party President Dr Wan Azizah Wan Ismail managed to hold on to Permatang Pauh—Anwar's seat since 1982—with a razor-thin majority of 590, after five recounts. Rumours had spread that she had lost. I was shocked and dazed as I followed it from London.

I wrote despondently on my blog that day:

'As the results churn out, it signalled a return to 1986—when DAP won twenty parliamentary seats, and PAS won one.

Could this be it?

Wait for the next few days, and we'll see the reactions and follow up on the Election Commission's (EC) messy handling and BN's improprieties.

Will it get anywhere? I doubt so.

---

[12] KEADILAN (2006), *Sham Democracy: A Report on Malaysian Elections* https://www.bersih.org/wp-content/uploads/2007/10/sham-democracy.pdf, Kuala Lumpur: KEADILAN, Accessed 7 August 2021.

But the struggle for change and a better Malaysia carries on.
It must carry on, no matter how difficult it may be.'[13]

Malaysian voters rewarded Abdullah's style. It was like having a domineering, hyperactive, and strict headmaster for as long as you can remember, and suddenly finding him replaced by someone less confrontational and focusing on building consensus, who says the right things. After all, it seemed that the opposition was fracturing and the *Reformasi* movement was losing momentum. Some also saw it as a repudiation of Mahathir.

The next few months were a time for reflection for the party faithful. Some had been arrested and detained, some had lost their jobs. A lot of money was poured into elections and the results were abysmal. Was there a future for KEADILAN?

Many compared KEADILAN to Semangat 46. Both parties were formed by senior UMNO leaders who fought against Mahathir. Both cooperated with the major opposition parties to challenge BN. Both failed to make much headway. Twice. The conclusion was that KEADILAN would soon close shop as Semangat 46 had done. Tengku Razaleigh Hamzah dissolved Semangat 46, and most of the members, including the founder, re-joined UMNO.

But unlike Semangat 46, KEADILAN is a multi-racial party. Our non-Malay members could not join UMNO. Neither would many of the Malay members, especially those from PRM, who came from a different political tradition than UMNO. Syed Husin Ali said that during PRM's cooperation with Semangat 46, the latter never saw itself in opposition. They would never challenge the police—unlike Anwar or KEADILAN.[14]

---

[13] Nik Nazmi Nik Ahmad, '1986 all over again', niknazmi.com, 21 March 2004, archived at https://web.archive.org/web/20040625165837/http://www.niknazmi.com/archives/000157.html#000157, Accessed 13 July 2021.

[14] Lim Hong Siang, 'Anwar berbeza dari Razaleigh' Merdeka Review, 21 September 2010, archived at https://web.archive.org/web/20100925110348/http://www.merdekareview.com/bm/news.php?n=11119, Accessed 5 July 2021.

During his imprisonment, much of Anwar's communication to the party leadership was in the form of letters in his hard-to-discern handwriting. But Anwar also entertained many supporters, taking the opportunity to read and reply to letters as a form of respite, alongside reading the Quran and Shakespeare! I wrote a letter to him via Nurul Izzah, trying to get a good word from him on my behalf to his friend Chris Patten, the former chairman of the Conservative Party, the last British Governor of Hong Kong, and the then newly minted Chancellor of Oxford University. His reply:

Saudara Nik Nazmi,
Thank you for the lucid letter.

I can't commend you enough for your endeavours in support of the *Reformasi* cause and your initiative—the excellent Keadilan website ('magnificent' according to Nurul Izzah!).
I would be happy to put in a good word to my friend Chris Patten, for you to pursue your Masters—BCL (Bachelor of Civil Law) at Oxford. Your performance of the highest distinction would naturally facilitate the acceptance. You'll have to update me as to the outcome of your undergraduate performance and advise me accordingly as to the timing of the recommendation letter to CP.
The present scenario is perplexing. It is deplorable enough that a man has been vilified and imprisoned from trumped up charges, and yet he has to suffer the ignominy of having to negotiate for his freedom! That seems to be the 'official rumour' circulated by the establishment apparatchiks.
Notwithstanding the grave challenges ahead, I remain optimistic that democracy and justice will prevail; and hoping to meet you soon.

Anwar Ibrahim.

KEADILAN then received a tremendous a shot in the arm: Anwar Ibrahim's sodomy conviction was quashed by the Federal Court on 2 September 2004. After five years in prison, he was released. I was back in Malaysia for my summer holidays and managed to attend the 'ceramah' at his Bukit Damansara home that night. I did meet one of the young professionals who were with me and Nurul Izzah, and campaigned together in the Indera Kayangan by-election. He told me that he returned to UMNO because Abdullah was a breath of fresh air. But for someone who believed in KEADILAN's yet-to-be-realized potential of a multi-racial party, that was not an option for me. The following day, Nurul Izzah invited me to sneak in and meet Anwar in person for the first time. He thanked me for my contribution to the cause but seemed to be in pain from his back injury.

Later, Anwar spent some time in the UK as a visiting fellow at St Anthony's Oxford as well as the US in the School of Advanced International Studies in Johns Hopkins University. I managed to organize a talk for him at SOAS London.

As I was already under observation by my sponsors, I decided to let Wan Mohd Firdaus moderate the session, while I mixed with the audience. Born to a Kelantanese family, Firdaus was a law student at Nottingham University and was active in UKEC and FOSIS. The event was titled 'Will Britain Betray Human Rights' and officially organised by SOAS Islamic Society, Federation of Students Islamic Societies (FOSIS), and Amnesty International.

British Politics

I also dabbled in British politics. Rafizi brought me to my first rally, protesting the invasion of Iraq.

Massive demonstrations took place around the world. In September 2002, 150,000 people assembled in London protesting the war. I attended several demonstrations, but the one I remember most was the one on 15 February 2003 where one million people gathered at Hyde Park to listen to Reverend Jesse Jackson and London Mayor Ken Livingstone. Similar demonstrations took place in 800 cities across the world on that day, and *the Guinness Book of Records* considered it the largest protest in human history. I had a Malaysian friend from Southampton who came down and wanted to have a tour of London—so I managed to persuade him that the best way to do that was to join the rally!

The protests were coordinated by the Stop the War coalition consisting of those on the left of the Labour Party, including former Cabinet minister Tony Benn, rebel and future leader Jeremy Corbyn, as well as figures from the Socialist Workers Party. The coalition worked with the Campaign for Nuclear Disarmament and the Muslim Association of Britain.

'But this march against war on Iraq means much more. It is the coming of age of a younger, more assertive and politically aware generation of Muslims,' wrote Ziauddin Sardar, the British-Pakistani author, in *The Guardian*, the day after the demonstration.

Just as *Reformasi* had provided a common platform for Malaysians of all faiths with a common desire for justice and a faith in reform, the invasion of Iraq brought together a cross-section of British society who were questioning the merits of the Iraq invasion. Thus, rather than being pigeonholed as only upholding Muslim causes, the community understood the need to put their issues in the broader context of British politics. Living separated life from the British community no longer made sense, as doing so meant being unable to voice issues that were close to Muslims— Iraq, Palestine, and so much more. Neither does doing this require Muslims to adopt the violent solutions promoted by Al-Qaeda and their absolutist supporters. The separation between Muslim civil society and mainstream British politics that took place since the controversy of Salman Rushdie's *Satanic Verses* came to an end.

The array of talks that we could attend on the campus was endless. I had the opportunity to attend a lecture by Tony Benn, who, by then, was like a godfather to the Labour left. He was a politician with a conscience, driven by conviction, and, at the same time, a powerful speaker.

In spite of the war in Iraq, I decided to join the Labour Students at King's. As mentioned, I was fascinated by how Blair managed to make Labour a winning party after years in the wilderness. In 2003, I received a call from the chairperson and she persuaded me to take up the position of treasurer. Later, I realized there were only two people who signed up. Considering how conservative King's historically was, this was no surprise. Eventually, the Student Union, which was controlled by Conservative Future, decided to deregister that year's Labour Students due to lack of members.

Nevertheless, I did join a few activities with Labour Students from across London. Unlike the intense protocol attached to Malaysian politicians, we met Labour dignitaries casually. I met Frank Dobson, who was Blair's first Health Secretary from 1997–1999 and then the official Labour London mayoral candidate in 2000. I also had the opportunity of meeting one person from Tony Blair's inner circle, Peter Mandelson, who was one of the original personalities to be described as 'spin doctor'. For many, he was referred to as 'the Prince of Darkness'. He would eventually become the First Secretary of State in Blair's successor Gordon Brown's cabinet. I managed to meet him for a second time when I attended the 2019 Doha Conference.

With other Muslim students, I was active in FOSIS. Fellow Malaysian Wan Mohd Firdaus brought me in. Established in 1963 (with active contribution from Malaysian students), FOSIS was formed to bring together students' Islamic societies from campuses across the UK under one umbrella. On one hand, we were advocating for access to prayer rooms and halal food on campus for Muslim students; but we were also concerned about how some were making the National Union of Students (NUS) a platform to bring in Israeli Zionist leaders. Muslim students were also concerned with what was happening in Iraq and allied with other student groups against the war.

I attended the FOSIS conference and even the NUS conference in 2004 as FOSIS began organizing candidates to run in universities across the UK to represent the universities at the NUS conference. I volunteered at the FOSIS booth in the 2004 NUS conference in Blackpool. As the conference ended and I searched for a bus or train to go back to London, Firdaus told me I could join the rest of the FOSIS team as a group of them would go back to London in a van.

I decided to take the offer and then realized that there were six of us, and it was a cargo van that could legally carry only three passengers. I was pleased when it was decided that I should sit in front with the driver and one more passenger. However, after dropping one of the passengers at the back in Manchester, it was decided that it was my turn to sit in the back. It was then that I appreciated the comforts we take for granted as passengers. I was also worried if we were caught by the British authorities and they found a cargo van carrying Muslim youths in the back (and unlike me, the rest of them had ample beards!). Fortunately, the journey back to London was uneventful.

The following year, I decided to run to be one of the delegates from King's to the NUS conference. I printed simple flyers on my computer and then distributed them in my lectures and mobilized my law juniors as well as my housemates who were studying medicine to distribute them. My poster spoke about how the NUS was more than just the discounts that you get with your student card. I spoke about the need for the Union to understand diverse student perspectives. As one would expect, turnout for voting for the NUS delegates was even lower than that for the Student Union, but I ended up as one of the delegates.

This time, I could travel comfortably by rail and sleep at decent hotels as I was an official delegate. FOSIS was just one of the groups that were active in NUS politics. Other than the student wings of the respective mainstream parties, various left-wing groups were active as well as a group that focused solely on fighting against tuition fees that were introduced by Blair and the Union of Jewish Students.

I made many friends from FOSIS, including two future journalists, BBC and then Al Jazeera reporter Hasan Patel and Al Jazeera producer Jamal el Shayyal.

In 2004, I also took part in a press conference competition held by the law firm Norton Rose. I had to take the role of 'Comical Ali' or Muhammad Saeed al-Sahhaf, the Media and Foreign Minister of Iraq during the invasion. His colourful personality and truth-defying pronouncements earned him somewhat of a cult following in the West. So, I had to put on a beret and was grilled by other students who posed as 'journalists'. I ended up as a runner-up in the competition.

My articles also attracted the BBC World Service to call me for comments—asking for my opinions on various developments in Malaysia.

At the same time, I was introduced to the centre-left newspapers *The Guardian* and *The Observer*. Reading *The Guardian* has become a daily habit of mine since then. On the weekends, I would gather my coins to buy the thick *Observer*, packaged along with magazines, DVDs, and other freebies. I would spend hours going through the weekend newspaper. I, of course, enjoyed the major bookshop chains there—WH Smith and Waterstones. But I also loved exploring rare, antique, and second-hand bookshops in Charing Cross, which was very near to King's.

2005 London Bombings

I also worked part time at a call centre for an automotive aftermarket intelligence company. When I was working there, we were hired to do market research for a lubricant company and we would cold-call a list of workshops from across the UK. I got my first lesson in trying to get a response from disinterested parties. To make matters worse, some of the car mechanics had thick accents and found it difficult to understand what I was trying to say.

My last day working there was 7 July 2005. I would graduate in that same month. The day before, it was announced that London had successfully won its bid to host the 2012 Olympics. As I was taking the Central Line from Marble Arch, where I was temporarily staying until my graduation, it grounded to a halt. The announcer did not mention the cause of the technical difficulty—which we experience from time to time on the centuries-old transit system. As I went up to ground level, I told myself that the city had much to do before the Olympics.

I later found out that three London underground trains and one double-decker bus were bombed that day. One of the underground trains was less than a kilometre away from where I was. I thought to myself that I could easily have been one of the 52 victims. Three of the bombers were children of Pakistani immigrants and one was a Jamaican convert to Islam. When 11 September 2001 took place in New York, I was in Malaysia and it felt far away. Now, I was near the site of the attack.

Where and when tactics such as suicide bombing could be applicable became a frequent, contentious topic during my time in the UK and after. I was passionate for the liberation of Palestine and against Western intervention in the Middle East. I had attended a series of anti-war rallies in London. My views are reflected by the well-known journalist Robert Fisk who wrote extensively on the region.

'We might be able to escape history. We can draw lines in our lives. The years of 1918 and 1945 created our new lives in the West. We could start again. We think we can recommend the same to the peoples of the Middle East. But we can't. History—a history of injustice—cloaks them too deeply.'[15]

---

[15] Fisk, Robert, *The Great War for Civilization: The Conquest of the Middle East*, London: Harper Perennial, 2006, p. 1285.

Yet, I also could not agree with those who resorted to attacks on civilians. I had personally got to know Muhammad Afifi al-Akiti when he started his studies in Oxford. He had studied in traditional madrasahs in Indonesia and Morocco. Today, he is a fellow at the Oxford Centre for Islamic Studies and a lecturer at the School of Theology, University of Oxford, as well as holding a position in the Perak Palace, similar to Mat Saman Kati. I would take the Oxford Tube, a bus service between London and Oxford, to have deep conversations with him. He authored a fatwa against suicide bombing after the 7 July 2005 bombings in London and argued clearly that Islam had always been against attacks on civilians.

I also remember the interactions we had at FOSIS with Hizb-ut-Tahrir, a global Islamist movement calling for a revival of the Islamic caliphate and implementation of the Shariah. They reject democracy, as in their eyes it gives sovereignty to the people, instead of God. Even Islamist parties participating in democracy are deemed as unbelievers. Thus, FOSIS, which was pushing for more Muslims to be active in NUS politics, was included in their blacklist. But when the NUS was pushing to ban Hizb-ut-Tahrir in 2004, they sought FOSIS to protect their existence on campuses.

Internships

Internships were still something new at that time and was not as widespread as they are today. But when in 2003 Wan Mohd Firdaus and I were able to obtain places in the corporate law firm Wong and Partners after our first year, we were excited. It is a member firm for Baker McKenzie International. The pay was RM800 a month, which was a lot for interns back then. That was about the same amount as what a law graduate earned during his or her pupillage back then. The office was in Menara Maxis KLCC at that time.

But that was only for a month. Afterwards, I joined Chooi and Co. in Jalan Sultan Ismail to work for Edmund Bon. He was making his name in human rights and constitutional law cases. After a month doing corporate law, this felt something closer to my interests. Primarily, I would assist Bon in writing articles, and he made it a point to put my name in in the pieces we submitted. I remember that there were a few pupils who assumed that as an intern, I would be at the very bottom of the food chain and wanted to pass some grunt work to me. The moment Bon found out about it, he told them that only he alone could assign me work! I also met Syed Ibrahim Syed Noh, a former JIM leader who was then the Chair of the Abolish ISA Movement, when Bon was handling one case involving an ISA detainee. Syed Ibrahim would be a future KEADILAN MP for Ledang in Johor.

In the following year, I was attached with the Asia-Europe Institute in UM as a temporary research assistant. Dr Patricia Martinez was a fellow there and she had quoted me in one of her papers. Since then, we were in contact with each other and when she said she had the budget for a decent allowance, I took the opportunity. The job involved me going to the Institute for Islamic Understanding and the UM Law library to go through various archives.

Studies

As can be discerned from my internships, I was losing interest in law. That is why this section comes last in this chapter! During my first year, all of us had to take the same subjects at King's: contract, criminal, and European and public law. The first two subjects seemed uninteresting and dull. European law was slightly more interesting, but it was quite complex. I did like public law, but admittedly did not put enough effort into it. I scraped through my first year, and passed contract with very little to spare. Thanks to the system in many traditional British universities, the first-year results did not count. I just had to pass it!

During my second year, I decided to take the remaining three foundation subjects so that I could undertake my Bar training in England (just in case): trusts, tort, and property law. That left me with one more subject to choose and I took human rights law. While I found human rights law interesting, again, my second-year results were abysmal.

I decided to buck up for my final year. I took an unusual combination of subjects, with a big part of it being assessed through dissertations. This meant that rather than being busy during the final exams, the work would be spread out throughout the academic year. My personal tutor, Jane Henderson, asked me whether I could cope with this. I assured her that I enjoyed writing.

Jurisprudence was compulsory, but dreaded by many as it was more philosophical and focused on legal theory. I found it interesting but challenging at the beginning. Initially, I struggled trying to understand John Rawls' *Theory of Justice*, in particular the part on 'the veil of ignorance' and 'the original position'. There was a feeling of satisfaction when I managed to make sense of it. There was a dissertation component to jurisprudence and I argued a middle path between the two legal positivists H.L.A. Hart and Hans Kelsen in analyzing Malaya's legal system after independence. As King's collection on Malaysia was limited, I used my University of London privileges to access the LSE and SOAS libraries. In SOAS, I found many interesting works on Malaysia, including letters to the Thai Palace, written by my ancestor Tok Semian as the Kelantan Palace scribe.

In history of English law, I was entirely assessed through two 8,500-word dissertations. Henderson was the tutor for this subject, and I decided on two topics: Winston Churchill's contribution as a Liberal Party cabinet member towards improving workers' rights through the Board of Trade, and another on the Bryce Report proposal on the House of Lords Reform. To undertake my research on Churchill, I spent some time at the Churchill Archives Centre in Cambridge and stayed with my KYUEM friend Loh Siang Ling.

I took another subject taught by Henderson: Soviet and post-Soviet legal systems. I enjoyed studying the legal system of a communist state with elements of civil law. It was entirely different from the English common law that we studied in England and which had shaped the legal systems in the Commonwealth, including Malaysia.

The last subject I took, which was partly assessed through final examinations as well as a 12,000-word dissertation, was advanced constitutional law. It was taught by Professor Robert Blackburn, who later would be Special Counsel to the House of Commons Political and Constitutional Reform Committee from 2010–2015. My dissertation was more on politics than law—looking at the shift in opinion in the Scottish and Welsh devolution from 1979 to 1997.

I thoroughly enjoyed academic research and writing, which made me briefly entertain the prospect of staying on to do my Masters (as I had mentioned to Anwar in my letter to him).

I had taken the right decision academically. I scored well in my final year—getting firsts for advanced constitutional law and Soviet and post-Soviet legal systems and second-class uppers for the other two subjects. I ended up with a second-class upper degree for my graduation, and my parents—my father in particular—was pleased. Someone remarked that had I worked just as hard from my second year, I could have graduated with a first class. But I was happy as, in spite of all my 'extra-curricular activities', I managed to get a good result. Not that it matters much now anyway.

My parents and Najihah, my third sister, came over for my graduation. As mentioned earlier, my father did not travel much, but he decided to be there for my graduation ceremony. We decided to make a trip out to Oxford and Bicester. Probably a legacy of colonization, Britain, to this day, features highly as a destination for Malaysians, and as many holidaymakers make shopping an important part of their itinerary, the outlet shopping in Bicester features high on the list of those who want to get lower prices on high street brands. For the shopping trip to Bicester, I decided to rent a car and drive for the only time in London.

Part Two

1. Plunging into Politics

First Marriage

Immediately upon my return to Malaysia in 2005, I got married. My first wife, Imaan Abdul Rahim, was one year my junior at KYUEM. I only got close to her in my first year in the UK, via the instant messaging app MSN Messenger. Originally from Penang, her father was a university lecturer and her mother was a former headmistress. Theirs was a high-achieving family. The children all obtained stellar results in the SPM. Her siblings played squash for Penang at the junior level; she on the other hand was proficient in piano and the violin. After her A-Levels, she read medicine at the University of Newcastle.

Both of us enjoyed reading and music, although I was more of a listener. We started going out during my first summer holidays back in Malaysia, when she was preparing to go off to the UK. I took the overnight train to Butterworth. Only after shivering in the second-class carriage did I realize how cold the train would get. I took the old ferry to the island and she fetched me to go sightseeing. When she was in Kuala Lumpur, I brought her to a talk I gave with MCKK old boy and old-time rebel Hishamuddin Rais in Bangsar. I guess she must have really trusted me because the venue looked very dodgy for a date!

Back in the UK, I visited her regularly in Newcastle, which is almost 400 kilometres away from London. At that time, I did not have a student railway card and took the seven-hour bus ride every time when I wanted to see her. In my third year, I finally got a railway card and could take the train instead.

A year after going out, we decided to get married. There was no grand or romantic gesture. I was on the phone with Imaan. She had just started her second year of medical school and I was in my third and final year of law school. She hesitated at first but soon was convinced of the idea. We then called our parents, who took some convincing, but eventually agreed on a wedding when I graduated and before she went back for her third year.

The solemnization ceremony and bride's reception were held in Penang. My reception was held in Kuala Lumpur. My parents invited the former Energy, Telecommunications and Post Minister—my father's old boss—Leo Moggie and his wife as the guest of honour. He had been the guest of honour at all of my siblings' weddings. I also tried very hard to get Anwar Ibrahim and Dr Wan Azizah Wan Ismail to attend. Unfortunately, Anwar had another event that same night, but Dr Wan Azizah did attend.

PNB

I also started working at PNB immediately after my graduation. They had sponsored me to do my A-Levels and law degree in London. The scholarship required me to serve the company for eight years.

PNB was created as part of the NEP to increase Bumiputera corporate equity in 1978. Today, it is one of Malaysia's biggest fund management companies. PNB manages certain unit trusts specifically for the Bumiputera community, while the rest are open to all Malaysians.

All the scholars, in addition to the new executive hires, were put into Management Trainee Program. In the first few months, we had to attend classes on finance and investment as we graduated from different disciplines. We were then rotated in different departments. I enjoyed the investment operations and research departments. The former was in high demand as it was the core department in PNB. During my time at investment operations, we were asked to choose a publicly listed company and do a presentation in front of our bosses. We decided to do AirAsia and got their red caps to wear in our pitch.

Eventually, I was assigned to the legal department. It was not surprising, as I was the only one with a law degree in the batch. But as mentioned earlier, I had no interest in the subject, in particular, the more practical aspects of law—as opposed to constitutional law and jurisprudence. PNB retained corporate solicitors and the department would liaise between other departments and our solicitors. I would be tasked to draft letters.

The staff was predominantly Malay. Our gross starting salary was RM1,800 a month—which after retirement and social insurance deductions left us with a little more than RM1,500. Many of our friends were earning more than that. Nevertheless, for those who were from middle-class Klang Valley families, it was still okay. We could still afford to eat out regularly. I stayed with my parents and either drove my father's reliable maroon Proton Wira, or took the LRT from Taman Paramount to Ampang Park. Most of my meals were taken at home. But I had a friend coming from a humble family who stayed with his sister. His sister was a clerk and he had to contribute some money for rent and utilities. He also sent money back to his parents and, sometimes, had to help out his family as someone who just came back from overseas. It was tough for him by the middle of the month.

Sometime in 2006, I got into trouble with my PNB superiors over an article I wrote, criticizing the government and UM's administration's response following a dramatic fall of the latter in the Times Higher Education Supplement world's top 200 university rankings. I started contributing opinion pieces for the mainstream newspaper *The Sun*. *The Education in Malaysia* blog, run by future DAP MPs Ong Kian Ming and Tony Pua, cited the part of my article where I wrote: '[t]he handling of the universities in dealing with this drop in rankings especially UM's administration can at best be described as confused, if not downright idiotic.'[16]

That phrase caught the attention of my bosses who called me up. They were quite polite—telling me it was okay to criticize, but certain lines must be drawn—such as calling the university administrators idiotic. By then, I had realized that both sides were wary—they were tired of managing me every time I got into trouble with the authorities, while I felt constrained at not being able to speak up like I wanted.

A Party Member at Last

I had long planned to be formally active in KEADILAN, and frankly, perhaps even become a candidate in some distant future—but, then, I was thinking of this happening after serving my bond with PNB. Today, I cannot pinpoint the exact moment when I actually decided to go for public office, maybe not at the point I started helping the party in 2001, but at some point before graduating in 2005, I had made up my mind.

What I knew by then was that I could not remain an armchair critic. I knew the status quo—where ordinary Malaysians of all races were left behind while the elites play up racial sentiments to remain relevant—was untenable, and that an alternative was needed. Merely writing or helping out the party leaders was not satisfactory enough, I wanted to roll up my sleeves and go to the trenches.

Upon my graduation, I joined the party as a member of the Kelana Jaya division. In 2008, the voters in the constituency

---

[16] Nik Nazmi Nik Ahmad, 'Stopping the (blush) slide in varsity rankings', *The Sun*, 16 November 2005, archived at https://web.archive.org/web/20060509211823/http://www.niknazmi.com/articles/index.php/archives/64, Accessed 13 July 2021.

were 42 per cent Malay, 38 per cent Chinese, and 19 per cent Indian. It had an MCA MP. It consisted of two state seats—the Malay-majority Seri Setia and the Chinese-majority Subang Jaya.

My parents' house was in the Taman Medan state constituency in the Petaling Jaya Selatan parliamentary division. While Taman Medan is a Malay-majority seat, Petaling Jaya Selatan had 45 per cent Chinese voters, compared to 40 per cent Malay, in 2008. But my uncle, Nik Mahmood was heading the party's Kelantan state chapter and invited me to be active there. At that time, it seemed that it was more likely for the party to win seats in Kelantan than in Selangor, but I declined. To travel frequently to Kelantan on my small salary was a big burden; additionally, I had grown up in the Klang Valley and spoke Kelantanese with an accent.

Kelana Jaya's division chief at the time was Malaysian Trades Union Congress president Syed Shahir Syed Mohamud. Syed Shahir was active in PRM, contesting a state seat for the party in his home state of Pahang in the 1970s and then for KEADILAN in Kelana Jaya in the 2004 General Election. Immediately on joining the party, the Kelana Jaya Youth leader Halimey Abu Bakar appointed me as the secretary of the youth wing, but before long, I was appointed as vice leader of the youth wing.

Relatively, Kelana Jaya was one of the more active and better organized divisions of the party. Among the first events we had was a gathering of party members in Syed Bistro in SS19, Subang Jaya. By then, the party no longer had an office or service centre to operate from, so meetings were often held in various mamak restaurants. Our agendas and minutes often had curry and tea-stains on them.

The division had a strong presence of PRM veterans. The children of Hamid Tuah—a land activist from the 1960s and 1970s—Ahmad Bungsu and Siti Nor were there. The son of PRM MP Karam Singh, Keshminder Singh was also in the committee. Faisal Mustaffa, who was in PRM Youth, was the division secretary and we would often carpool together as his family home was near mine. The 1999 PKN candidate for Subang constituency—which overlapped with the then Kelana Jaya boundaries—Irene Fernandez was also a member. Another group consisting of former UMNO grassroots activists such as Halimey were also active in the division. Many of the UMNO grassroots were either factory workers from the National Panasonic factory in Sungai Way or working with Malaysian Airlines at the Subang Airport. Then, there were a group of ordinary Malaysians, like future pastor Yee Siew Meng, who only became politicized due to *Reformasi*.

But party organization was still barebones compared to BN or even PAS. There was a revival in party morale with Anwar's release, but the poor results in the party's first two elections had sapped a lot of energy from leaders, activists, and donors. I remember volunteering for the first few events when we went to the farmers' market or 'pasar tani' in Kelana Jaya, distributing leaflets and selling the party newspaper. We had three or four members doing work on the ground. I contributed some money to put up banners with holiday greetings, and a few of us would hang them up in various locations.

It was a humbling lesson that grassroot politics matters. I had been involved in drafting speeches for party leaders, organizing events, and writing articles for a few years; but here, I was exposed to the more mundane side of activism. And a party can only do so much at the national level if our grassroots machinery was lacking.

There was a leadership training camp for KEADILAN Youth in January 2006. It was held in a dilapidated camp in Janda Baik in Pahang, where we slept in bunks. Party Secretary General and MCKK old boy Salehuddin Hashim, central committee member Johari Abdul, and youth leader Ezam Mohd Nor were among those who spoke at the training program. Four of us from KEADILAN Kelana Jaya carpooled to attend the event. As the party did not have much resources, we were supposed to pay for the event. However, many of our members did not have much of a budget either, so we paid a small amount in monetary form and were then expected to contribute specific raw food items that would be cooked for our meals: rice, instant noodles, and eggs, amongst others.

The Kelana Jaya KEADILAN Youth also had a healthier bank account compared to the division proper—the reason being that we had regular bowling tournaments either in USJ Summit (cheaper) or Sunway Pyramid (nicer venue but more expensive) where we collected a fee from participating teams. We would also distribute old copies of *Suara Keadilan* and 'ceramah' video CDs, which was on the tail-end of its popularity. Invariably, I would always end up last. I played just to make up the numbers.

Full-time Politics

I grew closer to Azmin Ali at this time. He was also heading the party's central election committee. He treated me to dinner at Alexis in Bangsar Shopping Centre, and tasked me to write a report exposing electoral abuses in Malaysia. He provided various pieces of evidence and materials which I then used for the write-up. It was released in September 2006 as *Sham Democracy: A Report on Malaysian Elections*.[17]

In early 2006, I was invited to attend the party's central leadership committee's meeting held at Anwar Ibrahim's Damansara residence. I was quite nervous to be invited to such a high-level meeting. Anwar asked me, a twenty-four-year-old guest at the meeting, for my ideas to face Abdullah Ahmad Badawi's UMNO. I said we need to focus on our strength, 'change', but also 'leadership', as many Malaysians had begun to perceive Abdullah's leadership as weak.

After the meeting, Azmin pulled me aside. He said Anwar wanted me to join his team. I replied that of course I was interested

---

[17] KEADILAN (2006) *Sham Democracy: A Report on Malaysian Elections* https://www.bersih.org/wp-content/uploads/2007/10/sham-democracy.pdf. Kuala Lumpur: KEADILAN. Accessed 7 August 2021.

in the offer—the problems lay in the fact that I was bonded to PNB for eight years. Azmin asked me how much would it be cost me to break my bond. I replied that it was almost half-a-million ringgit. The conversation ended after that.

In April 2006, I was dozing off when I received a call from Nurul Izzah Anwar. She was in the US. She said, 'Boss wants to talk to you.'

I tried to sound awake as Anwar asked how my family and I were. After the pleasantries, he went straight to the point.

'I want you to be in charge of my office. We will pay you a bit more than what you are earning now, and you can negotiate with PNB on the repayment. I will e-mail you the details.'

Soon, I received the promised e-mail from Anwar. The details were very brief. I discussed the matter with my wife, and then with my parents. They knew, from the way I spoke about it, that I had pretty much made up my mind. Ultimately, I knew I wanted to be in KEADILAN, and the opportunity of working for the party's founder as well as one of the most charismatic Malaysian politicians in history was too valuable to be wasted. Things might have been different if I were in a job that excited me, or that paid a better salary. Those are the 'what ifs' that we can ask so often because these are all in the past.

My mother was previously against the family being involved in politics, but *Reformasi* had changed her. She would take the lead in political conversations in her own circles. One thing that still concerned my family was how I would settle my bond with PNB.

When Anwar was back in Kuala Lumpur, I saw him in Damansara to finalize the terms. Initially, I planned to give a month's notice to PNB, but then, as Anwar wanted me to start as soon as possible, I decided to give a twenty-four hours' notice. In my notice, I clearly stated that I would settle any outstanding amount owed to PNB. I remember many of my colleagues (most of whom were not aware that I was planning my resignation for some time) being surprised.

Normally, my head of department, Zaida Khalida Shaari, would bring the entire department out for farewell lunches when an employee left, but she decided to have lunch with me alone at the Japanese restaurant in what was then the Nikko Hotel. She said that she had heard a lot about my activism and writing as an undergraduate, but she did not see that talent during my time at the legal department. She was curious about why I wanted to leave. I did not share much, other than saying that I had no interest in law.

I felt lost when I first started working for Anwar. At that time, it was basically just me, and we operated out of the study of his Bukit Damansara house. I came from a huge, established GLIC. True, I was pretty much at the bottom of the food-chain, but everything was provided for. In my new job—my official title was Private Secretary to Anwar—I was working on my own, coordinating with a jet-setting boss who was not the most organized of individuals himself! I had to figure out everything from the macro to the micro—to the point of taking care of my stationery! The good thing was that it was no routine nine-to-five job like the one I had at PNB.

As mentioned, Azmin was organized to the point of being obsessive. He tried to guide me as his successor (the so-called 'holder of the Red Diary' as during Azmin's time as Anwar's Private Secretary, they used the red *Economist* diary to schedule the latter's appointments; I used a plain black one as well as a computerized document), but he realized that I did not have the same degree of organization or detail that he had. There was one time when I made the mistake of double-booking Anwar: an event with the then Turkish PM Recep Tayyip Erdogan in Istanbul and a 'ceramah' with PAS in Kedah on the same day! Just as he got into his car, Anwar called me up, asked how my family was doing and then gave me the scolding of a lifetime!

Nurul Izzah also told me that Anwar complained that I was too reserved and quiet when I was with him. It always takes me time to warm up to people and I guess I felt intimidated by the party leadership. Even in Kelana Jaya, I preferred focusing on the Youth wing as I felt we were more focused on holding events, whereas at the Division level, there were too many petty arguments, but little in the way of action.

Questioning the NEP

I had started questioning the NEP when I began writing back in 2001. I called for non-racial affirmative action to replace the policy. I remember having passionate debates with my father, who had witnessed how bad things were for the Malays in his generation and was at the forefront of the policy's implementation. I was, on the other hand, a beneficiary of the NEP.

In August 2005, Anwar Ibrahim began publicly criticizing the NEP. When he sounded out key party leaders as well his friends, some were unsupportive. Even among those who believed in the merits of the criticisms (including the non-Malays), there were those who were wary about how much it would upset the Bumiputeras, in particular the Malays, who were repeatedly told that not only had this policy allowed them to succeed, but that it was part of the constitution and, thus, should not be questioned.

Nik Mahmood Nik Hassan asked me for some help to draft a motion for this, calling for the formulation of an alternative to the NEP, to be brought to the 2005 party congress. We had a discussion with Abdul Rahman Othman, the party treasurer, at his home in Subang Jaya. I could sense his unease that the party would take that line. Eventually, we proceeded to work on the motion without him. In 2007, he left the party.

The motion was passed by the party congress—calling for a new deal that would shift away from race-based affirmative action. What was significant was that this emerged from a Malay-majority party.

In 2006, the Malaysian Economic Agenda was launched. By that time, I was already working full time with Anwar. The agenda was centred on a commitment to justice, the core of KEADILAN. It was launched as a seven-page document written by Anwar:

'On the positive side, the NEP has produced upward social mobility for certain sub-sectors of the majority Bumiputeras. Thanks to the preservation of special Malay rights, such as in the exclusive granting of foreign tertiary scholarships throughout the seventies, eighties and early and mid-nineties to Bumiputeras that fulfilled minimum academic requirements, the NEP has been instrumental in creating a sub-class of Bumiputera professionals and engineering an urban Bumiputera middle-class . . .

'Unfortunately, such upward mobility has not disseminated equally throughout the rank-and-file of ordinary Bumiputeras. The economic cake may have grown, but the lion's share has been cornered by the ruling elite . . .

'Indeed, as of 2005, Malaysia lived down to its empty slogan of 'Malaysia Boleh' by setting yet another record, this time for having the worst income disparity gaps in Southeast Asia, behind even Indonesia and Thailand, as measured by its Gini coefficient of 0.47. According to the World Bank, individual inequality in Malaysia as measured by the Gini coefficient is the second worst in all of the Asian countries for which data is available. Only Papua New Guinea ranks worse . . .

'Also important, if we are to move on, is to stop resting on our laurels and be brave enough to acknowledge how we lag compared to our true rivals. Malaysia's league of competitors should be Singapore, Taiwan and South Korea, which share a similar long history of development . . .

'Aid, especially better educational aid that is intellectual, entrepreneurial and vocational, needs to be given out to the poor and underprivileged regardless of race and religion, whether to the Tamil labourer on the plantation, the small-town Chinese shopkeeper or the Malay farmer, all of whom probably desire a better, and easier life for their offspring.'[18]

This had a major impact in shifting non-Malay support towards Anwar and KEADILAN. While criticism of the NEP was not new, it was largely led, predictably, by non-Malays. But this was a Malay leader trying to change the narrative, including, with Malay audiences. While he cited Gini coefficients and investment data in forums in the city, in PAS '*ceramahs*' in the kampungs, Anwar would talk about the injustice of a Chinese girl from the kampung with excellent SPM results being denied a place in the university, while the children of the Malay elite got into places despite having mediocre marks.

The Mahathir-Badawi Crisis

After stepping down as premier, Mahathir declined to remain in the cabinet in the same way his sparring partner Lee Kuan Yew did in Singapore. He promised to completely leave politics after twenty-two years at the top. From the beginning, however, tensions emerged as Mahathir tried to push Abdullah to announce Najib Razak as his Deputy. Eventually, Abdullah did, but that was just the beginning. The tensions continued to simmer. Mahathir's knack of picking fights with Malaysian premiers continued. There was speculation that he was unhappy that Abdullah led UMNO and BN to stellar results in the 2004 election so soon after taking over, eclipsing not just the disastrous 1999 election, but Mahathir's best performance four years prior to that.

The new PM had also cancelled a few mega projects that were launched during Mahathir's era, including a new bridge to Singapore, the double-tracking of Malaysia's railway line,

---

[18] Anwar Ibrahim, *A Malaysian Economic Agenda*, Kuala Lumpur: KEADILAN, 2006.

and the privatization of the Bakun hydroelectric dam—projects close to the former premier's heart. In February 2004, a Royal Commission was set up to look into the Malaysian police. Also, Anwar was released from prison, and that was because Abdullah did not interfere in the court's affairs; that was saying something to Mahathir, who was responsible for the judicial crisis in the 1980s. From Mahathir's perspective, the praises that his successor enjoyed from the Western media for Anwar's release certainly did not help Mahathir to trust Abdullah. In many ways, the break with Mahathir was over a perceived ideological repudiation of the fourth premier's UMNO Baru and return to the old UMNO of Tunku Abdul Rahman, Abdul Razak Hussein, and Hussein Onn.

In December 2005, I received an invitation from a think tank chaired by Abdullah Ahmad to attend a talk by Mahathir. A Kelantanese from the Kok Lanas in Kelantan as well as an MCKK old boy, he was one of PM Razak Hussein's Young Turks. He was a key aide to Razak from the 1960s onwards. But after the latter's demise, Abdullah Ahmad was detained under the ISA due to a power struggle within UMNO. He was only released when Mahathir became PM and became a close associate of the fourth premier. Abdullah Ahmad had coined the term 'Malay Supremacy' (that does not exist in the constitution) during a lecture in Singapore in 1986; the term has since been used to describe an extreme interpretation of the consensus forged by the Federal Constitution.

After two uncontroversial questions were answered by Mahathir, I raised my hand and was invited to take the microphone. 'When you were PM, I was very critical of many things, but for better or for worse, I could see that the country was heading in a certain direction. I think many young people share my view in saying that under the new PM, we cannot see where our country is heading. What is your comment on this?'

'Now you're trying to get me to say bad things about the current administration, but I made a pledge not to be critical of the government,' Mahathir began, and said that the current administration has some direction: Islam Hadhari and the emphasis on agriculture, for example. He was being sarcastic, of course.

However, he then admitted that at most, the present government could only present a fuzzy picture when it came to what their actual objectives were and he could not find a firm direction where it was heading. 'When I find the answer, I will tell you.'

I wrote this on my blog that day:

'While enjoyable, one cannot but feel how Mahathir's speech actually exposed the many weaknesses and inconsistencies of his tenure. Again, as I acknowledged, he provided direction and vision to the country, and result is an incredible transformation that was not dreamt of by previous generations. For that, he deserves a lot of the credit . . .

Yet when he mentioned on the need for checks and balances and criticisms in the country; or the AP issue (which he said justifies a departure for his non-criticism pledge since it involved a 'blatant abuse of power'); or the failure of privatisation—one cannot help but cringe.

Coming from a man who did so much to destroy the judiciary, parliament, electoral commission and media; one who used the ISA without reservation in 1987 and 1998 (and other years as well) against anyone who were critical and influential in the country; and one who set the ball rolling in the first place in privatisation—this spin of being a critical, liberal ex-statesman in the same manner as his old nemesis Tunku Abdul Rahman seems too superficial.

Tunku had his weaknesses and shortcomings, and like most people, was not the perfect democrat either—but he was personally convinced of the need for check and balance as well as a strong parliamentary institution, backed by free and fair elections.

Mahathir spoke so much, and rallied so many global citizens against the injustices on the international arena. In many instances his verbal quips were misguided, but the overall critique was laudable. One may ask however: why didn't he accord the treatment he expects and demands internationally to critics back at home?

Another more long-standing question—it's fashionable now in the establishment to (indirectly. at least) criticise the excesses of Mahathir, just as it became fashionable post Tunku to criticise his shortcomings—but why don't we cut the chase and be more open to criticisms against even the sitting administration?'[19]

His differences with Abdullah soon came out in the open by 2006. What seemed amazing for those of us born after Mahathir became PM was that he could attack his successor despite not having tolerated such criticism when he was in charge. Of course, as someone who followed Malaysian political history, I realized that this was not new—Mahathir came to fame as a strident critic of the first PM, Tunku Abdul Rahman, and was criticized by both Tunku and the third premier, Hussein Onn, during the split of UMNO. But for many others, this appeared unprecedented.

Abdullah's inner circle was a group of mostly youthful Malays—highly qualified and critical of Mahathir's legacy. Known as the 'Fourth Floor Boys' (as they occupied the fourth floor of the PM's Department building), they were informally led by his son-in-law, the Oxford-graduate, Khairy Jamaluddin. He was only in his late twenties at that time. In some ways, they spoke about reform, but as the PM's gatekeepers, they developed a reputation for arrogance and faced a party with strong vested interests, hostile to any ideas of change.

---

[19] Nik Nazmi Nik Ahmad, 'Questioning Mahathir' niknazmi.com, 10 December 2005, archived at https://web.archive.org/web/20060307125219/http://www. niknazmi.com/wordpress/index.php/archives/136#more-136, Accessed 14 July 2021.

Ignoring how his own children benefited during his premiership, Mahathir made both Khairy and Kamaluddin—Abdullah's son—as his target over their business dealings. Mahathir complained about the lack of press freedom when his gripes about the PM was not widely reported! He started a blog and began appearing in *Malaysiakini*, which emerged to get around the limitations on the press during his time as premier.

Differences with Abdullah over Mahathir's pet project—the national carmaker Proton—worsened the situation. The Proton CEO was sacked and a financially-distressed Italian motorcycle manufacturer owned by Proton was sold-off. Mahathir also attacked the increase in the awarding of approved permits for imported cars. He argued it was killing the national carmaker. He focused his attacks on Rafidah Aziz, the Minister of International Trade and Industry—who was previously a close ally of Mahathir. It later emerged that Rafidah's family were among those who benefited handsomely from the award of the permits.

Mentari Project

At the end of 2007, having learned more about the Kelana Jaya constituency where I was active in, I put a word out on my blog asking for anyone who was interested to work with me on a community project to come forward. I thought of doing something along the lines of the Kalsom Project, on a small budget but over a longer run. Someone replied in the comments section saying that she was interested.

I met up with the said person, Mawarni Hassan. She was a former teacher who graduated from Canada and served in the examinations syndicate. Having just left the government service, she and her children wanted to do something for the community.

We met at a McDonalds at the city centre to plan further. Along with Mawarni and her children, I gathered a group of my friends who had just graduated. I was fortunate to have Mawarni as she was an experienced educator and manager. We decided on doing a voluntary tuition project. We charged RM10 per family to get their commitment, as we feared making it free would mean parents not taking it seriously. However, when there were families who could not pay, they were not pressured to pay. Many who could not pay the fee insisted on paying in kind in the form of refreshments as they did not want their children to get a free lunch!

Finally, we settled on doing it in Desa Mentari in the Kelana Jaya constituency. A massive low-cost housing project that was built in the early 2000s, it was part of the BN state government's 'zero squatter' policy. The government wanted to move the squatters that flourished during the early days of industrialization to a proper environment, while at the same time, unlock the land they occupied for development. Desa Mentari is located next to Kampung Lindungan near Old Klang Road. The residents hailed from Kampung Gandhi in Kampung Penaga and other squatter villages and longhouses nearby. The Malays were the majority in Desa Mentari, with a substantial Indian minority. These squatter colonies were so abandoned by authorities that not only was it beset with poverty, but it was rife with crime, gangsterism, and social ills.

In 2001, a racial riot took place that started in the nearby Kampung Medan and spread to these localities. These were the squatter areas where my La Salle friends came from. Six people died, twenty-four hospitalized, and almost 200 people were arrested. When I became politically active in the area, I got to know those who were detained by police during the incident.

Mahathir decided to introduce his PPSMI policy in 2002, demanding that science and mathematics be taught in English in all national schools. Ostensibly, it was supposed to improve the command over English. During the British era, there were four streams of schools in the country, each with a different language as their medium of instruction: English, Malay, Chinese, and Tamil. Upon independence, primary schools teaching in all these languages were allowed to remain, but secondary schools had to adopt only English or Malay. In 1969, the government declared that from the next year onwards, students entering the first standard in English primary schools would use the Malay medium instead, ensuring the end of the use of English medium from all levels of national schools by the early 1980s. Thus, I studied all subjects in Malay.

Standard one and form one students would start learning under PPSMI in 2003, and it would be fully implemented by 2008. This policy attracted a lot of opposition from various backgrounds. Malay nationalists opposed a policy deemed undermining to the status of Malay as the national language. Chinese and Tamil educationists were concerned about its impact on vernacular education. Social activists feared that the working and rural classes would be adversely affected as they generally had a poor command over English. What was raised by the third group obviously was relevant with the Desa Mentari community.

We reached an understanding with the PAS kindergarten in the 10th floor at Block 8: we would pay a small amount and use their space over the weekends for our project, which we named the Mentari Project. We photocopied some 2,000 pieces leaflets promoting the tuition and distributed it to the letterboxes in Desa Mentari.

The first class was in January 2008. I was a bit disappointed that only a small number of students—less than twenty—attended. I joined Mawarni, her children, and my friends in facilitating the classes. As long as it was primary school children, I was fine. If I had to teach additional mathematics—or worse, biology or chemistry—that would be a different matter altogether! But the number of students grew every week. The students called us 'Cikgu', or teacher.

The approach that we crafted for the students was dynamic. We tried to make learning fun through games as well. We focused on English, Malay, science, and mathematics. Some parents were complaining that they used to be able to assist their children in lower primary in science and mathematics, but are now unable to do so because the language of instruction was English.

The Mentari Project also emphasized field trips. Over the years, the students from the project were able to go to the Petronas Twin Towers, including its science centre, the aquarium at the Twin Towers, and various theme parks. For children with middle-class parents or well-funded Parents Teachers Associations, these trips were taken for granted. But some of the children in Desa Mentari had never set foot inside these nearby attractions. Many of us were young professionals and were able to share our experiences in doing well at school and furthering our studies, including at foreign universities, and the children were excited to be able to engage with us. At the same time, we learned just as much, if not more, from the children, who faced bigger challenges than we did.

One of the big challenges is male underachievement. This is a global phenomenon, of course, but witnessing it up close in the confines of low-cost housing with the faces to boot, beyond the abstract statistics, was a revelation. I personally remember a boy who I first met in the Mentari Project when he was in primary school. He participated actively in class, asking and answering questions. He got almost all As, including English, in his UPSR exam, ahead of many girls in the program. However, in secondary school, he began mixing with the wrong crowd and was soon playing truant, not just at the Mentari Project but even at school. He did not sit for his national form three exams. On the other hand, many of the girls diligently continued attending the project and went on to not only finish secondary school but to get diplomas and even degrees! The absence of positive male role models was a factor in many cases similar to this.

Law and Order

Anwar Ibrahim released the VK Lingam video in 2007. VK Lingam was a controversial senior lawyer with friends in high places and was caught in the video having a telephone conversation in 2002 with the then senior Federal Court Judge Ahmad Fairuz Abdul Halim. The conversation focused on their concern over the promotion of judges by the Chief Justice at that time as well as the need for Fairuz to be promoted all the way to be Chief Justice. By March the following year, Fairuz was appointed to the position.

The video, he said, proved that he was a victim of a broken judicial system. Fairuz had been one of the three Court of Appeal judges that dismissed Anwar's appeal against his corruption charge. The result was massive: the Bar Council rounded up 2,000 lawyers to march to the Palace of Justice to demand a Royal Commission to investigate the matter. The Commission's report left many issues unanswered.

Criminal cases also caught the attention of the public, including one involving two girls from working class families. Nurin Jazlin Jazimin, who was eight, was kidnapped after going to a night market in Wangsa Maju in August 2007. Almost three weeks later, parts of her naked body were found in a bag in Petaling Jaya. It was believed that she was sexually molested with a cucumber and an eggplant, and her privates were infected, which led to her death. Sharlinie Mohd Nashar, four, was reported missing after playing with her older sister in a playground just 200-metres from her home in Petaling Jaya, near where Nurin's body was found. After her sister was unable to find her, she informed her parents and they found her doll at the playground. Until today, Sharlinie has not been found.

National party

In 2005, I attended my first KEADILAN congress in the Istana Hotel Kuala Lumpur and I have not missed one since. That was a marked upgrade over the party's congress the previous year that was held at a Chinese temple in Ipoh due to difficulty in getting hotels and convention centres to agree to host the party.

The 2005 congress was the one where I helped draft the motion to dismantle the NEP.

During *Reformasi*, Ezam Mohd Nor and KEADILAN's youth wing had captured the imagination of the public. His fiery speeches, reminiscent of Anwar, and bold challenges to the authorities attracted a lot of public attention. But since the detention of Ezam and other key leaders under the ISA, the dismal results of the 2004 election, and Abdullah Ahmad Badawi's shift of style from Mahathir Mohamad, the party's youth wing was struggling to make a headway—even with Anwar and Ezam's release from detention. Speculation intensified from 2005 about Ezam rejoining UMNO. I had helped out when he formed Gerak—an anti-corruption NGO that year.

In 2007, Ezam, who had grown distant from the party, turned forty, the age limit for the youth wing. Shamsul Iskandar Md Akin, a practicing lawyer, replaced Ezam. Shortly afterwards, he appointed me as one of its national committee members.

So, I started travelling across the country on my own, driving a Proton Waja. It was owned by Nazifah, my fourth sister who was working overseas. In return for taking care of her bills in Malaysia, I was allowed to use the car. For me, it was definitely an upgrade from my parents' Wira; it had a CD player. I had tons of original CDs as well as dubbed CDs to accompany me during my journeys.

I remember speaking at my first proper 'ceramah' at Anwar's original family home in Penang in front of Dr Wan Azizah. I was fumbling as I felt nervous and thought that I was speaking for too long. It turned out that I had spoken for barely three minutes when I finished my speech! I went to a FELDA settlement in Keratong in Pahang to speak. It was my first time at a Federal Land Development Authority (FELDA) plantation. These plantations had become strongholds of the BN coalition. While the hold of BN over urban Malay voters had waned with more education and industrialization, in FELDA, the smallholders considered their prosperity dependent on UMNO. I learned a lot by venturing out of my comfort zone.

One of the KEADILAN Youth vice leaders was S. Kesavan. He has a good command of Malay and was a charismatic speaker. In one meeting, he declared his intention of running in the Hutan Melintang state seat in Perak. MIC had won convincingly over KEADILAN's Malay candidate in the constituency in 2004. Kesavan bravely declared that he would not get married until he had won in an election. The rest of us broke into laughter and I said, Kesavan, you probably will be single for a long time!

True enough, when we visited Hutan Melintang, we saw how challenging it was. Located at southern Perak, it is separated from Selangor by the Bernam River. There is a fishing village there that leads to the sea. There are large plantations also. As we went around distributing political leaflets, a Chinese lady at the fishing jetty stared at the KEADILAN flag.

'Is this a new party?' she asked.

'No, this is Anwar Ibrahim's party.'

'Oh, you guys are still around?'

It was not a promising sign for the party and Kesavan's chance of getting married.

But the party was improving. In Sabah and Sarawak in Borneo, local parties traditionally dominated the political scene. But most were part of the BN coalition. A normal line of attack against national opposition parties are that we are 'Malayan' parties, that did not understand the unique Sabah and Sarawak culture, which were in many ways more integrated and less racialized compared to in the Peninsula. These attacks were not only levelled at PAS as Islamism is rather alien to the local population, but also against the DAP (which had made some inroads there) and KEADILAN.

In the 2006 Sarawak state election, KEADILAN's Dominique Ng won in Padungan, the city centre of Sarawak's capital Kuching. The seat was previously contested by DAP and KEADILAN had to fight hard to get them to give way. Nationally, this meant that

KEADILAN finally had its first non-Malay and Borneo legislator as it progressed in fulfilling its potential as a truly multi-racial national Malaysian party. The party lost narrowly—by less than 100 votes—in the Muslim Bumiputera seat of Saribas.

Former corporate leader Abdul Khalid Ibrahim joined the party in July the same year and was immediately appointed as the party's Treasurer General. I was tasked to go to his house—a large bungalow in Bukit Damansara built to imitate a Malay palace—and personally get him to fill the membership form. It was significant as his experience in the corporate world gave the party credibility with the business sector.

I joined a trip to Pesantren Sunan Drajat in East Java in Indonesia with Anwar, Khalid, and a few other party leaders soon after this. The *pesantren*, or madrasah, was a centuries-old site that had been built by one of the nine saints who brought Islam to Java, Sunan Drajat. It surrounds his tomb, deep inside the Javanese heartland, two hours from Surabaya. As mentioned earlier, the main Nik family in Kelantan is related to another of the nine saints, Sunan Ampel.

'The saints spread Islam by incorporating the culture of the Javanese, not by opposing it,' said Kiyai Haji Abdul Ghofur, the founder of the *pesantren* to us. 'They adopted shadow puppets, the gamelan orchestra and the *silat* art of self-defence in spreading Islam. This peaceful approach created the largest Islamic community in the world. Doesn't that tell us something?'[20]

As KEADILAN was pushing for a shift from the NEP, Khalid Ibrahim joining the party helped reassure the Malays. He served PNB as CEO from 1979–1994. As mentioned earlier, the company was closely linked to Bumiputera economic empowerment and the NEP. Khalid was involved in the famous Dawn Raid on the London Stock Exchange in 1981, when

---

[20] Nik Nazmi Nik Ahmad, *Moving Forward: Malays for the 21st Century* (2019 ed.), Shah Alam: Marshall Cavendish, 2019, p.96.

PNB surprised the market by acquiring the majority of shares in British-owned Guthrie Plantations. After leaving PNB, he was CEO of Guthrie from 1995–2003.

In the following year, a by-election took place in the Ijok state seat of Selangor, not far from Khalid's birthplace. KEADILAN nominated him for the seat against BN's MIC candidate. Ijok was a backwater constituency, with the Malays barely making half of the population and Indians making for almost 30 per cent. The largest town was the rustic Batang Berjuntai—which means 'dangling branch', a reference to the railway line to the coal mine Batu Arang that was damaged during World War II. But the name also was a double entendre as in Malay it could mean a dangling phallus. I remember passing the highway going back to MCKK and trying to make sense of the name as a teenager!

I made a few trips to campaign in Ijok at that time. BN had massive and intimidating operation centres. We were tasked to take care of the Bukit Badong district and, at first, settled on a shophouse next to the trunk road as our operation centre. A rent amount was agreed, and we duly paid it. The next day, we were informed that someone from BN had paid double the agreed amount just to keep the shophouse out of our hands. Finally, we found a house deep inside the oil palm plantation that could be rented out. During the campaign, more than a dozen of us slept on the living room floor at times, including Saifuddin Nasution Ismail, the former KEADILAN Youth leader who was then appointed as the party's first strategic director.

While we did focus on some local issues including how Ijok was left behind from Selangor's economic development, much of the focus was on national matters, including the recent Scorpène submarine corruption scandal and the resulting murder of the beautiful Mongolian translator, Altantuyaa Shaariibuu.[21]

---

[21] More on this can be found at https://www.theedgemarkets.com/article/altantuyas-name-appears-number-times-scorpene-submarines-after-sale-services-contract-says.

The result was disappointing as BN won with almost the same margin as it did in the 2004 election.

Blogs and Social Media

In April 2007, while I was visiting Imaan in Newcastle, I finally decided to create an account on Facebook. My friend Nawar, who was studying in the US, had prodded me to join Facebook after it was open to the public in September 2006, but I had put it off. Previously, in addition to my blog, I had used Friendster, launched in 2003. I wrote on my blog in May 2007:

> '[the] Ijok [by-election] took my mind off Facebook for a while, but I still check the site regularly. Don't know how long the Facebook craze will last, what's certain is that it has not captured Malaysia (yet!).'[22]

This Facebook 'craze' certainly lasted a long time!

Blogs also gained prominence in Malaysia during this period. Famous bloggers included IT consultant Jeff Ooi and former *Malay Mail* executive editor Ahiruddin Attan. Two years later, both were sued for the contents on their blogs by the parent company of *The New Straits Times*. Oxford graduate and former IT entrepreneur Tony Pua started a blog as well and eventually joined the DAP.

2007 was also the year my colleague at Anwar Ibrahim's office—Nathaniel Tan—was arrested by the police. One late afternoon in July, I received a call that he was arrested by the police who went to the office and said that they were investigating something 'related to the Internet'. It turned out to be relating to a corruption allegation on the Deputy Home Minister. A vigil

---

[22] Nik Nazmi Nik Ahmad, 'Facebooking', niknazmi.com, 1 May 2007, archived at http://web.archive.org/web/20070501235621/http://ww.niknazmi.com/wordpress/, Accessed 27 July 2021.

was organized which we attended along with Anwar. My wife and I dropped by when he was brought to the magistrate, and we caught sight of him in his orange lockup jumpsuit.

We also managed to get Anwar to start a Malay blog. He adapted quite fast, engaging with readers' comments by answering many of them individually. For him, the world had changed rapidly. When he was imprisoned, bulky handphones were only available to a small circle in the country and the Internet was still basic and underdeveloped. Now, he started using a Blackberry to access the Internet and e-mail us throughout the day.

The fractured nature of the media market—where the elites read the English media, while the other communities largely consumed media in their own languages—also ensured the BN administration could dominate politics effectively through divide-and-rule. Messages were crafted effectively for different audiences. Normally, the BN component parties would rally their own communal members through the vernacular press, but together they would preach messages of unity and moderation.

But the government's commitment to the freedom of the Internet, the maturing of a generation fluent in the national language, and the rise of bloggers as citizen journalists meant that the old methods of controlling the media through command and control as well as divide and rule began to weaken.

Expanding Office

Anwar's office grew steadily. We moved to Khalid Ibrahim's old bungalow in Petaling Jaya, near the UM campus. Anwar's office was in the master bedroom, while two other bedrooms became offices that were shared between the other members of the staff. There was a reception below and a meeting room. The walls were repainted, and small repairs were done, but otherwise the house remained as it was.

The new staff consisted of many young graduates: Nurul Izzah joined after graduating from her master's program at Johns Hopkins University; Sim Tze Tzin completed his undergraduate engineering degree at UTM and later furthered his studies and worked in California; Nathaniel Tan who was a Harvard graduate and blogger. The chief of staff, Ibrahim Yaacob, was much more senior. He is the son of the first mayor of Kuala Lumpur. Another senior staffer was former foreign service officer and academician Din Merican.

I helped Izzah start a blog and kept persuading her to run in the upcoming election. She agreed to some 'ceramah kelompok' at flats in Lembah Pantai and I agreed to be one of the speakers. I had no such thoughts myself. But unbeknownst to me, Tze Tzin was making plans to run in Penang. Ibrahim Yaacob was also planning to run in Setiawangsa. Such was the dearth of willing and capable candidates at that time that many of us doubled as aides and candidates.

Rising Racial and Religious Tensions

Racial rhetoric escalated in UMNO after the 2004 election. UMNO Youth—led by its chief Hishammudin Hussein and vice chief Khairy Jamaluddin—were aggressively propping up the concept of Malay Supremacy. Hishammudin brandished the traditional Malay dagger, the *keris*, in the UMNO General Assembly in 2005. It reminded the non-Malays of the 13 May 1969 riots and attracted a lot of criticisms, but he did it again in the following year. It was an attempt by the right wing in UMNO to focus on a new NEP and Malay agenda. The dream of the liberal and united 'Bangsa Malaysia' espoused by Vision 2020 by Mahathir in 1991 seemed to have come to an end.

Another issue which heightened tensions was the 'Lina Joy' saga. She was born Azlina Jailani to a Malay Muslim family. She converted to Christianity. Malaysian identity cards openly state whether one is Muslim or non-Muslim. She tried to change her religion on the card through the National Registration Department but failed as she did not have the necessary documents from the Shariah Court. She filed a suit in the High Court in 1999.

Eight years later, the Federal Court ruled that Lina could only leave Islam through the Shariah Court. Some Muslim activists celebrated this as a victory for Islam, while non-Muslims felt that this trampled upon the rights of the non-Muslims.

Anwar Ibrahim stated that the decision was correct in terms of procedure, but it did not bar anyone from applying to leave the religion through due process: the Shariah Courts. At the same time, he said that the authorities had to build public confidence in the Shariah Court system.[23] At the crux of it, the authorities failed to foster understanding between Muslims and non-Muslims and this meant that religious tensions could flare easily.

The concerns of the non-Muslims were understandable. There was the case of army corporal M Moorthy. Army records showed he had converted to Islam and applied to change the details on his military identity card. That was not done and his family reported that he was a practicing Hindu until his death. When he died a year later, it became a legal issue as the religious authorities tried to stop his wife from claiming his body. He was finally buried as a Muslim, but even the Shariah Lawyers Association President Muhamad Burok criticized the religious authorities for not communicating with Moorthy's family, which might have resulted in the Shariah Court granting him a Hindu funeral.

After the Lina Joy ruling, it seemed that parties like DAP and PAS had a ready template for their statements by appealing to their core supporters: non-Muslims for the DAP, Muslims for PAS. On the other hand, I remember that Anwar and KEADILAN's leaders would discuss things long and hard to come to a position on the matter. While our position perhaps angered both sides, we felt it was the best for a diverse country like Malaysia.

When all was said and done, in light of all these traumas, the moderation that PM Abdullah Ahmad Badawi had promised under Islam Hadhari came to nought.

---

[23] The entirety of Anwar's statement can be found at https://www.malaysiakini.com/news/68160.

Bersih 1.0

Two rallies took place in November 2007 that had a major impact on the election the following year. The first was the Bersih rally on 10 November. 'Bersih' was initially a coalition of opposition parties and NGOs calling for free and fair elections in Malaysia. The coalition used KEADILAN's *Sham Democracy* report—which I authored—as one of the main supporting documents in making a case for electoral reform in Malaysia.

Bersih demanded for the authorities to clean up the electoral roll; the use of indelible ink; the abolition of postal votes for military and police personnel; and free and fair access to media for all parties.

That morning, I had breakfast with Din Merican and a few colleagues before taking the Light Rail Transit (LRT) towards the Central Market in Kuala Lumpur. There was heavy police presence as well as ordinary Malaysians wearing yellow Bersih t-shirts underneath their jackets. We waited at the McDonald's nearby. We later joined the crowd and walked towards the National Mosque. Inside the mosque, it was packed to the brim, as if it were the congregation for Friday prayer (but also a reminder to the *Reformasi* demonstration there before Anwar Ibrahim's arrest in 1998).

After prayers, we marched to the National Palace as the leaders were planning to hand over a memorandum to the king's representative. Near the Palace, we could see the riot-control force of the police with their water cannons. The leaders spoke to the crowd and Anwar arrived on a motorcycle to beat the traffic. After that, we made our way back on foot to Central Market. I bumped into KEADILAN Youth members from Kampung Berembang, a squatter village that had been demolished recently in Selangor bordering Kuala Lumpur.

I had attended a few massive anti-war demonstrations in the UK, but attending something for my own country and in my own country was truly satisfying. The estimated crowd was 30,000–40,000 people. I had not missed a Bersih rally since.

Hindu Rights Action Force

Fifteen days after the 2007 Bersih rally, the Hindu Rights Action Force (HINDRAF) rally took place. A day before, three lawyers leading HINDRAF were arrested under the Sedition Act. HINDRAF's support had steadily grown due to several incidents where authorities had demolished Hindu temples in the country. But there were deeper grievances: the Indian-Malaysian community formed 7 per cent of the national population in 2010. However, linguistic, religious, and class differences complicated matters. The Tamils are dominant but there are Malayali, Telugus, and Punjabis as well. As of 2010, over 86 per cent of the Indians in Malaysia are Hindus. Christians make up 6 per cent, and Muslims slightly more than 4 per cent.

With the introduction of the NEP, while the Bumiputeras have access to affirmative action and the Chinese community continued to derive support from their business community, the smaller Indian minority could not depend on either. On many economic measures, the Bumiputeras remain behind the Indian community. However, the latter, particularly the Tamils, suffer gross inequality. The tensions between Malays and Indians burst out in the open with the Kampung Medan riots in 2001, and simmered beneath the surface until it erupted again with the HINDRAF protests.

Conservatively, around 30,000 Indians of the Hindu faith marched to the British High Commission in Kuala Lumpur to hand in a memorandum protesting the introduction of Indian indentured labourers to British Malaya. An estimated 5,000 riot-police personnel were mobilized. Early in the morning, the first teargas cannisters were launched towards the crowd, many of whom had brought photos of Mahatma Gandhi with them. The protestors marched with the rallying cry of 'Makkal sakti' or 'People power.'

2. The 2008 General Election

In February 2008, I invited Anwar Ibrahim to speak in Desa Mentari. Besides the Mentari Project which was just initiated, we decided to open a BA operations centre there. Having one allowed us to strengthen our outreach in the high-density residential area. We split the rent between KEADILAN and PAS Kelana Jaya, and much of the KEADILAN rent came from my pocket.

We had obtained the necessary police permit, spent money on thousands of handbills and multiple banners to inform people on the event. About 3,000 people came. When I arrived with my parents, there was already about 30 uniformed policemen around. In an effort at provocation, UMNO organized a futsal tournament nearby. Worse, bags of vomit, faeces, and urine were also thrown from the flats above, leaving a strong stench just as the event started. The police intervened when Anwar arrived. Anwar spoke briefly before leaving. A young woman, who was an UMNO member, said to me, 'If only we had this many police when Sharlinie went missing!' My father complained, 'What's happening to this country?'

After the event, Yahya Sahri, from KEADILAN Selangor, spoke to me about contesting in the upcoming election. This was not something new, but this time, the person was seriously persuading me by telling me that they had not found someone for one of the state seats under the Shah Alam Parliamentary constituency. He pestered me a few times until I decided to answer jokingly, 'If you want me contest, at least allow me to contest in my constituency, where I am active and had been working in the grassroots'. I was referring to Seri Setia, where Desa Mentari was.

'Your son said he is willing to run in this constituency,' said Yahya to my parents. 'So, I am asking both of you to give your blessings for him to run here.' My parents laughed politely.

A few days afterwards, Yahya called me up and said, 'You can't say no now. The party wants you to run from Seri Setia.'

Selangor

BN had swept Selangor during the 2004 General Elections, winning 54 of the 56 seats in the State Assembly. DAP managed to win two seats. The young Selangor Chief Minister, Dr Khir Toyo, had consistently campaigned on the slogan of 'Zero Opposition' and he nearly achieved this in 2004. That chimed in nicely with the state government's 'Zero Squatter' policy that drove its development projects.

In November 2007, Khir courted controversy by awarding the Hulu Selangor municipality council and land office brooms when they fell short of achieving revenue targets. This drew condemnation from the civil service union as being insulting. Khir had made a fatal error: civil servants had traditionally been one of the pillars of support for BN. He also attracted criticism for approving development projects on state land and forest reserves.

Nevertheless, Selangor still seemed sure for BN due the coalition's dominant performance in 2004. The disappointing results of the Ijok by-election, when KEADILAN fielded a star candidate, added to the lack of optimism. The Alliance Party and BN had dominated its State Assembly every single election since Independence except in 1969. At that time, it was initially a hung assembly but eventually, the cooperation between Gerakan and the Alliance allowed the status quo to be maintained in Selangor.

Seri Setia

The Seri Setia state seat then was part of the Kelana Jaya federal constituency. It was 54 per cent Malay, 18 per cent Chinese, and 28 per cent Indian in 2008. It was one of the bigger Indian constituencies in Selangor and Malaysia—other seats with a lower proportion of Indian voters were contested by Indian candidates. However, Seri Setia was a traditional UMNO seat. In 2004, Seripah Noli Syed Hussein from UMNO defeated PAS candidate Mastura Muhamad with a majority of more than 11,000 votes.

Geographically, the seat was small, but had a big population as it spanned parts of two cities—Petaling Jaya and a small part Shah Alam. This included much of the Kelana Jaya locality, which is a mix of luxurious bungalows, upper-middle class double-storey terrace houses, modest single-story terrace houses; the factories in Sungai Way; the low-cost flats in Desa Mentari, Kampung Lindungan, and Desaria; and a mix of apartments and terrace houses in PJS10 and PJS8. There was also Glenmarie—the only Seri Setia electoral district under Shah Alam. Much of this area were plantations and tin mines earlier. The former plantation workers of the Seaport estate settled in Kelana Jaya while the former Glenmarie estate workers were housed in a small section of their former estate. A golf club and massive bungalows dominate the neighbourhood. The former Sunway mine workers reside in PJS10. The tin mines, that used to be the engine of the country's growth, mostly closed down after the collapse of prices in the 1980s.

I was still undecided about contesting in Seri Setia. I e-mailed Anwar, who was overseas at that time, and he replied that he was leaning towards allowing me to contest. But if I had the courage to do so, then I should. I spoke with my parents and my wife. Having crossed the Rubicon by leaving PNB to work for Anwar, I felt this conversation was easier—although we did discuss about how much money would be needed to run in the election. My wife, who was in her final year in Newcastle and would be graduating in the summer, also preferred to be with me for my maiden election.

I knew one of the local party veterans, who had been with the party since the beginning of *Reformasi*, was eyeing the seat. That was one of the reasons why I did not put my name forward for Seri Setia. But the party was trying to find young and credible candidates. I arranged to meet with the man at a *mamak* restaurant in Kelana Jaya. I began by saying: 'Sir, the party approached me about running in Seri Setia. I heard you are interested in the constituency as well. If you are, then I would be happy to withdraw . . .'

He immediately interjected, saying that I was too young and new in the party. He also said that maybe when I was older, I could try my luck to run, but this was his turn.

My sense was that, initially, he was not too interested in running but got riled up when I expressed my interest. After a long conversation, I felt we were going nowhere and we ended up returning to our homes without reaching a conclusion.

I, then, gathered a few close friends, including those from MCKK and KYUEM at my house to discuss things further. Many said I should offer myself for the Kelana Jaya Parliamentary seat—but that was a no go as the party was planning to run Loh Gwo, who shot to fame for filming the VK Lingam scandal. Nationally, the party was trying to ensure a diverse line-up of candidates and Kelana Jaya was one where the party could field a Chinese candidate. Meanwhile, Syed Shahir Syed Mohamud, the KEADILAN division chief who had contested the seat in 2004, was sent to the federal seat of Pandan in 2008.

I finally made a decision to run. The paperwork involved was immense, and I took all the way to the eve of the Nomination Day to fill the various forms. A structure was agreed upon to coordinate between the local party, PAS as our coalition partner as well as my family and friends who volunteered.

Then, there was the issue of fundraising. Candidates running for state constituencies have a campaign spending limit of RM100,000 while those running for federal constituencies can spend RM200,000. In reality, no one audits this and people get around the limits through various ways. But at that time, for many in the Opposition, there was no question of ever reaching the upper limit. Personally, I had been working for just three years and was still trying to resolve my scholarship issue with PNB that was worth almost RM400,000. I had bought a small condominium and had a small amount of savings. I was still driving my sister's Proton.

I remember having a chat with one of the leaders in KEADILAN Youth, Amirudin Shari, and another of our comrades in 2007. Both of them had made plans on running but said that they were supposed to set aside a small amount money since 2004 but did not do so and were scratching their heads about finding the funds. Amirudin and I were later Selangor State Assemblyman and EXCOs, although he went on to become the Chief Minister of Selangor later!

My parents, siblings, uncles, and aunt chipped in. I visited a few relatives. While they knew I was working for Anwar, they were surprised that I was running in this election. The party helped as well. It was generally a lean, no-frills operation.

There was also the issue of Subang Jaya, the other state constituency under Kelana Jaya. In 2004, DAP was supposed to run in Subang Jaya. Unfortunately, DAP's candidate did not turn up, giving a walkover to Lee Hwa Beng from MCA. This had made Syed Shahir—the KEADILAN candidate's—task at the Federal seat extremely difficult from the beginning. As I was teaching at one of the Mentari Project sessions, I contacted Tony Pua, asking whether DAP had a proper candidate. If not, KEADILAN would be interested.

'Don't worry,' he replied. 'We do.'

That was to be Hannah Yeoh, who would later be the Speaker of the State Assembly and then Federal MP as well as a deputy minister during the PH government. Less than a week before Nomination Day. Tony linked me up with her team and we met the next day at 11.00 p.m. at the McDonald's in Taipan USJ (formerly UEP Subang Jaya).

We decided to divide our scarce resources on polling agents and counting agents. KEADILAN's volunteers would focus in Subang Jaya to help Gwo Burne and Hannah, along with the DAP team. Meanwhile, as at that time DAP did not want to have anything to do with PAS, the Islamist party committed to assist in Seri Setia and they made up the bulk of my machinery there.

A small event was also hosted in Kelana Jaya at the house of Izham Hashim, who was the local PAS deputy chief at that time. Roslan Shahir, the PAS division chief, was in attendance along with much of their machinery. Roslan introduced me as the candidate and it was a relief at that time seeing their acceptance. Ironically, Izham would later quit with the bulk of the division committee during the 2015 PAS schism. Izham contested under the AMANAH banner in the 2018 election at a Selangor state seat and was duly appointed EXCO. Roslan remained in PAS.

On the day, the parliament was dissolved (most State Assemblies also follow suit when the federal legislature goes to the polls). Both the Minister of Works and Malaysian Indian Congress (MIC) President Samy Vellu as well as Selangor MB Khir Toyo came to Seri Setia. Malaysia's guidelines on caretaker governments were grey at best; thus, they both utilized government resources as campaigning tools. Khir Toyo was there at the ground-breaking ceremony for a new mosque in Kampung Lindungan, then both Samy and he were at a separate event for the site of the new Seaport Tamil School next to the mosque. Samy had to face a hostile crowd, which indicated how deep the anger of the Indian community was at the MIC.

Election Campaign

Nomination Day was on 24 February 2008—less than three weeks after the idea of me contesting was first broached. Those twenty days passed quickly and before I knew it, I was the KEADILAN candidate for Seri Setia. This also meant that Anwar Ibrahim was ruled out from contesting as he would be eligible to do so only on 14 April, five years from the end of his corruption sentence. Anwar not only negotiated for KEADILAN, DAP, and PAS to put a single candidate in each seat (ensuring straight fights with the BN, so we would not split the vote); but without being bound to his own seat, he travelled across the country to campaign for the three parties.

Election nomination days in Malaysia are always festive. This is when candidates submit their nomination papers with a proposer and seconder. They will, usually, also mobilize a crowd to accompany them. My parents and the rest of my family, along with friends, joined the party faithful. I remember seeing loyal PAS members donning KEADILAN t-shirts. Gwo Burne and I marched towards the nomination centre in the old district and land office in Subang Jaya (now demolished) as we joined Hannah, her husband Ram, and her supporters before making our way in.

My proposer was Yusof Amin, the deputy chief for the division. He used to work for Malaysia Airlines and had been involved in the UMNO grassroots before making the switch during *Reformasi*. He was one of the founders of KEADILAN in Kelana Jaya. My seconder was Hadzrin Shah, who was in my batch in MCKK, before joining me at KYUEM. He later furthered his studies in Australia and was working with his sponsors.

As we made our way into the hall, we could see BN's crowd. It was certainly bigger, but I believed our crowd matched theirs in passion and energy. I finally met my opponent for the first time, incumbent Seripah Noli Syed Hussein, who was also a State EXCO. She had a long political career. I greeted her and she said we were like grandmother and grandson!

When it was announced that all the candidates qualified to contest, I remember feeling relieved. But of course, the battle had just begun.

I focused on crime, cost of living, and the issue of affordable housing as some of the main issues for my campaign. As an unknown underdog, I challenged Seripah Noli to a debate on the issues. Predictably, she ignored the challenge.

The Internet featured heavily in my campaign. We redesigned my blog to be a campaign website. The first post had information about my nomination day details to get people out. I had also started a 'Friends of Nik Nazmi' group on Facebook about a week before nomination day, and a few of my friends guessed what the agenda behind this was. We also organized a day to get my friends and supporters to blog about me. My e-mail inbox and phone were flooded—I could no longer reply to each message because there were so many. I also did a campaign video on a shoestring budget—shot at my parents' house in Petaling Jaya (where I was still staying as a 26-year-old in a long-distance marriage) as well as Desa Mentari. We had Rage Against the Machine playing in the background. It was put on YouTube as well as distributed on video CDs as almost everyone in my constituency, including those in the low-cost flats, had VCD players.

I extended my fundraising appeal online and managed to get a decent number of small contributions from the public. At the same time, we allowed people to register as volunteers via the website.

All these innovations did create a buzz online as well as get me press coverage (including international sources, although the mainstream local press coverage was limited), but I knew that in elections, no matter how good you are in the air-war—the political battle in the old and new media—you need to win the ground game.

My team told me I had to upgrade my wardrobe. While I obviously had sufficient office attire, I could not wear my tight t-shirts or faded jeans. With my scrawny underweight body and my youngish-face, dressing my age would not instil confidence. I took time off to go to the mall to buy big batik and linen shirts— the stereotypical uniform of Malaysian legislators. Interestingly, as I grew older as a politician, I suddenly could afford to try to look younger.

The typical schedule throughout the thirteen-day campaigning period would begin with prayers at a mosque or a surau, then a walkabout at the 'pasar tani', breakfast at one of the stalls or mamak restaurants, knocking on doors in house-to-house visits, a press conference, lunch with the campaign team or with another group of constituents. I mastered the art of shaking hands with voters and kissing their babies. There would usually be a lull in the afternoons when I could go back to my parents to refresh or even take a power nap—except on Fridays, when I would go to one of the bigger mosques to offer my Friday prayers. In the evening, I would visit a night market, attend evening prayers, and at night, visit a few electoral districts for 'ceramah kelompok'. We had a few big 'ceramah' throughout the campaign period in Seri Setia. Sometimes, to ensure I could attend the morning prayers at the mosque, I would sleep in the office, on the floor.

One of the amusing things that happened to me was that a few Malay parents that I met over the campaign trail came to me and said that their daughters were single. I answered politely that I was married and that my wife was overseas!

I had Tony Pua, Hannah Yeoh, and Azmin Ali campaigning for me. Nurul Izzah was supposed to come as well, but she had to focus on her constituency and her sister, Nurul Nuha, came instead. I still remembered Nuha peppering her speech with Japanese words and I was wondering whether the audience was still listening! In return, I also spoke at Tony and Hannah's constituencies. The highlight was Anwar Ibrahim speaking in Sungai Way on an old lorry with a wooden body, common on Malaysia's roads.

Due to the HINDRAF movement, there were many Indian-Malaysian volunteers. It made a difference as Seri Setia's Indian community made up almost 30 per cent of the voters then. I met many former Indian Progressive Front (IPF) activists. The party was formed by a former MIC senior leader and MP,

M.G. Pandithan, in 1990, after accusing the MIC leadership of practising caste-based politics. IPF was influenced by the Dravidian movement which sought equality for the so-called backward castes. IPF joined Tengku Razaleigh's coalition and Pandithan contested the 1990 election with the opposition. He lost and tried to bring IPF back into BN, but this was vetoed by MIC.

One of the activists was Moses, who—just as I was about to speak at a 'ceramah' in Desa Mentari—handed me a piece of paper with the transliteration of a Tamil greeting in the Latin script: 'Sagothara sagotharigaleh unggaluku en manamarnthe vannakkam' (சகோதர சகேததரிகளே உங்களுக்கு என் மனமார்ந்த வணக்கம்).

I got used to the beautiful tradition of being honoured with flower garlands by the community.

In the working class areas, I gave my speeches entirely in Malay. In the middle-class neighbourhoods, most of my speech was still in Malay, but I peppered it with English. There are subtle differences between the two. In many Chinese working class and rural neighbourhoods in other constituencies, for example, they would prefer Mandarin (or the dominant Chinese dialect in the locality). If you cannot speak Chinese (like me), they would prefer Malay over English.

Hannah joined Loh Gwo Burne and me at the BA Operations Centre in Desa Mentari for a press conference during the campaign. Her team made sure that we concealed any PAS flags and logos during the event.

8 March 2008. Polling day finally came. I would be lying if I say that I was not nervous; but as an underdog, I was relatively relaxed. As I told the press later and as cliched as it sounds, I came hoping to win but was prepared to lose. I did not have much to lose anyway. I remember a friend of mine, wishing me luck and saying that he would try to get me a job afterwards when I lost!

I joined my parents to vote. As I was in the UK during the last election, this was not only my maiden election as a candidate, but my first time exercising my rights as a voter! The team brought me to visit the different polling centres. After greeting the voters, we lunched at a popular Kelantanese restaurant in my constituency, before continuing the visit. The polling centre in Desa Mentari was tense and the riot police had been mobilized. It rained at around 4.00 p.m., while voting was still taking place. I am not superstitious, but it definitely helped in 'cooling off' the situation.

I returned home afterwards. Reports from the Indian-dominated polling centres of Glenmarie and Desaria suggested that a big surprise was in the air. I was winning big there. I thought I could get some rest, but it turned out that I had to freshen up again. My team suggested we follow the results together from a big screen outside my operations room.

There, we tallied results from the different polling districts from our counting agents. It was still close, until about 9.00 p.m., when I received conclusive word that I had won. We switched to the various TV stations, which were still not reporting about any significant opposition gains. Interestingly, Sabah and Sarawak, where BN dominated, had their results certified and reported early. But the news that was shared via our mobile phones and the Internet told a different story. I called my parents and asked them if they wanted to be at the tallying centre when my results were officially announced. They agreed to it immediately.

We waited and waited. In spite of all the reports from our counting agents stating that I had won comfortably, the EC refused to certify the results. It was already 1.00 a.m.—four hours since it was confirmed that I had won. Along with Hannah Yeoh and Gwo Burne—they had also won—we went to our supporters to calm them down.

> 'We've waited for this for fifty years, let's be patient a bit longer,' I said at the end of my speech. 'They cannot silence the voice of the people forever!'

The crowd clapped excitedly.

Hannah told the elderly or those with young children to just go home. But they did not budge—including my parents.

Just after 3.30 a.m., our victories were finally certified. I teared up a bit despite myself. I had won on the ticket of a political party that was born on the streets. For a decade, people had not given our multi-racial politics a chance. I won in a multi-racial constituency that was a fortress for the ruling coalition previously. From one parliamentary seat, KEADILAN now had thirty-one seats, consisting of Malays, Chinese, and Indian MPs, becoming the biggest opposition party. At twenty-six years, one month, and twenty-eight days, I was also the youngest candidate and elected legislator in *that* election.

One of my earliest comrades in *Reformasi* and then colleague at Anwar Ibrahim's office, Nurul Izzah, defeated Shahrizat Jalil—Minister of Women, Family and Community Development—in Lembah Pantai. In fact, the opposition won all the seats in Kuala Lumpur except for Setiawangsa. Many other cabinet ministers and BN senior leaders lost. Samy Vellu—who was jeered when he campaigned in Seria Setia—lost to Dr Jeyakumar Devaraj, a PSM leader who contested under the KEADILAN banner. Samy had been an MP for the Perak constituency of Sungai Siput and MIC President since the 1970s.

PAS extended their hold in Kelantan, and the opposition seemed on their way to winning majorities in the state assemblies of Kedah, Penang, Perak, and Selangor. In Selangor, Seri Setia was one of the thirty-six seats won by the PAS, KEADILAN, and DAP—from only two DAP seats in 2004. Reflecting on the victory three days later, I wrote:

> 'I know this is a once-in-a-lifetime opportunity. KEADILAN, PAS and DAP must use this golden opportunity to prove the viability of a multi-racial progressive movement in Selangor, Perak, Kedah, Penang, Kelantan and the Parliament and

build on it. We must put the people ahead of the party. Otherwise, just as the people showed the courage to vote out so many BN representatives in this election, they will do so to us in five years' time.'[24]

I could not help but think of how fortunate I was. Many opposition activists contested in many elections, suffered one defeat after another, before finally scoring a maiden win. Even then, they would be opposition legislators. Some spent years in detention. Here I was, in my first try, the youngest candidate in the election, scoring a victory and being part of a new state government. Most importantly, 2008 was the second time in the country's history that the ruling coalition had lost its two-thirds majority. The first time was in 1969. Yet, this time around, it was a multi-racial wave and it was peaceful.

---

[24] Nik Nazmi Nik Ahmad, 'Reflecting on 8 March 2008', niknazmi.com, 11 March 2008, archived at http://web.archive.org/web/20080513113650/ http://www.niknazmi.com/wordpress/?p=711, Accessed 27 July 2021.

3. Serving Selangor

On 9 March 2008, I did not get much of a rest, having waited for the official results until the early hours of the morning. After going home at 6.00 a.m., I had to attend the wedding of a resident in Desa Mentari at noon. I was even asked to grace the 'merenjis' or sprinkling of scented water ritual on the bride and groom. I winged it as I did not have that ritual in my wedding, not to mention being asked to grace the ceremony before!

By the end of the day, all the KEADILAN state legislators were instructed to be 'quarantined' at Holiday Villa Subang Jaya. Officially, it was to ensure our security if BN wanted to buy us over. In reality, the leadership had heard stories regarding Badrul Hisham Abdullah, the KEADILAN State Assemblyman for Port Klang. The fact was that there was a lack of good candidates in quite a few seats and Badrul was one such person who was roped in to contest after the division leader refused. He hardly campaigned but won with a comfortable majority.

We heard rumours of some individuals approaching him to withdraw even before the election. Now that he won, and that the BN state government had fallen, the effort to get him to cross over went into overdrive. We spent three days at the hotel and we were instructed to keep our location confidential from everyone. The party provided talks on the basics of being a legislator and instructed us to brainstorm about our plans for the state.

The first night, we shared rooms. I shared my room with Amirudin Shari, who won the Batu Caves seat. On the second night, we were given individual rooms and those with spouses could bring them (but not the children) on the third day. I was thinking about unsettled payments, unwashed clothes, a long list of items that I had to take care of at home, and starting a proper office as an elected representative.

While we were there, Khalid Ibrahim, the party's candidate for Chief Minister, told me he wanted me to assist him. The first job at hand was to ensure his swearing-in took place as planned. I helped in the drafting of the letter from the leaders of the three parties—KEADILAN, PAS, and DAP—to the Selangor Palace, confirming their support for Khalid. Despite the break-up of the BA, these three parties had come back together as a loose alliance. Finally, on 13 March 2008, Khalid was sworn in at the Istana Bukit Kayangan before Sultan Sharafuddin Idris Shah as the Chief Minister. He would lead a new coalition to run the state with the largest economy, almost a quarter of the country's GDP.

We then visited the State Secretariat building in Shah Alam and met the State Secretary, the State Financial Officer, and the State Legal Officer. The three of them were the most senior civil servants in the state government and sat in the EXCO (i.e., the state cabinet) *ex-officio*. I can still recall vividly how awkward that first meeting was. The civil servants had never experienced a different political party governing the state before. The next agenda was the appointment of the State EXCOs. It was a delicate balancing act between political parties, race, and gender. KEADILAN had won fifteen seats, DAP had won thirteen, while PAS had won eight. Four out of ten EXCOs were women.

Finally, my position was formalized in the state government. Khalid appointed me as his political secretary and I took my oath of secrecy in front of the EXCO on 26 March 2008. The position is provided for under the Selangor state constitution. It was first introduced at the national level in 1963 for cabinet ministers and the state constitutions were amended to allow the appointment of a political secretary to the Chief Ministers. In Selangor, it was first filled in 1964. My rise in politics was swift indeed. I was thrown into the deep end of the pool and I had to learn fast. When I had a private lunch meeting with Anwar, he told me before I left, 'Many people are envious of you in the party. Do your work well.'

There is no proper job description for the position, but in practice, it meant heading the political operations for my principal. Yahya Sahri, who formally asked me to contest, was appointed as a special officer. I recruited a few other individuals—*Malaysiakini* journalist Arfa'eza Aziz as press secretary, and, towards the end of the year, future think-tank CEO of Institute for Democracy and Economic Affairs (IDEAS) Malaysia, Tricia Yeoh, as a research officer. I was also provided with an old Proton Perdana as an official car. I was still using my sister's car and only bought my first car—a Honda CRV—in 2009.

I remember having to chair meetings for organizing events and taskforces that would involve various department heads. The first few times were nerve-wrecking. I felt I was being judged as a twenty-six-year-old who was trying to preside over high-ranking government officers who were almost two decades senior to me. But I became more confident and comfortable as I spent more time in the position.

On 11 May, I was invited to speak at a concert—Harmonic May Rockestra—where my two favourite local rock bands were performing: Butterfingers and Hujan. The bands performed with an orchestra at the Chinese Assembly Hall in Kuala Lumpur. As the date was close to 13 May, the organizers wanted me to speak against racism, inspired by the recent election results. Nevertheless, I felt nervous trying to speak to revellers who were probably wondering who this scrawny politician was, spoiling their fun. But when I mentioned how I was a Butterfingers fan from the days of their first album, *1.2 Milligrams*, the crowd immediately warmed up to me.

Aftermath of Political Tsunami

KEADILAN, DAP, and PAS formalized their opposition coalition by calling themselves the 'Pakatan Rakyat' on 1 April 2008. PAS downplayed its Islamic State agenda. It also leveraged on its PAS Supporters Club which consisted of non-Muslims. While not members of the Islamic party, they were able to tap into the non-Malay anger towards the government, particularly the Hindus. This was relative progress on one hand, but on the other hand, having two-classes of membership was revealing, as it implied that the non-Muslims were essentially second-class citizens.

PM Abdullah Ahmad Badawi's undoing was that in spite of his spectacular 2004 win, he failed to build a strong grassroots organization. Along with the groundswell of public anger, it created a perfect storm against his government four years later. Dr Mahathir Mohamad's criticisms on Abdullah reached a climax after the disastrous elections. The fourth premier called for his chosen successor to quit. Two months after the election, he announced that *he* himself was quitting UMNO. Mahathir's old rival Tengku Razaleigh Hamzah announced that he would be challenging Abdullah in the next party elections.

UMNO Youth leader Hishammudin Hussein, who had courted controversy for his *keris*-kissing antics over the past few years, apologized and acknowledged how it had cost BN its support from the Chinese community. UMNO-owned *New Straits Times* criticized Hishammudin in an editorial after the election.

But Abdullah did not sit still. Zaid Ibrahim, the outspoken UMNO lawyer who defeated my uncle Nik Mahmood in Kota Bharu in 2004, lost this time around. Abdullah appointed him as a senator and then to the cabinet as the minister in the PM's Department for Legal Affairs and Judicial Reform. The bad electoral results probably helped to steel Abdullah to resurrect his planned reforms. But it had another bonus—it would put the spotlight back on the man who had started the mess after all: Mahathir. Zaid stated that the government had to apologize for the 1988 judicial crisis. Ultimately, it still fell short of what many demanded. Many had likened Abdullah's attempts at reforms to be similar to Mikhail Gorbachev's *perestroika*: an effort to change the system from within that unleashed other forces that ultimately undermined the system itself.

In June 2008, Abdullah announced that he would resign and hand over power to his deputy, Najib Razak, at an unspecified date. When the government arrested a Selangor DAP leader under the ISA, along with two others, in September, Zaid resigned from the cabinet.

Return of Anwar

A major gathering was held in Kampung Baru, the Malay enclave in Kuala Lumpur on 14 April 2008, the day when Anwar Ibrahim was legally allowed to contest in elections. This was exactly nine years since his corruption conviction and would be his first speech to the public after the election. An estimated 20,000 Malaysians crowded at the Sultan Sulaiman Club. At the same venue in 1946, Malay nationalists gathered to fight the British proposal for a Malayan Union and decided to form UMNO. Then, during the 13 May 1969 racial riots, Kampung Baru was one of the sites of the clashes between the Malays and the Chinese.

This time, however, Anwar continued his attack on Malay Supremacy:

'We are here to counter the massive propaganda campaign by Umno leaders, who are talking on Malay supremacy . . . [But] what we desire for is a new Malaysia is supremacy for all Malaysians.'[25]

The mood of the public was electric as Anwar spoke of upholding 'Ketuanan Rakyat' or the People's Supremacy to replace UMNO's Malay Supremacy. I regretted not bringing my DSLR

---

[25] Azreen Madzlan, 'Kampung Baru hails 'Ketuanan Rakyat'', *Malaysiakini*, 15 April 2008, https://www.malaysiakini.com/news/81390, Accessed 30 July 2021.

camera along. The club was also part of the country's footballing history: At one time, it was a famous amateur football club where the likes of Malaysian footballing legends Mokhtar Dahari (internationally, the third highest goal scorer in the world), Abdul Ghani Minhat, and Khang Hung Meng plied their trade.

State Assembly

The swearing in ceremony for Selangor State Assembly persons was done in April 2008. One assemblyperson could not attend—M Manoharan, who was one of the HINDRAF leaders detained under ISA and who contested under the DAP banner. Imaan was still in the UK, so I brought my parents along. My father faced some difficulty in entering as he was wearing the full Malay costume instead of a lounge suit, but eventually they allowed him in. The legislators wore the 'Number One dress', a uniform that originated in the British army as a ceremonial uniform. Those with medals and titles from the palace had to wear them. Most of us in the government wore empty uniforms as we did not have any medals or titles! There were quite a few other young legislators, including my political neighbour Hannah Yeoh (29) and my KEADILAN Youth comrade Amirudin Shari (28).

Previously, the DAP had always complained about wearing these uniforms when the MCA did so, claiming that it is a waste of public funds. Not only that, the uniform in Malaysia came with the 'songkok', traditionally seen as a Malay Muslim headgear. This time around, as they were part of several state governments, they decided to wear it without making a fuss.

In fact, the previous state Opposition Leader from DAP, Teng Chang Khim was elected as the Speaker. The Speaker introduced the Select Committee on Competency, Accountability and Transparency (SELCAT) to hold the administration accountable. While it began by investigating the abuses of the previous BN administration, it soon took the PR administration to task as well, as I would experience later.

In 2009, the issue of BTN grabbed the headlines. As elaborated previously, I had attended it in 2003 as a PNB scholar and personally experienced how it was merely a partisan brainwashing program paid for by the taxpayers' money. State civil servants as well as students from the two tertiary institutions owned by the state government were required to attend the program. Generally, the content differed if the participants were mostly non-Malay as the racial element was somewhat downplayed. But I heard a few cases where the speakers did not realize that non-Malays were there and used strong racist language, which made the minorities feel uneasy. We raised it in the assembly, pressuring the state government to stop sending civil servants and students there. The EXCO in charge of education, Dr Halimah Ali from PAS, accepted our arguments, and shared the experiences of her children when attending BTN.

By November that year, the issue made it all the way to the Federal Cabinet, and the PM reportedly said, 'This must end.' A conflict erupted between those who wanted to reform the program and those who defended the status quo. An UMNO online forum attacked Amirudin and me as 'shameless Malays' who attacked a Malay institution.[26] When Dr Mahathir—who was responsible for the overt politicization and racialization of the program—tried to defend it, Cabinet Minister Nazri Aziz from UMNO responded:

'Don't think that people outside do not know about the syllabus based on patriotism for Malays. . . . They all know what the syllabus is all about so who are we to say that it did not happen? You want to lie? You make people laugh. I mean there are people who attended the courses who came out very angry. There were many instances of the use of words like 'Ketuanan Melayu'. It is ridiculous . . . Do they want to say that

---

[26] 'BTN Rasis', MyKMU, 27 December 2009, archived at http://web.archive. org/web/20091227151432/http://forum.mykmu.net/modules.php?name-Forums&file-viewtopic&t-33530, Accessed 7 August 2021.

Malaysia belongs only to the Malays and the government is only a Malay government?'[27]

Unfortunately, the issue remained unresolved until the end of the BN era at the Federal level.

The State Assembly passed Malaysia's first Freedom of Information Enactment in 2011. In the same year, another PR state, Penang, passed their Freedom of Information Enactment. To date, these are the only two states that have passed such legislation.

But the passing of the legislation was a rollercoaster ride. Civil society had worked hard to push for the legislation. Khalid Ibrahim had pledged to focus on freedom of information. When PR won in Selangor and Penang, the two states announced that they would enact Freedom of Information legislation. But in the new Selangor Menteri Besar's interview to commemorate 100 days of change, he expressed the concern that such a legislation might be redundant as it would be in conflict with the federal Official Secrets Act.[28]

However, after criticisms from civil society, the state government began to look at the implementation of Freedom of Information in greater detail. Elizabeth Wong, the EXCO from KEADILAN, was not only a blogger but also civil society activist previously. She was tasked with leading the implementation of the legislation. In the first meeting, the Centre for Independent Journalism made the case for the legislation, stating that over seventy countries at that time had some form of 'right to know' legislation or another.

---

[27] Asrul Hadi Abdullah Sani, 'Nazri calls Dr M a racist for defending BTN', *The Malaysian Insider*, 7 December 2009, archived at https://web.archive.org/web/20091212223732/http://www.themalaysianinsider.com/index.php/malaysia/45724-nazri-calls-dr-m-a-racist-for-defending-btn, Accessed 3 August 2021.

[28] Beh Lih Yi, 'Selangor on track with pledges', *Malaysiakini*, 16 June 2008, http://www. malaysiakini.com/news/84569, Accessed 1 August 2021.

In July 2010, the Freedom of Information Bill was presented
at the State Assembly. Unfortunately, this was drafted by the State
Legal Advisor, who is an officer of the Federal Attorney General's
Chambers, and was very much watered down from the expectations
of campaigners. In my arguments to the BN, who rejected the bill
as they did not want similar legislation at the Federal level, I said
any opposition party should welcome this as a tool to hold the
PR government to account! The PR backbenchers pushed for
amendments to embody the spirit of the bill. The BN legislators
argued that it was in conflict with the Official Secrets Act.

Eventually, the State Government agreed to form a Select
Committee chaired by PAS State Assemblyman Saari Sungib
to look into amending the bill. This was the first time Selangor
adopted a select committee to amend a bill. Hannah and I were
among the members. The two members of the opposition in the
Select Committee did not attend a single meeting. We managed to
bring it closer to the vision of the civil society campaigners and eight
months after the first tabling of the bill, it was passed in April 2011.

Settling into a Routine

I maintained the office I rented in Kelana Jaya to be my service
centre. At that time, I felt more comfortable working with people
who were in my age group, and at 26, it did not leave me with
much choice. We allocated one day to hold my designated 'meet
the people' session where my constituents could walk in and meet
me. In the UK, these sessions are called 'surgeries'. In Malaysia
however, the term '*klinik*' (Malay for clinic) is used. I am not sure
how this happened, but I am pretty sure there is a link! People
will come to see politicians for everything. Much of it is welfare-
related, but some of it is also to certify documents for government
procedures. Or, sometimes, they would come in with a business
proposal or maybe an idea for reform. Fortunately, my experience
as Anwar Ibrahim's private secretary gave me some experience in
how to deal with this.

Patronage is also a big thing in Malaysia. Government legislators are provided with a budget (and the opposition either gets nothing or a smaller allocation). Thus mosques, churches and temples; residence associations and youth NGOs; parents-teachers associations and a motley crew of organizations would come knocking on my door to ask for funding. I was still new and I did not budget properly. I kept approving requests for funds until my allocation ran low. In 2009, the same problem occurred. I was summoned along with one EXCO and another backbencher to explain this to SELCAT in February 2010. Fortunately, my answers satisfied the committee.

> 'During a press conference after the inquiry, SELCAT chairman Teng Chang Khim said [Ronnie] Liu was "average" in answering the questions thrown by the committee but commended Nik Nazmi and Shuhaimi [Shafiei], describing them as "superb".
>
> "Nik Nazmi adhered to the guidelines by using 30% of his allocations for small projects and is very familiar with his account . . . " he said.'[29]

I took a short respite in July 2008 to attend Imaan's graduation as a doctor. We took the opportunity to do some simple travelling in the UK and managed to catch up with my close friends Loh Siang Ling and Khairul Shahdan. We also went on a budget flight to Istanbul where we visited the historic sites. I thoroughly enjoyed the kebabs and managed to buy pages of Ottoman manuscripts that contained miniature paintings.

Upon returning to Malaysia, Imaan had to wait for a bit before being called up to start her 'housemanship' or practical training with the Ministry of Health at HKL. We stayed at my parents'

---

[29] Yuen Meikeng, 'Pakatan reps under scrutiny', *The Star*, 1 February 2010, https://www.thestar.com.my/news/nation/2010/02/01/pakatan-reps-under-selcat-scrutiny, Accessed 1 August 2021.

place while waiting for the condominium that I had bought to
be completed. Both of us had busy schedules, but hers was more
challenging. Often, she was expected to work for over thirty hours
at a stretch when on-call. We moved into the condominium in a
newer part of Petaling Jaya, Kota Damansara, in early 2009.

Fulfilling Our Promises

Heading into the 2008 election, KEADILAN and PAS,
technically, were still cooperating under BA and presented a joint
manifesto in Selangor. DAP had their own pledges to their voters.
These policies were done without much access to government data.
Now that we were governing together, we had to balance policy
priorities and fiscal realities. I attended a meeting in the evening
with a group of civil servants led by the State Financial Officer.

During the Royal Address to the State Assembly in 2008
(which is written by the government of the day to set out the
executive's policy priorities), the term *'merakyatkan ekonomi
Selangor'* or 'creating a people's economy' was coined. The policies
announced, which originated from the BA manifesto, included
cash gifts for those attending universities; elderly death benefit;
twenty cubic metre free water every month for residential
consumers; and a ninety-day maternity leave for civil servants
of the state. But there were other new policies: a special fund for
estate workers and their families and financial grants to Chinese
and Tamil vernacular schools as well as independent Islamic
religious schools.

All eyes were on the PR states to see what policies they
could introduce now that DAP and KEADILAN were no longer
opposition parties. A lot of attention was on Selangor due to the
financial and economic strength of the state, on whether we could
be both popular with the public and yet credible with the business
community. At the end of the day, however, state governments in
Malaysia have very limited power under the Federal Constitution,
particularly in the peninsula.

Anwar: Deja vu and Return to Parliament

On 29 June 2008, slightly less than three months after the historic election, Anwar Ibrahim's aide Saiful Bukhari Azlan made a police report alleging that the former had sodomized him. It was like 1998 all over again.

My staffer at that time, Najwan Halimi (now a Selangor State Assemblyman), had warned me about Saiful before the accusation, as he knew him as a staunch BN supporter. Najwan was suspicious about Saiful's motives in working for Anwar. I had raised it with Anwar. During the election, when four staff members contested, a vacuum was created that allowed individuals like Saiful to be hired.

Anwar declared that this was an attempt to stop his comeback, now that he was eligible to run. Photographs of Saiful with Deputy PM Najib Razak and other UMNO leaders were released. A doctor's report was released showing that there were no signs of Saiful having been sodomized. In August, Anwar pleaded not guilty to sodomy when he was charged.

Dr Wan Azizah had also resigned as MP for Permatang Pauh, which she had held since 1999, in the same month. Anwar contested from the seat he first won in the year I was born—in 1982. I spent days there during the by-election, to campaign for Anwar. He won convincingly—with a majority of over 15,000 and 66.6 per cent of the popular votes. August ended with Anwar being sworn into parliament after a ten-year absence and being elected as the Opposition Leader.

Paying back PNB

A few days before being nominated in the 2008 elections, I received a letter of demand from PNB's lawyers for me to pay back my scholarship.

I had two agreements with regards to my PNB scholarship: one for my A-Levels and another for my undergraduate studies. In May 2008, I cleared out my savings and sent a cheque for

RM50,000 to settle the first agreement as one of the guarantors was a friend of my father and I did not want to trouble him further. I proposed to settle the amount owed for my undergraduate studies—just over RM340,000—in instalments of RM2,000 per month or just over 14 years. PNB, perhaps realizing that I was now an opposition legislator who could not afford to be declared bankrupt (as I would be disqualified), refused my proposal to settle the RM340,000.

In July, I received a summons to appear in court along with my guarantors—my father and Nazifah, my fourth sister. Five months later, PNB pushed for a summary judgment, bypassing the need for a trial. After discussions with my family members, we finally decided to mortgage a property that my mother owned in Petaling Jaya. I made the proposal in May 2009. Finally, PNB agreed.

'That is a relief,' was my immediate reply to my lawyer. It could easily have gone wrong. My combined salary as State Assemblyman and political secretary ensured that I could afford to pay the instalments. But even then, I was fortunate that my family had some property that I could mortgage to raise the money. Some had advised me to challenge the legality of the agreement. Others told me to just ignore PNB until the court ruled on the issue. But in my resignation letter itself and in all my correspondence with my sponsors, I had always stated my intention to pay. I believed that it was the right thing to do as they did pay for my studies and I did not fulfil my eight-year bond.

Engaging in Forums

In August 2008, UKEC invited me, along with two new MPs: Khairy Jamaluddin and Tony Pua, to speak at a summit in a forum on the role of youth after the 2008 election. That was the first time I shared a stage with Khairy. Tony was thirty-six while Khairy was thirty-two. There was a lot of interest in the new batch of young politicians. In June the following year, International Islamic

University of Malaysia (IIUM) invited Khairy, their alumna Nani Abdul Rahman who was working at a GLIC, and myself to an economic forum that attracted a huge crowd. In 2011, I appeared in IIUM again, this time with Mukhriz—Mahathir's son—a deputy minister at that time, and senior academician Professor Khoo Kay Kim, discussing meritocracy and the special position of the Bumiputeras.

Without events like these, there was no way opposition figures like me could go into public universities or even government schools—except vernacular schools, which are slightly more open. When the parents or schools request for funds, we had to hand it outside of school premises, even though we were elected representatives, simply because our parties were in opposition federally. It did not even matter that we were governing the state these schools were in!

A funny incident occurred soon after I was elected. I was attending an event at a local Tamil school. The headmaster saw me driving my own car and asked me, what time would the 'Yang Berhormat' (or 'the Honourable', a title used for legislators in Malaysia following the British Parliamentary practice) arrive. I answered that I was the State Assemblyman. He sheepishly replied that he thought I was a staffer, due to my age!

In 2009, I was invited to officiate the Islamic Students Association annual meeting in UM. The association was closely associated with PAS at that time. As I was on the way to the campus in my official Political Secretary car, the students called me to inform that the campus was on the lookout for my vehicle to stop me from entering. A student arranged for me to reach the UM Mosque and handed me a student jacket and helmet. Then, I had to ride on the back of his motorcycle into the campus. Campus student affairs staff as well as the security came, recording my speech as I denounced their intimidation of the students. It was another example of the desperate and dramatic measures that the authorities undertook to perpetuate the old politics of command and control.

I was invited to speak at the Malaysian Islamic Student Group annual conference in 2008. It was held at Houston, Texas. As this was a student organization, they could not pay for my flight, but I was to be provided a room and food at the conference. I thought it was a good opportunity to engage the students and decided to take part. The UMNO representative that had been invited claimed that it was too expensive while the PAS representative was busy campaigning for a by-election. I decided to fly from Singapore to Houston via a stopover at Moscow.

As I was the only politician there, during my session, I shared the floor with a representative from Ikatan Muslimin Malaysia (ISMA). I was not familiar with the organization at that time. I was surprised in my session to hear the ISMA speaker talking about the dangers of political change to the survival of Malays and Islam. I responded by reiterating my conviction that Islam has always rejected extreme racialism and emphasizes justice and mercy for all!

The University of California, Berkeley invited me to speak on new media and Islam in October 2009. The panellists included Pakistani-American author Haroon Moghul among others. Author Wajahat Ali moderated. Since I would be in the Bay Area, I received another invitation from Stanford University to talk on multi-racial politics in Malaysia. Whereas the Berkeley event was a forum with many speakers, in Stanford, I would be the only speaker. I was quite nervous but I remembered Sarah Maxim, who invited me to Berkeley, telling me, 'Hey you are the expert. You know more about Malaysian politics than them.'

My session at Stanford gave me the confidence to engage not just with the Malaysian community but also foreign universities in my trips abroad. I enjoyed my trip to the Bay Area—I managed to check out the second-hand bookshops in Berkeley.

Hannah and I were selected to attend a program by CPA held for two weeks in London in 2010. This was Hannah's first trip to London, so we decided to go a week earlier to explore the city on our own. I also travelled to four cities to meet with Malaysian students. The other participants—from across the Commonwealth—were amazed at how young (and tiny) the two of us were. We were hosted by the outspoken Speaker of the House of Commons, John Bercow, as well as Liberal Democrat Minister of State, Jeremy Browne. Future New Zealand Deputy PM and Minister of Finance in Jacinda Ardern's cabinet, Grant Robertson was also a participant at the program. I remember hurrying off with Hannah to Bayswater to satiate our craving for Malaysian food.

The following year, I took my maiden trip to Australia with Imaan, where I combined speaking at universities in Canberra, Melbourne, and Sydney with a brief holiday. It was only with the trip that I realized how big the Malaysian community was in Australia, having had an Anglo-centric perspective all this while!

MACC and Teoh Beng Hock

In May 2009, I was summoned by the Malaysian Anti-Corruption Commission (MACC) for an investigation over a function held by the state government in 2008 where the Chief Minister was accused of channelling contributions to his federal constituency outside Selangor. I attended the investigation in their Shah Alam office. The investigating officer was polite, but for whatever reason, typed with one finger at a time, which prolonged the process of investigation. In the background, I could hear other officers playing table tennis. It was as if I was undergoing a process of mental torture. I had to stop myself from just asking the officer to allow me to type my own testimony, as that would probably be much faster. It lasted a few hours.

Although a few other people were called to be investigated, nothing happened. Two months later, however, the harassment took a fatal turn. Thirty-year-old Teoh Beng Hock was an aide to one of the DAP EXCOs in Selangor. I did not know Beng Hock well, but we met each other in meetings and would greet each other at the office lobby. On 15 July 2009, he was summoned to the same MACC office on the 14th floor for an investigation involving the purchase of Malaysian flags worth RM2,400 by his boss. He was questioned for nine hours and released at 3.45 a.m. He was found dead at 1.30 p.m.

The shocking news caused a storm. Not only had I been investigated just a few months back, but Beng Hock was also a colleague. Led by Anwar Ibrahim and the other PR leaders, we gathered near MACC Shah Alam to protest a day after the body was discovered. A Royal Commission of Inquiry was formed, and in its report two years later, it claimed that the death was due to suicide as a result of the aggressive interrogation techniques of the MACC officers. Initially, the coroner and the High Court had ruled that Beng Hock's death was neither a homicide or suicide. However, in 2014, the Court of Appeal ruled that 'a person, or persons' were responsible for the death 'accelerated by an unlawful act or acts of person unknown, inclusive of Malaysian Anti-Corruption Commission officer'.

Defections

KEADILAN suffered terribly from defections in 2010 as five MPs left the party for various reasons, costing us our position as the biggest opposition party. A year before, in Perak, three State Assemblypersons—two from KEADILAN and one from DAP—crossed over to BN, leading to the collapse of the PR State Government after less than a year from its formation. Not long after the fall of Perak in 2009, rumours surfaced that Port Klang State Assemblyman Badrul Hisham had gone missing. He did re-emerge but eventually it was decided that as the Menteri Besar's Political Secretary, I would take over the management of Badrul's constituency, including his allocation. Complaints kept piling up about his performance, or rather the lack of it. In October, he finally declared that he was leaving the party and in the following year joined UMNO.

As mentioned earlier, the spate of defections from 2009-2010 was largely due to the limited quality of candidates that the party had in the 2008 election. Many of the notable leaders from the beginning of *Reformasi* faced financial and legal pressures from the struggle as this multi-racial, big tent party was trying to find its feet. After two disappointing elections, Anwar and the leadership looked high and low for credible candidates, but this was easier said than done in 2008. Many loyal and capable people continued to assist the party but were not willing to run.

But how should the issue of defections be treated? To be honest, many opposition parties, including KEADILAN, have been open to defections when it is in their favour. UK PM Winston Churchill began his career as a Conservative MP, then became a Liberal MP (including as a Cabinet Member), before returning to the Conservatives.

But of course, not all politicians are Churchill (who himself has a problematic legacy, to say the least). Also, we have to acknowledge that legislators sometimes have to leave their parties over matters of principle. My stand has always been clear: the constitution and laws should be amended so that any MP who wants to leave his or her party must step down and a by-election held so that the legislator's constituents can confirm or reject the decision to switch. Shahrir Abdul Samad resigned his Johor Bahru seat following his conflict with PM Dr Mahathir Mohamad in 1988 and successfully won the constituency as an independent in a by-election (but he eventually re-joined UMNO).

Fatherhood and Port Dickson

In 2010, we discovered that Imaan was pregnant. As first-time parents, both of us were excited. It helped that she was a doctor, otherwise we would probably be panicking at every single unexpected thing. We had planned to go on a trip to India but cancelled it as she would have been heavily pregnant during the trip. In her third trimester, instead of driving herself, I would send

Imaan to Kuala Lumpur Hospital (HKL) and then have breakfast at the nearby McDonald's while doing some work.

On 24 March 2011, I dropped Imaan off at HKL and headed to Petaling Jaya for an interview that I had to do. Suddenly, I got a call from Imaan saying that she was going into labour! I fetched her from HKL and then brought her to the private KPJ Damansara hospital. By the afternoon, she had given birth to a healthy 3.4 kg boy. I was overjoyed.

We had decided to name him Nik Ilhan. We were looking for a name beginning with the letter 'I', following Imaan's name, as he would inherit what is actually my surname, Nik. In a conversation over lunch with my friends from A-Levels, I had asked them for ideas and one of them suggested Ilhan, after the Turkish footballer İlhan Mansız. While it is a male name in Turkish, meaning 'ruler', it is actually a female name in Arabic! A good example would be Ilhan Omar, who became one of the first two Muslim women in the US Congress.

Not long after Imaan completed her maternity leave, she received her first posting as a medical officer to Port Dickson in the state of Negeri Sembilan. It was about ninety minutes from Kuala Lumpur. Originally a part of Selangor, in 1880, it was handed over to Negeri Sembilan. It had been a port to transport coal and tin ore. Presently, it has two oil refineries. While there are nicer beaches elsewhere in Malaysia, its proximity to the Klang Valley makes it a traditional holiday haunt for the city folk and tourists who do not want to travel far from Kuala Lumpur.

Imaan was given a government house built in the late 1980s or early 1990s within the vicinity of the hospital. It was spacious but a bit run down. Having worked in the Klang Valley, this was a different experience. The idea was for Imaan to be based there with Ilhan and the Indonesian helper we hired, while I would spend either Thursday to Saturday or Saturday to Monday every week there. The reason was that I had engagements in my constituency during the weekends. We spent time in the beach. Our parents who came to visit would push Ilhan on his stroller in the hospital compound or try the seafood eateries.

But it was difficult to fit it all in and, eventually, Imaan decided to take the difficult decision of getting us all back to our condominium in Kota Damansara while she commuted to Port Dickson daily.

Sarawak

I made my first trips to Sabah and Sarawak after being elected as a State Assemblyman. My initial journey was to Sarawak in October 2009, organized by one of KEADILAN's pioneers in the state, Abang Zulkifli Abang Engkeh. I went with two comrades from KEADILAN Youth: Amirudin Shari and Teja Assemblyman, Chang Lih Kang, to the small town of Saratok. There, the predominantly Christian Ibans make up slightly more than half of the population, followed by the Muslim Malays and a small Chinese minority. At times, the three of us split to different venues and I focused only in Malay kampungs.

There was a lot of curiosity about us. The three of us were young opposition legislators, and while Sarawak was a state blessed with natural resources, poverty and a lack of infrastructure remain as serious problems. Partly, this was due to a peninsula-centric development by the federal government, but the state's own leaders were notorious for plundering Sarawak's resources.

Sarawak was on our radar because of the looming state elections there, which ended up being held in 2011. I was assigned to the Nangka state constituency in Sibu. While the parliamentary constituency has a Chinese majority, almost half of the voters in Nangka are Muslim Bumiputera. Many traditional wooden houses on stilts remain, as the Igan River that borders the constituency frequently floods. I spent two nights in Nangka to assist the campaign in the third week of March. Four days after my return to Kuala Lumpur, Ilhan was born.

But less than two weeks later, after sending Imaan and Ilhan to her hometown in Penang, I made my way to Sibu again. I rented a big but old kampung house in Nangka. The idea was for female campaigners to occupy the upstairs rooms while male campaigners were to take up the ground floor. However, there were a few sightings of 'unknown creatures' that made everyone avoid the top floor!

KEADILAN increased our presence to three seats, including— for the first time—two non-Muslim Bumiputeras: lawyer Baru Bian from the small Orang Ulu community, Lun Bawang, and businessman Ali Biju of the Iban community. Ibans are the dominant ethnicity among non-Muslim Bumiputeras in the state. But Norisham, the young candidate for Nangka, fared badly, like other Muslim Bumiputera candidates. There was a fear among the Muslims that the position of Chief Minister, which the Muslims had held since 1970 in spite of being a minority in the state, would be lost as Pakatan Harapan (PH) had campaigned for Baru Bian as Chief Minister.

Sabah

I took my maiden trip to Sabah in 2010, invited by Darell Leiking. Back in 2008, Darell had messaged me, wanting to learn more about KEADILAN. He organized a trip for me and Nurul Izzah to Sabah during the harvest festival in the state. Darell is a Kadazan lawyer. He comes from a political family.

The party first contested in Sabah in 2002. Our membership in the state grew steadily to the point that, today, Sabah has the second biggest KEADILAN membership after Selangor. We had a packed itinerary with the party leaders from the state and then a dialogue with young professionals. But we were also exposed to the beauty pageant or *Unduk Ngadau* celebration that is part of the traditions of the harvest festival.

I fell in love with Sabah and Sarawak. While both the territories and the peninsula share the same characteristics of the Nusantara or maritime Southeast Asia, and experienced one form of British colonization or another, Borneo is shaped by its large number of non-Malay Bumiputeras, both Muslim and non-Muslim: Ibans, Bidayuhs, Melanaus, Orang Ulus, Kadazan, Dusun, Murut, Bajau, Brunei, Suluk ... the list goes on. Intermarriage is common across ethnicities and faiths, so it is common for a Muslim in the two states to have relatives who are Christians and vice versa. Things which are deemed 'sensitive' in the peninsula are less so there. But they were also abandoned by the federal government while their own state governments were beset with corruption. Infrastructure like highways, water, and the Internet—taken for granted in much of the urban and semi urban areas in the peninsula—are sorely lacking.

Trouble in the Office

I soon settled into my job as Political Secretary to Khalid Ibrahim. I learned a lot from him and his corporate approach to governance. Khalid's tactic of portraying himself as a 'non-politician' impressed the public, who were tired of the old shenanigans and wanted things done. In many ways, this happened.

But let's face it: as a Chief Minister he *was* a politician. The 'non-political' persona he tried to craft was, ironically, imminently political. It was the identity he wanted the masses to associate him with. As his Political Secretary, I had to be the buffer when his division leaders or the state party (of which he was the chair) complained about him.

Yes, there were the usual request for projects, but there were also genuine proposals to strengthen the party. I would bring these complaints and views to him, and he would dismiss them, often with condescending views about 'politicians'. He would share similar views on civil servants too—sometimes to their faces. There was one time he tried to show off by calculating a sum in his head and challenged the civil servants to do so on calculators.

He got it wrong, but none of the senior civil servants wanted to say anything; so, I had to raise my hand and correct him instead.

One Wednesday, while I was at a meeting at the iconic A&W Petaling Jaya, having a root beer, I received a call from the party asking where Khalid was. I said I thought he was at the Political Bureau—a meeting of the party's most senior leaders held weekly. I had made sure the meeting was put in his schedule—but he was absent.

This went on for quite some time, in spite of reminders from the office and myself. He would have one excuse after another for avoiding party meetings. Expectations were not only high in KEADILAN Selangor, but at the national level as well. The national party leadership would convey concerns to Khalid as the party's first and sole head of a state government, which he would try to stonewall as much as possible. Eventually, I was tasked to attend to represent Khalid at the Political Bureau meetings. But this did not resolve the problem as when I conveyed what was discussed, he would often sit on it, or just ignore it altogether. Worse still, he would utter disparaging remarks about the party.

At the end of 2009, Anwar Ibrahim was appointed as the Selangor Economic Advisor to allow him (and the party) to have a better grip on things in the state. But this only delayed the inevitable. It came to a point that I found the stress too much. I, also, had to attend to my constituency as a first-time, young legislator. I conveyed this to Anwar, and he called me to his house to talk things over with Azmin Ali and Rafizi Ramli. Publicly, I maintained my professionalism as I tendered my notice to Khalid. In mid-2010, I officially stepped down.

In August 2010, I was appointed as the party's Communications Director. This provided me an official place on the Political Bureau as well as an 'official' reason for resigning from the Menteri Besar's office, although some media were reporting that there was tension between Khalid and me.

Rafizi's Return

Since Rafizi Ramli returned to Malaysia, he had been focusing on corporate life and politics took a backseat. He served his sponsors, Petronas, and rose rapidly in the national petroleum corporation. He, then, joined a pharmaceutical GLC as general manager. After the 2008 election, Anwar approached him to get him to help.

Finally, as Anwar took on the position of the Selangor Economic Advisor in November 2009, Rafizi was appointed as the CEO of the Economic Advisory Office. Soon, Akmal Nasir, who was in form one in MCKK when I was in form five and had just graduate from the University of Wisconsin-Madison, e-mailed me expressing his interest in helping out the state government. As there was no place in the Chief Ministers's office, I recommended him to Rafizi, who took him on. He would, eventually, join me in the KEADILAN Youth committee, replacing me as the wing's leader and also becoming the Johor Bahru MP.

In the following year, after the party elections, Rafizi was appointed as the Strategic Director for KEADILAN. This provided a lot of room for Rafizi and me—as strategic and communications directors respectively—to collaborate. There was a lot of excitement as young leaders were not only given a chance to be elected as legislators but also to be appointed to key leadership roles.

We launched a campaign called 'Demi Rakyat' ('For the People') in 2011. I was tasked to lead the video campaign. One of the videos featured various personalities—from social media influencers to activists and celebrities: singer Yasin Sulaiman who had consistently been a strong and public supporter of Reformasi; comedian Man Kadir who happened to be a grassroots leader with the party, and Atama Katama, a vocal Kadazan rapper.

The highlight was a campaign video of Anwar shot on the LRT, at a mamak restaurant and a mosque in my constituency, where he led the afternoon prayers and gave a short talk to the congregation.

In 2012, we launched a campaign for lowering car prices. Malaysia's car prices had been shaped by the protectionist automotive policy designed to protect Proton and Perodua, the two local automotive companies. In that year, 53 per cent of households in Malaysia had an income of RM3,000 a month or less, and almost 72 per cent owned or used a car. Loans for private cars reached over RM134 billion, the second highest category of loans after residential housing. Even the smallest car at that time, that were used by ordinary Malaysians, was taxed at 60 per cent for excise duties and 10 per cent sales tax. The smallest Perodua car that was sold at RM40,000 actually included RM16,500 in duties and taxes.

KEADILAN pushed for a comprehensive transportation policy to be incorporated by PR, including support for the automotive industry to be competitive and export-driven as well the construction of efficient intra-city and inter-city public transport to reduce the dependence on cars. On the other hand, we wanted a gradual reduction of car duties and taxes as well as a transparent bidding process for the controversial approved permits.

We launched the official campaign in August, complete with car stickers bearing the '*Turunkan harga kereta*' or '*Cut car prices*' logo. There was not much of a budget, so I procured a run-down Proton Tiara and wrapped it in the logo and colours of the campaign. I drove the car to the main toll plaza in Kuala Lumpur, heading north to the North-South Expressway at Jalan Duta. Fortunately, it did not break down and we distributed the car stickers to the commuters. The campaign grabbed the attention of the public and I saw cars across the country displaying the stickers.

Immediately, the government signalled that they were looking at reducing car prices. We launched the sale of the campaign's t-shirts and car stickers online and embarked on a nationwide tour with other PR leaders to promote the campaign. The Malaysian Automotive Agency issued a statement supporting the campaign to reduce car prices gradually. In the BN manifesto for the 2013 election, they pledged a gradual 30 per cent reduction of car prices.

The Cancellation of PPSMI

In 2009, then Education Minister Muhyiddin Yassin announced the cancellation of the teaching and learning of science and mathematics in English (PPSMI), beginning in 2012 and to be completed by 2014. The teaching of science and mathematics would revert to Malay in national schools, and Mandarin and Tamil in vernacular schools. While the introduction of the policy attracted criticism from Malay nationalists, vernacular educationists, and social activists, its cancellation was vehemently condemned by much of the urban middle class.

My rejection of PPSMI was not purely nationalistic, but pragmatic. As the policy was rushed by Mahathir, many of the teachers were not ready to teach in English, which left an adverse impact on the students. Through my close interaction with the rural children in Projek Kalsom and the urban poor in my constituency, including through the Mentari Project, I knew that the teaching of science and mathematics needed to be done in a widely-understood language. Research has shown that younger students fare better in science and mathematics if the language used is one that is familiar to them.[30] Also, the goalposts of the policy seemed to keep shifting: if the intention is to improve the command of English, then that should be done through English as a subject!

Yes, English is a dominant global language, but in a globalized era, languages like Mandarin, Arabic, French, Russian, and Spanish matter too. So, the traditional bilingual obsession is a bit outdated.

---

[30] Martin, Michael O.; Mullis, Ina V.S.; and Foy, Pierre, 'Students' Backgrounds and Attitudes Towards Science', TIMSS 2007 International Science Report: Findings from IEA's Trends in International Mathematics and Science Study at the Fourth and Eighth Grades (Chapter 4), Chestnut Hill, MA: TIMSS and PIRLS International Study Center, Boston College, 2008.

Religious Tensions

Since PR was formed in 2008 and BN suffered the loss of their usual two-thirds majority in parliament, racial and religious issues were played up consistently by the UMNO. I had a habit of sharing my statements and contents on various mailing lists and e-mail groups (as it was common then) which would normally provoke passionate exchanges with those in this list.

In 2011, there were a few pointed exchanges about apostasy from Islam. Under classical Islamic jurisprudence, the ultimate penalty for apostasy was death. However, today, a number of mainstream scholars have argued that there is a lack of a proper consensus in classical Islam on the punishment for apostasy.[31] There has also been references to the Quranic commandment of no compulsion in religion to reject the need for capital punishment. In Malaysia, as Islamic law is a state matter,[32] different states have different punishments for apostasy. The spectrum being: permitted under certain conditions, illegal and subject to various non-capital punishments; and illegal and subject to capital punishment (which in this case cannot be exercised due to the Federal Constitution that limits the scope of Shariah punishments).

I got riled up by the exchanges on one of the e-mail lists when people were writing that the blood of apostates is fair game in Islam. Yet, traditionally, the punishment for apostasy has always been in the hands of the ruler or political authority, not a free-for-all. I wrote about the life of Algerian freedom fighter Emir Abdelkader, or Abdul Qadir al-Jaza'iri. John Kiser's biography of Abdul Qadir *Commander of the Faithful* left a deep mark in

---

[31] Alalwani, Taha Jabir, *Apostasy in Islam: A Historical and Scriptural Analysis*, Herndon: IIIT, 2011;

Brown, Jonathan AC, *Misquoting Muhammad: The Challenges and Choices of Interpreting the Prophet's Legacy*, London: Oneworld, 2014.

[32] Under the Federal Constitution, legislatively Shariah courts are placed under the State List, whereas the civil courts are under the Federal List.

me. That was the first time I had heard about Abdul Qadir, but having read the book, I was amazed at why no one had told me his story before. Simply put, he was a Muslim Mahatma Gandhi or Nelson Mandela!

The French were driven by *mission civilsatrice*—imperialism that was supposedly not merely a purely exploitative economic exercise, but a civilizing mission to 'enlighten' the non-Western peoples. As Edward Said argued in *Orientalism*, Europe had always had a complicated history with the 'Orient'. There has been a lot of civilizational engagement with the 'Orient', but it also is the main representation of the Other.[33] Islam was seen to have gained ground due to the sword, whereas Christianity, as upheld in the West, supposedly spread peacefully due to divine providence.

Yet, in Algeria, France pursued a genocidal policy from its invasion in 1830. In the first three decades of colonization, an estimated 500,000 to 1 million locals died.[34] Ironically, in Abdul Qadir's jihad that was waged against the French from 1830–1847, he combined guerrilla tactics—that were initially successful—with a sense of chivalry and mercy towards his powerful opponents. He released prisoners that he could not feed. When a priest was sent to negotiate with him to release a French prisoner, Abdul Qadir asked why he did not ask to release *all* the prisoners instead, which he duly did. He eventually surrendered.

Abdul Qadir was exiled in France where he attracted admirers as the tale of his exploits reached Europe. Some of the French soldiers who experienced his humane treatment in Algeria visited him. He engaged in discussions with various personalities and expressed his interest in improving relations between Islam and Christianity. He attracted notable supporters who championed better treatment for him. Finally, in 1852, he was allowed to leave

---

[33] Said, Edward W., *Orientalism*, New York: Random House, 1979, p.1.

[34] Kiernan, Ben, *Blood and Soil: A World History of Genocide and Extermination from Sparta to Darfur*, New Haven: Yale University Press, 2007, p.364.

for a Muslim land other than Algeria. Six regiments of the French Army that had vanquished him before paid their respects to him. Abdul Qadir decided to go to the Ottoman Empire, finally settling in Damascus.

In 1860, a conflict erupted in Damascus, originally between the Druze and the Christians, but then spread to pit the Muslims against the Christians as well. The Christians, who heard of Abdul Qadir's reputation in Algeria, came seeking refuge in his residence. He was not the only notable Muslim personality who protected the Christians, but his heroics against the French also allowed him to engage the Muslim community in his efforts to protect the Christians. Eventually, a mob of Druze and Muslims reached Abdul Qadir's residence to protest. He argued with them, using the full force of his mastery of religious knowledge. Eventually, when the mob argued that Abdul Qadir too had killed Christians, he rebuked them by saying:

> 'You are fools! The Christians I killed were invaders and occupiers who were ravaging our country. If acting against God's law doesn't frighten you, then think about the punishment you will receive from men . . . It will be terrible, I promise. If you will not listen to me, then God didn't provide you with reason—you are like animals who are aroused only by the sight of grass and water.'[35]

Abdul Qadir was credited for saving thousands. After the riots subsided, he was hailed as a hero internationally. The Ottoman Sultan, Abdulmejid I bestowed on him the Order of Medjidie and his former adversaries, the French, awarded him their highest distinction, the *Légion d'honneur*. At the same time, he was honoured by the Vatican and was given a pair of pistols from

---

[35] Kiser, W. John, *Commander of the Faithful: The Life and Times of Emir Abd el-Kader*, Rhinebeck: Monkfish, 2008, p.299.

Abraham Lincoln, the then US President. He received a supportive letter of fellow Muslim freedom fighter and Sufi Imam Shamil of Daghestan, who fought the Russians. Imagine the global reach of his exploits, in the days before the TV or Internet!

Standing up for my constituents

I managed to lobby the state government to establish a kindergarten focused on the poor in Kampung Lindungan. The state authorities cooperated with an NGO to run the kindergarten. Costs were kept low to make it affordable. The ground breaking ceremony was performed by Khalid Ibrahim in September 2010. It opened two years later, with eight classrooms. Until today, pre-school is not compulsory in Malaysia and suffers from a lack of government-owned kindergartens. Even government-owned kindergartens are managed by different ministries: the Education Ministry, the Rural Development Ministry, and the Department of National Unity and Integration.

In 2011, the residents of Kelana Jaya began mobilizing against a proposal to redevelop the Perbadanan Kemajuan Negeri Selangor (PKNS) Sports Complex. This consists of a large field used for football and cricket, tennis courts, and a hall used for events. PKNS is a Selangor state agency that was responsible for developing much of Kelana Jaya. Residents surrounding the development received notices of plans for a high-density mixed development on the site with a gross development value of RM2 billion. This was made when I was abroad, but immediately upon my return, I met the PKNS officers to be briefed about the project, which was a collaboration with a private developer. I then met the Save the People's Field committee that was formed by the residents. I roped in Derek Fernandez, a lawyer who also served as a City Councillor in Petaling Jaya, to advise me.

The neighbourhood involved consisted of the rich and the upper middle-classes. It was traditionally an UMNO stronghold, but they voted strongly for me in the last election in line with the revolt of the multi-racial urban middle classes against UMNO. I called a press conference to express concern at the spate of high-density developments in the vicinity; the old factory in Sungai Way where many of my local party comrades had worked was torn down for commercial redevelopment.

Yet another mixed-development consisting of a mall, a hotel, and condominium was being built further up the already heavily congested Damansara Puchong Expressway. PKNS had requested for the land title in 2006 with plans for development—during the BN era. We were also informed, looking at the necessary documents, that the complex was zoned as a commercial land, and this was confirmed by the Chief Minister in the State Assembly.

I set a date to have a townhall session with the residents and called for Khalid to reconsider the project. Over 150 residents attended the session. The Petaling Jaya City Council rejected the first application from PKNS to develop the field. Not long after, Khalid requested PKNS to engage with the residents on the project. During the engagement, the PKNS General Manager attended. This engagement was quite heated and after the traffic consultant admitted that there was no solution to the traffic situation, PKNS deferred the project until that issue was solved.

But the issue escalated in 2012 when—through their sheer persistence—the residents committee discovered that the zoning for the complex was, in fact, for open field and recreation, and not building and commercial! It was as if the local plan was free for anyone to put their desired zoning. This simple stroke changed the value of the land from RM20 per square feet to RM500 per square feet. I pushed for a SELCAT hearing and it was duly called. The session revealed three versions of the local plan. The Speaker, who chairs SELCAT, declared his regret for the actions of the City Council officials which led to the discrepancy, but could not decisively conclude that there were elements of fraud. SELCAT recommended that the relevant planning document be cancelled.

In a provocative move, PKNS appealed on the rejection of the development application to the State Appeals Board. In my speech at the State Assembly debating the SELCAT report on the matter, I called on PKNS to withdraw their appeal. I told the residents that I would use the Freedom of Information legislation to get more details on the matter.

On the day of the Board meeting, we were informed that PKNS withdrew their submission. I urged the state corporation to be more sensitive. Why was a state corporation behaving like another private corporation, merely focusing on its bottom line?

When asked by the media if I thought that the project would continue, I said no. This provoked a response from Khalid, who declared that I had no right to say so! Khalid probably found that I was a nuisance, but for me, I was only doing something morally and legally right, and wanted to stand up for my constituents.

Bersih 2.0 and 3.0

Bersih 2.0 was held on 9 July 2011, four years after the first gathering. The issue of gerrymandering and malapportionment in Malaysian elections was brought up again. In 2008, BN had won 51.4 per cent of the popular vote, but 63.1 per cent of the seats. This time, former Bar Council chairperson Ambiga Sreenevasan chaired Bersih and civil society took the lead. The demands these times were, among others, cleaning the electoral roll; reform postal voting; the use of indelible ink; free and fair access to the mainstream media; stopping corruption; and stopping dirty politics.

Bersih was planning to go to the streets, but after meeting the king, agreed to organize it at a stadium. PM Najib Razak had also promised the use of a stadium. However, the request to use the Merdeka Stadium was rejected by the authorities. The decision, thus, was to march to the stadium anyway. Bersih was declared an illegal organization, as were donning and distribution of yellow Bersih t-shirts. These draconian moves were undertaken via legislation that was used to combat triads and criminal gangs!

Police set up roadblocks in the city. One night before the event, I decided to stay at Concorde Kuala Lumpur with my driver and comrades from KEADILAN Kelana Jaya. I watched *V for Vendetta* all over again. On the day of the protest, Amie Rashidi, who studied with me in KYUEM, decided to join me and we merged with the crowd at the intersection of Jalan Pudu and Jalan Imbi, with the idea of making our way to Merdeka Stadium. It rained heavily in the afternoon as thousands started to gather. Uniformed and plainclothes policemen were everywhere and we saw water cannon trucks and riot police driving past the crowd.

Eventually, we got cornered. We managed to find our way to KLCC while being chased by the police, where a few leaders were speaking to the crowd. An estimated 50,000-strong, multi-racial crowd gathered in the streets, albeit divided at various spots due to the intimidation by the authorities. At KL Sentral, the main railway station of the city, Ambiga, Anwar Ibrahim, Dr Wan Azizah Wan Ismail, PAS President Abdul Hadi Awang, and National Laureate A. Samad Said were part of a trapped crowd attacked by the police with teargas. The cannisters hit Anwar's bodyguard and PAS MP Khalid Samad. Teargas was also fired into the Tung Shin Hospital at Jalan Pudu, not far from where I was.

Rashidi and I were soaked in sweat and rainwater. Later that evening, my cousin was getting married and my uncle sent me a message as the rally died down, asking me to try to make it even if it was straight from Bersih. Rashidi was apprehensive at first, but I persuaded him, and after stopping by at a mosque to pray and freshen up, we dropped by in our post-rally state and entertained a range of questions from the guests.

Bersih 2.0 also saw gatherings organized throughout the world by Malaysians. Almost 1,000 people gathered in Melbourne. There were other gatherings throughout Australia, and also in the UK, New Zealand, Singapore, the US, Japan, Egypt, and Indonesia— totalling thirty cities worldwide. A printed copy of *The Economist* which reported on Bersih was censored: parts of the article on the rally had duly been blackened out—including the section on the death of Baharuddin Ahmad after inhaling teargas. Yet, the article was fully available online!

The following week was the State Assembly sitting. I submitted an emergency motion to debate Bersih 2.0—urging the federal government to stop arrests and obstacles to the group as well as for the state government to guarantee the use of premises owned by it without police obstruction, in line with the Freedom to Assemble as provided for under the Federal Constitution.

A Parliamentary Select Committee was set up to deal with electoral issues following Bersih 2.0. Other than engaging with local stakeholders and agencies, the committee also went to the UK, Germany, and Denmark to look at their electoral systems. The report was tabled and passed in Parliament, but without the opposition's minority report. 18 recommendations were unanimously agreed upon, including cleaning up the electoral roll of dubious voters, allowing for political parties to submit complaints or feedbacks on the roll and on political party funding. However, four more recommendations were only agreed to by the government backbenchers.

Bersih was not satisfied. In April 2012, Bersih 3.0 was organized as a sit-in at Dataran Merdeka. It was joined with *Himpunan Hijau*, or 'Green Gathering', a movement protesting a rare earth plant built in the state of Pahang. I took the LRT from Kelana Jaya with a few friends to the city centre. Eventually, I walked behind the old Kuala Lumpur Railway Station with its Moorish domes. A growing crowd in yellow was gathering and the police made a line to stop us from reaching our destination. By this time, I was a relatively senior political leader in the party by experience, and many in the public recognized me. I had a responsibility to lead from the front. I tried to find a different route, avoiding the human barrier made by the police, but as most of the crowd decided to go ahead *through* the police line, I joined them. The barrier of policemen crumbled easily as we outnumbered them, but everyone was peaceful, otherwise.

We made our way to the Central Market. About 300,000 Malaysians of various races gathered in Kuala Lumpur this time, painting the city yellow. Observers stated that the rally was peaceful and had a carnival-like atmosphere until the police used water cannons and shot teargas cannisters at the gathering directly. Police brutality was indiscriminate and more widespread, according to the Bar Council.[36] The uncompromising stand of the authorities with such a big crowd made for a dangerous cocktail. We had prepared ourselves with bags of salt and bottles of water to be used to moderate the effect of teargas. The Al Jazeera crew was roughed up as they tried to record a protestor being assaulted by the police. The BBC also protested when their coverage was partially censored by local satellite broadcaster Astro. Solidarity gatherings in over eighty cities took place in support of Bersih 3.0. Clearly, this gathering showed how far Bersih had evolved in garnering attention for electoral reform in Malaysia.

---

[36] Bar Council Malaysia, *Final Report of the Malaysian Bar on Bersih 3.0 rally held on 28 April 2012 in Kuala Lumpur,* https://www.malaysianbar.org.my/cms/upload_files/document/Final%20report%20of%20the%20Malaysian%20Bar%20on%20the%20BERSIH%203.0%20rally%20held%20on%2028%20April%202012.pdf, Kuala Lumpur: Bar Council Malaysia, 2008, Accessed 8 August 2021.

4. The 2013 General Election

Parliament was dissolved by PM Najib Razak on 3 April 2013. There was a lot of expectation on and excitement for the opposition, PR. KEADILAN launched a campaign bus and trailer that travelled across the Peninsula as Anwar visited cities and towns to make the case for change. At every visit, he was greeted by tens of thousands of Malaysians. While this is a natural part of political campaigns in the West, in Malaysia, it was a novelty in 2013.

KEADILAN and PR adopted the rallying cry of '*Ini kali lah!*'. This was a Sabah Malay expression meaning '*The time has come!*' and the title of a folk song from the state. The coalition—led by Rafizi Ramli, Tony Pua (DAP), and Dr Dzulkifli Ahmad (PAS) introduced the Orange Book as the PR manifesto for the election. This included an emphasis on a shift of focus from Bumiputera equity to household income for the poorest Malaysians, an affordable higher education policy, the restructuring of monopolies in public utilities, and preservation of basic subsidies for the people as long as corporate subsidies remain unchanged.

In Kelana Jaya, Gwo-Burne was dropped in favour of Wong Chen. Born in Petaling Jaya to Kelantanese Chinese family, he received his early education in Kelantan. After being educated in the UK, he started his legal career in Kota Bharu. After five years, he moved to Kuala Lumpur and became an established corporate lawyer during the rapidly growing years of the 90s. Like many of his generation, his conscience was pricked during *Reformasi*, though he only started helping out KEADILAN after 2008.

We got to know each other then and was tickled that he spoke Malay with a Kelantanese accent. Initially, there was a talk of fielding him in the rural Pahang seat of Bentong. It was not an easy seat, but Wong Chen started the work and I visited Bentong to attend some events to promote him. Then, the party decided to move him to the safer seat of Kelana Jaya. I organized for Wong Chen to sit down with the other State Assemblyperson in the constituency—Hannah Yeoh. We were three law graduates (Wong Chen was the only one still practising) with kids around the same age and got along well.

But tensions remained. As recently as February 2013, PAS leaders had been telling their KEADILAN counterparts that they preferred UMNO's Tengku Razaleigh Hamzah as the candidate for PM. He was seen as a maverick and there were always talks that he could emerge as a compromise candidate. The move was led by PAS President Abdul Hadi Awang. The differences between the conservative wing of the party—led by Hadi, and the moderate wing—led by the spiritual leader Nik Aziz Nik Mat had been simmering since the formation of PR in 2008. There were demands for a 'unity government' between UMNO and PAS due to the perceived threat to Malay Muslim polity following gains by the opposition. But since *Reformasi*, PAS had attracted many Malay professionals while the 2008 wave had also brought in many moderate PAS Members of Parliament, who won in the peninsular west coast, outside the Islamic party's strongholds. These seats had many urban Malays but a substantial number of non-Malays as well.

Seri Setia

Compared to five years earlier, when voters backed me partly due to a protest vote against BN, this time, I went in as an incumbent with a track record to be evaluated. There was greater coordination with Wong Chen's team as the MP candidate, as well as Hannah's team, now that we were all in the PR coalition. I also had a better idea of what to expect in an election campaign. I realized that my decent cooking skills acquired from my time as a university student in London could be put to good use to engage the mothers and the homemakers in the constituency!

At the same time, unlike five years before, when Imaan was still in the UK and Ilhan was not yet born, this time she joined me for much of my campaigning and our two-year-old boy even joined me on nomination day. My parents and family members joined the throng of supporters for Wong Chen, Hannah, and me.

Anwar Ibrahim took the time to campaign for Wong Chen and me in Kampung Lindungan. Anwar and the other leadership were focusing on the more marginal seats that KEADILAN and the coalition needed to win in order to get a majority. The only available slot was during the morning, not the usual evening or late-night 'ceramah' that we are used to in Malaysia. Even then, the field was full when he introduced Wong Chen, Hannah, and myself to the voters in what we called a *'teh tarik'* session. To live up to the title, a 'tea-pulling' session was done at the end!

National Campaign

The conservative Malay-Islamic group that I crossed swords with in a Malaysian Islamic student event in the US in 2008, ISMA, entered the election under the ticket of the old PAS splinter party, the Pan-Malaysian Islamic Front. They focused on putting Malay-Muslim candidates in Malay majority and plurality seats where BN and PR fielded non-Malay candidates. Malay-Muslim right wingers had always focused on two elements: one, using medieval Islamic jurisprudence to declare that it is not permissible to appoint non-Muslim leaders; or two, that it could be done only for areas where non-Muslims are the majority. This was an atavistic worldview that did not reflect the diversity of views of classical scholars, nor was it grounded in modern democratic reality.

But on the Internet, these views not only spread but thrived. As in many parts of the world, we found it ironic that the Internet that was such a liberating medium in its inception, enabled polarizing views to exist in a bubble, merely reinforcing, instead of challenging, prejudices.

PR was also beset by intra-party contests, particularly between KEADILAN and PAS, across the country. PAS President Abdul Hadi Awang raised the issue that KEADILAN had a history of defections, and also accused some of the candidates of being 'communists' (referring to a PSM candidate standing on the KEADILAN banner) and 'drug addicts'. But Hadi took matters even further when he campaigned for a DAP member in Pahang who contested as an independent against the KEADILAN candidate.

During the campaign, I took one night off to go to Kelantan to campaign for Nik Mahmood Nik Hassan. Nine years after his first run, my uncle was back on the hustings. This time, he was contesting the seat of Tanah Merah. While KEADILAN won the seat in 2008, our family's roots were in Kota Bharu, and from the beginning, we knew it would not be straightforward. When I spoke to my uncle, he also said that there were tensions between the PAS party machinery and the KEADILAN team on the ground.

I also spoke in Damansara Perdana, in Tony Pua's constituency. Addressing the largely multi-racial, middle class crowd in English, I emphasized the need to build on the successes of the 2008 election. While we had garnered majority support from Malaysians in the Peninsula, we needed to get support from Sabah and Sarawak this time around. Malaysia deserved a government of all talents. The Petaling Jaya and Subang Jaya PR Parliament and State Assembly candidates organized a massive grand finale 'ceramah' at the Petaling Jaya Stadium in Kelana Jaya, which happened to be in my constituency, on the last day of the campaign. A crowd of 50,000 Malaysians of all races gathered in the field to listen the candidates. Imaan took a photo and asked me, 'How does it feel to be rockstar?'

On election day, while I took nothing for granted, there was a sense of confidence in Kelana Jaya and Seri Setia, as well as in retaining Selangor. My family, friends, and supporters gathered at the tallying centre to wait for the official announcement. I managed to win Seri Setia with an increased majority of 4,663 compared to 2,863 previously. My popular vote increased marginally from 55.8 per cent to 57.1 per cent.

But it turned out that this was *not the time*, contrary to our battle cry. There was only a gain of seven seats for PR—all from DAP. Nevertheless, PR did win the popular vote of 50.9 per cent, while BN's popular vote was only 47.4 per cent. This was the first time that the ruling coalition did not win the popular vote. Despite defending my seat and the state government, the failure of the coalition to win at the federal level was a massive disappointment. I felt a sense of void.

5. Troubles on Many Fronts

Allegations of fraud as well as anger at malapportionment and gerrymandering that had been raised by Bersih all these years intensified with the 2013 election results. The indelible ink that was long demanded by Bersih was introduced for the first time, but it was easily removed and the authorities claimed it was so due to the 'halal' regulations. But the public noted that Indonesia and Afghanistan did not have the same problems with their ink. There was also a sudden, questionable increase in voters in rural and semi-urban constituencies. It was calculated that in 2013, one rural vote was equal to six urban votes.

Immediately, PM Najib Razak blamed a 'Chinese tsunami'. Less than a week before the forty-fourth anniversary of the 13 May riots that took place after the third national election, it seemed that the BN leadership was willing to rile up racial sentiments as an excuse for their bad performance in the polls. UMNO-owned *Utusan Malaysia* put up a headline 'What more do the Chinese want?'[37], while MCA-owned *Star* reported on how the Chinese would be the real losers for rejecting BN. This was the worst kind of disinformation. It was true that Chinese votes for the PR increased. Yet, other than in Kelantan and Kedah, the

---

[37] The original Malay headline was 'Apa lagi Cina mahu', which carries with it a more crude and rough intonation then the English translation. ('Apa Lagi Cina Mau?', Utusan Malaysia, 7 May 2013.)

votes for PR increased in all states, including Perlis, Pahang, and Terengganu where Malays make up more than 70 per cent of the population. With the Chinese forming less than a quarter of the national population, it was clearly an 'urban tsunami' that gave PR the majority in popular vote.

Anwar Ibrahim tweeted on the morning after the election, 'Wear black.' The party leadership decided to organize a gathering—again in the Petaling Jaya Stadium. I liaised with the state and local authorities to book the stadium as well as inform the police on the same day about what eventually came to be known as the 'Blackout 505 Rally'. Previously, whenever I organized 'ceramahs' or rallies, I would get one of my staff to write the letter to inform the police about the event, as required by the law. This was to minimize my risk should the police take action. But I knew that this time it would be different, and I took the responsibility of writing to the police in my own name.

More than 100,000 Malaysians came to the rally that night. People filled the football field, as well as the terraces to the brink. Nearby, at the Paradigm Shopping Mall, black t-shirts ran out at many retail shops as customers were looking for something black to wear at the stadium. It came to a point that the toll to the North Klang Valley Expressway was jammed with the volume of traffic and cars parked by the roadside. People walked for kilometres in the rain to show their support; but I also had friends and family caught in the jam who complained to me about it! In my speech, I said that the call for change transcended race, as opposed to what Najib and UMNO were arguing. The annoying part was that since the 2010 football World Cup in South Africa, the vuvuzela had made an appearance in Malaysian political rallies and protests as well; it can be a struggle to get your voice heard above all the noise!

As expected, the next day I received a summons to appear in court. I was charged at the Sessions Court in mid-May under Section 9(5) of the Peaceful Assembly Act for failing to give a

10-day notice to hold the rally. If found guilty, I was liable to a maximum fine of RM10,000, which would mean I would lose my seat. From the beginning, I declared that this was a political persecution which went against the talk of national reconciliation that was being mooted by Najib in the aftermath of the election. I pleaded 'not guilty' and my legal team focused on challenging the Peaceful Assembly Act, arguing that it violated the right to Freedom of Assembly guaranteed under the Federal Constitution. PR organized 'Blackout 505' rallies across the country, attracting huge crowds and I spoke at a few of the events.

Deputy Speakership

PR won 44 seats in the Selangor State Assembly. KEADILAN actually lost one seat, while PAS made a gain of seven seats and DAP two seats. This meant that the composition was 14-15-15. Khalid Ibrahim maintained his position as the Chief Minister, but it was largely due to the backing of the two other parties, not his own, as his support within KEADILAN continued to erode. Frankly, I was hoping for a place in his cabinet as a State EXCO, as I had been a member of the political bureau since 2010. Instead, my name was proposed for Deputy Speaker; while Hannah Yeoh from the DAP was to be appointed Speaker.

Hannah made history as the first female Speaker of any federal or state legislature in Malaysia. Hannah was thirty-four, while I was thirty-one, making a young combination for positions traditionally held by more veteran politicians. In true British tradition, we had to wear robes not only for the swearing-in ceremony but also when we presided over the State Assembly sessions.

At the end of 2013, I launched the Young State Assembly person Program, where young students could apply to have a feel of being a legislator at the State Assembly. They would be introduced to the legislative process while being able to voice their views and understand policies affecting the younger generation in the state. This became a fixed program in the state calendar and the real Speaker and Deputy Speaker would preside over the debates while State EXCOs would at times appear to reply to the young participants as 'the government'. In 2014, the Youth Parliament of Malaysia was inaugurated and I like to think the program I founded was its forerunner.

Overall, it helped that PR had a comfortable majority in the State Assembly, so the sessions were generally straightforward. But it was still a massive learning experience. In November 2013, during a heated debate in which a BN State Assemblywoman was told to retract a misleading statement, the Opposition Leader Mohd Shamsudin Lias rose to defend her. The controversy was an old issue that had been explained by the state government. After failing to properly explain which part of the Standing Orders he was referring to, he ignored my instruction for him to sit. I told him that if he was unhappy with my decisions, he could put in a motion. Both sides began to shout loudly. Finally, I had to instruct Shamsudin to leave the State Assembly for a day.

But I was not being one-sided. In 2014, Azmin Ali, who was KEADILAN's Deputy President and chair of the backbencher's club in Selangor, was critical towards the state government's handling of the state's water supply, a perennial problem. Former Speaker Teng Chang Khim, who was now a State EXCO, stood up to interrupt Azmin. I told Teng to allow backbenchers and the opposition to speak as they had limited time, and as a member of the government, he could answer at the end of the debate. Teng tried to raise a point in the Standing Orders (which treats all members equally) but I wouldn't let him.

'Yes, I understand that Sungai Pinang (Teng) was the Speaker before, but I am the Speaker for this session,' I said to Teng. Twice, he tried to read the Standing Orders but I asked him to sit each time.

In November 2013, while I was presiding, Khalid Ibrahim announced in his speech that the State EXCO had agreed on pay increase for the Chief Minister, the State EXCOs, the Speaker, the Deputy Speaker, and the State Assemblypersons. I struggled to maintain a straight face as I heard that as Deputy Speaker, I would enjoy the highest increase in terms of percentage: 373 per cent increase to RM15,750 per month! While the EXCO had discussed and approved the matter, the government backbenchers, and even the national party leadership were not consulted and were, understandably, not in favour of such a huge hike. As the move attracted brickbats from the press and the public, we struggled to defend the move before a society that had endured low wages for so long.

Traditionally pay for legislators in Malaysia, at the federal or state level, were relatively low. This created different problems: those without personal financial means found politics expensive to pursue; professionals were reluctant to leave their high-paying jobs; or it exposed legislators to corruption. The pay increase of State Assemblypersons was certainly justified: it was RM6,000 earlier and now increased to RM11,250. Even a pay increase for the Deputy Speaker was somewhat understandable—now the State Assembly was sitting for much longer and doing more work than what it did during the BN era, and it was only right that there was increase. But selling a 373 per cent pay rise to the public was a bit difficult. I received many sarcastic and angry messages when the news broke out. Finally, the PR leaders, while accepting increase for the State Assemblypersons, pushed for a reduction in the increase for the other positions.

In April 2014, US President Barack Obama visited Malaysia, becoming only the second serving US President to visit the country. Fifty years previously, Lyndon B. Johnson paid a visit. There was a FELDA settlement in Negeri Sembilan that he stopped by and it was renamed after him. A townhall session was held between Obama and the Malaysian youth and I was among those invited to attend. I had followed Obama's career closely since his famous 2004 DNC speech and read his books.

His background—having a Muslim father and growing up in Indonesia, eventually becoming the first African American US President—was inspiring. He had also modernized political campaigning and was adept in social media. Unfortunately, he was also close to our PM Najib Razak, seeing the latter as a valuable Muslim ally in the war on terror.

The townhall was held at Tunku Chancellor Hall UM. The security was manned by US Secret Service Agents, wearing suits, sunglasses, and ear-pieces, just like the ones you see in Hollywood movies. In his speech, Obama said, 'The most important thing that I learned as a young person trying to bring about change is you have to be persistent, and you have to get more people involved, and you have to form relationships with different groups and different organizations.'

But it was the action of a few UM students, protesting the Trans-Pacific Partnership trade agreement as well as US support for the Egyptian Field Marshal Abdel Fattah el-Sisi who overthrew the popularly-elected President Mohamed Morsi, that attracted headlines. They raised the placards in the middle of Obama's speech, and Obama deftly commented on it in his speech, before the security asked the students to sit and remove the signs. Later, the UM management took disciplinary action against the students, while the US Embassy announced their respect for the students' right to protest.

Hannah and I, along with the BN Assemblyman Shahrom Shariff, were invited to join the Young Political Leaders visit to Australia in mid-2014. We managed to meet Foreign Minister Julie Bishop and Speaker Browyn Bishop, while also speaking to the Australian media. In addition, we spoke to the Malaysian students in Canberra. As usual, the authorities had warned students about attending events with the opposition, and action was taken against one of the students who spoke on our panel in Canberra. But compared to my time as a student, more students defied these directives and became politically active.

South Africa

In September 2013, I attended the CPA conference in Johannesburg, South Africa. After the conference, Imaan and Ilhan, who was thirty months old, joined me for a short break in Cape Town. As you can imagine, Ilhan proved to be a handful on the flights. We wanted to take the opportunity of my trip to visit a city that we have heard so much about. We visited Robben Island to see Nelson Mandela's tiny cell from 1964–1982 that was described vividly in his autobiography *Long Walk to Freedom*. How he survived being imprisoned for 27 years under the racist apartheid system, but, then, upon being elected as South Africa's first post-apartheid President, embraced his tormentors, was truly inspiring.

We stayed in a bed-and-breakfast in Bo-Kaap. This was the Malay quarter in Cape Town. The Malays were brought to the Cape by the Dutch from across maritime Southeast Asia in the 17th century. It was the Malays who brought Islam to the Cape, and the 'kramats'[38] or tombs of the community leaders are located across Cape Town. We dropped by a few of the tombs. I could only reflect on how difficult it must have been for them a few centuries ago being sent to a foreign, distant, and cold land. Yet they remained steadfast in their faith and principles in facing the colonial power.

But the African National Congress (ANC) had deteriorated over the years as their dominance as liberators had allowed complacency and corruption to set in. I was always intrigued by this. I managed to visit South Africa again for work over the years and met with Mmusi Maimane, the country's Opposition Leader from the Democratic Alliance. I, then, organized a call by Maimane to call on Azmin as the Selangor Chief Minister when

---

[38] Kramat comes from the Malay word 'keramat'. Tombs of venerated saints are called keramat. Keramat in turn comes from the Arabic word 'karamah' كرامة which means 'dignity'.

he visited Malaysia. South Africa shows that no political party has a monopoly on virtue and those that started as forces of freedom ended up holding the country back.

Kajang Move

As Khalid continued to ignore the party leadership, the State Assemblyman for Kajang resigned in January 2014 to make way for Anwar Ibrahim. The idea was to safeguard Selangor as a stronghold for PR and to be a launchpad for the coalition nationally, in the same way Turkish President Recep Tayyip Erdogan and Indonesian President Joko Widodo successfully governed Istanbul and Jakarta to prove their mettle before running to run the country.

However, on 7 March, the Court of Appeal swiftly overruled Anwar's early acquittal over the Saiful Bukhari sodomy allegations, thereby disqualifying him from running in the by-election. Party President Dr Wan Azizah replaced him. She won handsomely over the MCA/BN candidate.

Tensions between the party and Khalid continued, including over a deal taking back the state water companies. Eventually, Wan Azizah was named as the KEADILAN and DAP's candidate for Chief Minister while Khalid was sacked from the party. Khalid was able to hold on to PAS support—except for two Assemblymen who were eventually sacked by PAS. This further soured relations between PAS on one end and KEADILAN and DAP on the other. I felt a tinge of regret on losing Khalid, whom I considered a father figure, but as someone who also struggled with how he so cavalierly dealt with the party, I knew that we had no choice.

PR Youth tried to find a solution to the problem and the three parties youth leaders collectively met with the senior counterparts in turn. When we met PAS President Abdul Hadi Awang, he signalled that he clearly wanted to retain Khalid as Chief Minister and would monitor any 'weaknesses'. Later, I revealed this to the press and stated that this was clearly at odds with the intentions of the majority of Selangor's state assemblypersons, who wanted Khalid removed.

Nevertheless, the Selangor Palace was not happy with the nomination of Dr Wan Azizah based on the argument that she would be a proxy for Anwar. There has also been no female Chief Minister in any state in Malaysia. An UMNO lawyer argued that her menses would prevent her from being appointed to the position!

This was the level of despicable politics that was being practised in Malaysia and that female politicians had to face to break the glass ceiling. I still remember how Wan Azizah responded in the 2004 election. Her challenger from UMNO, Pirdaus Ismail, was a graduate in Islamic studies and the imam for the National Mosque. Pirdaus ridiculed her ability to be an MP, when she could not even lead prayers (under orthodox Islam, only male imams can lead a mixed-congregation). A pious Muslim, Wan Azizah replied, 'Let him lead the prayers while elect me to the constituency!'

It became clear at that time that Azmin Ali had been working on getting the position for himself quietly, and eventually he was named as Chief Minister in spite of not being nominated by the majority of State Assemblypersons. Wan Azizah graciously pulled out and Azmin became Menteri Besar.

Running for Youth Leader

I decided to contest for the party's Youth Leader position in 2014. This party election would be the first time where the age limit is lowered from forty to thirty-five. KEADILAN also conducted party elections on a one-member-one-vote basis since 2010, the first major party in Malaysia to do so.

I worked closely with Saifuddin Nasution, Nurul Izzah, and Rafizi Ramli. Saifuddin was running for Deputy President against Azmin Ali; Izzah and Rafizi were going for the Vice Presidencies. I launched a campaign with a multi-racial line-up for the Youth

Wing. At the same time, I treated Azmin Ali to dinner in Bangsar to inform him of my intent to contest, although I knew he was backing my old friend Amirudin Shari. Azmin himself was defending his position as Deputy President against Saifuddin as well as my former boss Khalid Ibrahim.

A debate was organized in Johor between the candidates for the leader of the Youth Wing's post. Some pointed out how messy it was for KEADILAN to conduct its party election so openly, and indeed, there were some unfortunate incidents. The bottom line, however, is that as a mass-based party, making the leadership accountable to all the members is the best way forward. This weakens the control of party warlords. Although having millions of members, only a few thousand delegates will determine the party leadership. Thus, while little is seen in open campaigning, the campaign takes place behind closed doors which makes it unaccountable and corrupt, while challenging the status quo becomes difficult.

I travelled across the country, meeting party members from Kota Kinabalu, Sabah to Kota Bharu; Bahau in Negeri Sembilan to Batu Pahat, Johor. We even came out with a rock theme song for the campaign. While race-based parties tend to swing to the right during party elections (and tack to the centre during general elections), racial and religious rhetoric had no place in KEADILAN. The main factions tend to have multi-racial support. The racial power-sharing model of the Alliance and BN was breaking down, and clearly, a multi-racial party was the way forward.

The result turned out to be a close one. I obtained 4,509 votes against Amirudin's 4,259 votes: a majority of 240 votes. The rest of the committee were dominated overwhelmingly by Amirudin's line up. Azmin and Izzah successfully defended their positions, while Rafizi was elected as Vice President for the first time.

During that year's Youth Wing congress, after the new committee was officially announced and invited to the stage, I was about to deliver my maiden speech as the Youth Leader. However, almost everyone from the other faction walked out in protest at Amirudin's defeat, which was strange, because they accepted their own victories despite claiming the party polls were flawed. The press was in full attendance. I was furious but tried my best to control myself. I pledged to unite the Youth Wing and asked the members to evaluate us over the next 100 days. Eventually, after a stormy meeting, we did a public show of unity at the party's main national congress, but the tensions persisted not just in the Youth Wing but the entire party and would have serious long-term repercussions.

State EXCO

As the new Chief Minister, Azmin Ali appointed his EXCO, which consisted of a few new faces, including Amirudin and myself. I was given the portfolio for education, human capital development, science, technology, and innovation. In reality, although Malaysia is a Federation, much of the power lies with the centre. National schools and public universities are all under the purview of the Federal Government.

Nevertheless, the Selangor state government under PR had provided grants to Islamic schools, Chinese and Tamil vernacular schools, mission schools, and Chinese independent schools. Chinese independent schools are secondary schools which chose to continue teaching in Mandarin after the government made secondary schools teach only in English or Malay after independence.

Students at the Chinese independent schools sit for the Unified Examination Certificate (UEC) examinations—equivalent to the A-Levels. The qualification is recognized throughout the world: in China, Singapore, the US, and the UK, among others. It is also recognized in many Malaysian private universities. However, local public universities do not recognize the qualification, resulting in a longstanding campaign by

Chinese educationists to have the UEC recognized, which Malay nationalists naturally oppose. By the time I became State EXCO, the two private institutions under the state government, UNISEL and Selangor Islamic University College had recognized the qualification. Today, a few state governments have recognized the UEC too.

This debate is a longstanding one in Malaysia, and tends to overlap with the country's cultural wars. The importance of upholding Malay, not only as the national language but also as the most widely spoken language among all the races and classes across the country, must never be overlooked. But, when it comes to calls by certain segments (sometimes by the pro-English middle classes, other times by Malay nationalists) to close down vernacular schools, I strongly disagree. The government should strive to make national schools the school of *choice*. I also think it's strange that people who oppose vernacular schools also overlook the liberalization of government policy for enrolment of Malaysians to international schools and the mushrooming of various private and international schools, including Islamic ones.

I was appointed to several boards related to my portfolio. I was chair of University of Selangor's (UNISEL) board of governors and a member of its board of directors; chair of the Selangor Public Library Corporation, and a trustee of the Selangor Foundation. At UNISEL, we introduced the Sagong Tasi scholarship for the indigenous Orang Asli. It was named after Sagong Tasi, who along with other family heads from the Temuan tribe, were asked to vacate their homes due to a development project. The Courts had ruled in favour of Sagong Tasi against the state government and recognized the indigenous ownership of the land. But after the PR victory, the state government withdrew their appeal to the Federal Court on the case.

As State EXCO, I made several trips abroad. One memorable trip was to Jordan in 2015. I visited a project established by Malaysian students in Mafraq for Syrian refugees. It was called

'The Tears of Syria in Jordan'. I was amazed by their initiative, but more importantly, was inspired by their compassion. It has since expanded to assist Syrian refugees in Turkey, Lebanon, and Malaysia. Today, it operates schools, provide assistance during winter, and the Islamic festivals. I visited the refugee camp and went into their shelters. I couldn't help but feel sad, particularly for the children who suffered the most. I even carried a few of them around the camp.

I was also invited to deliver a speech to the World Affairs Council. Two former Jordanian PMs, Dr Abdul Salam Majali and Dr Adnan Badran, were in attendance. I stated in my speech:

> 'As noted by Indian essayist Pankaj Mishra in *From the Ruins of Empire: The Intellectuals Who Remade Asia*: from the heydays of European imperialism to the hegemony of American capitalism, Muslims maintained a strong adherence to our faith and traditions. When many fathers of independence in the Muslim world—or the Third World in general—tried to replicate one form of Western model or the other, it failed miserably—simply because such models were the product of the unique historical contexts of their societies. It was out of these deadlocks that the search for a solution from within began to gather momentum.
>
> 'The challenges of terrorism or literalism however emerge when the desire for a quick fix leads to answers that may appear authentic but are unable to incorporate our tradition of moderation or the challenges of today's world to its core.
>
> 'Our task—and opportunity—is to prove both sides wrong. We can prove to the literalists that religion can make a positive contribution to modern, plural democracies. We can also show liberal fundamentalists that religion can contribute to the discourse to reform capitalism and modernity; that the health and happiness of our countries depend on something more than mere socio-economic development.

'Let us retell the forgotten stories of moderation to the younger generation—the stories of Salahuddin al-Ayubi and Abdul Qadir al-Jazairi—heroes whose chivalry and dedication to justice made them legends even amongst their foes. Let us celebrate the thinkers and scholars such as Ibn Khaldun, Ibn Sina and al-Khwarizmi whom without their contribution the modern world would have been a very different and poorer place.'

Chairing the Selangor Library was enjoyable for a bibliophile like me. It was run by Mastura Muhamad, who, with impeccable integrity and a desire to make libraries in the state world-class, had overseen significant improvements in the organization since taking over in 2009. When I was chair, the corporation had over ninety libraries state-wide, including the iconic Shah Alam Library. As they had a budget for a community library, I managed to get them to work with the Petaling Jaya City Council to repair an abandoned community hall in Kampung Lindungan that was overtaken by drug addicts. This was turned into a new library using old shipping containers, and featured a media room, meeting facilities, and computer labs for the use of the community.

There was also a greater realization about the importance of technical and vocational education. The state government had one technical college back then, the INPENS International College. In addition, we collaborated deeply with the Selangor Human Resources Development Centre, which is an agency set up in collaboration with industries in the state. This allowed students to get an early exposure to technical working environments as well as the involvement of major investors in the training of skilled workers. This included a range of fields such as big data analytics, solar panel installation, and cloud computing.

In line with the Federal Cabinet, the State EXCO meetings are usually on Wednesday, after the Chief Minister's audience with the Sultan. This came from a relatively modern tradition in the UK: constitution expert Vernon Bogdanor claims that the weekly audience only started with Queen Elizabeth II.[39] Additionally, we would celebrate the Sultan's birthday annually in December with a dinner, praying with him during Hari Raya Aidilfitri, and attend his Hari Raya celebration afterwards along with other royal functions and events.

Balik Kampung

My parents, wife, Ilhan, and I went back to Kota Bharu in 2014. Tok Wan Jah had passed away at the age of ninety-six in 2012, a year after Ilhan was born. This was Ilhan's first 'balik kampung' and we spent the night in Tok Wan Jah's house in Kubang Pasu. Ilhan enjoyed himself running on the wooden floors. I also showed him the surviving portion of my paternal great grandfather Wan Musa's house—estimated to be more than a century old—and my paternal grandparents' neighbouring house which is rented out to a kindergarten. I had never stepped inside the house as they had passed away before I was born. We also visited our family's cemetery in Banggol.

Three years later, we returned to Kota Bharu, but this time, we stayed at a hotel instead. Tok Wan Jah's house was also rented out, but we managed to show it to Ilhan, who could not remember much from his earlier trip. Ilhan and I also took the opportunity to visit the Kota Bharu War Museum, which could do with better maintenance, but still contained many interesting artefacts from World War II. Ilhan inherited both my father's and my own interest of history. Like most boys, he is more fixated on World War history and memorized each tank and gun model.

'Balik Kampung' typically suggests going back to one's hometown or village. But as people become more mobile across

---

[39] Bogdanor, Vernon, 'The Audience: May I speak freely, Your Majesty?' *The Telegraph*, 6 March 2013, https://www.telegraph.co.uk/culture/theatre/ 9912902/The-Audience-May-I-speak-freely-Your-Majesty.html, Accessed 30 August 2021.

the generations, it will mean journeys across family trees and across generations as we seek to trace our roots. While this can be inward looking, the reality is that in a diverse, trading country like Malaysia, this journey will expose us to the many intermarriages and colourful histories that shaped our families. Part of my family originated from Tak Bai, which today falls on the Thai side of the border and reputedly has Chinese and Mongolian blood; while through his mother, Ilhan has Thai and Indian blood. In the journey back in 2012, I spent time working on my father's biography, and asked him to repeat stories from our family history so that it would be preserved, especially for Ilhan and his children.

Anwar's Second Imprisonment

The country's apex court, the Federal Court, upheld Anwar Ibrahim's conviction for the second sodomy case on 10 February 2015 and he was ordered to serve his five-year sentence immediately. KEADILAN Youth had organized a gathering outside the court. The mood in the opposition, which peaked just prior to the 2013 election in anticipation of taking over the federal government, was now gloomy and pessimistic with Anwar's imprisonment and the tensions within our coalition.

Nevertheless, after discussing with the comrades in PR Youth, as well as various youth NGOs, we decided to organize protests called '*KitaLawan*' or 'We Fight'. The protests were held every Saturday in Kuala Lumpur. On 21 February, the first arrests began.

The next day, while I was enjoying dinner at home with my family in Shah Alam, I was informed that suspicious plain clothes individuals were lurking around the house. Knowing that I would be next, I savoured the curry dinner slowly. Eventually, approximately ten policemen arrested me for the *KitaLawan* rallies. I was brought to the Jinjang police station in Kuala Lumpur. I was released at around 2.00 a.m. with Imaan and my supporters waiting.

Exactly two weeks later, on 8 March, the police summoned me to the Dang Wangi police station to give a statement on the latest *KitaLawan* rally. At the end of the interrogation, they informed me that I was being arrested under the Penal Code and would be held in the Jinjang Detention Centre. I was allowed to have lunch with my parents, wife, and Ilhan as well as my second sister, Nazli, and her husband. For many in the opposition, particularly among the *Reformasi* and KEADILAN activists, being imprisoned was seen as a badge of honour. Now, it was my turn.

As I wrote in *9 May 2018: Notes from the Frontline*:

'If courting arrest and worse was the price of making a stand, so be it. And it was nothing compared to what other leaders had or were facing. How on earth does one 'play by the rules' when those very rules were made unfairly and enforced selectively? Our ultimate objective was not merely winning state governments after all, but Federal power.'[40]

Of course, being imprisoned was nothing glamorous. Arriving at Jinjang that afternoon, I was told to strip naked and change to a well-worn purple remand uniform. Fortunately, I got a cell to myself. There was a partially open shower and toilet and I was provided with a small 'Good Morning' towel, toothbrush, and small packets of soap and toothpaste. The toothbrush was broken in half to make it less hazardous. I was not allowed books or my phone, and had to resort to looking at the sky through the small slits in the wall. I asked the lockup guards about prayer times. Food was a packet of rice with fried fish and watered-down curry that looked more like Tom Yum.

Every time someone was arrested, we would usually have a vigil outside. I was disappointed not to hear any of the speeches or

---

[40] Nik Nazmi Nik Ahmad, *9 May 2018: Notes from the Frontline*, Petaling Jaya: SIRD, 2018, pp. 3–4.

songs, but knowing that there was a vigil going on for me outside was uplifting. I found out that Imaan came and spoke to those who gathered. I could not sleep properly due to the hard surface.

The next morning, Eric Paulsen, my lawyer, met me before the remand hearing. I had expected to be released, but he warned me that there was a chance that I would not be. I later found out that it was a rookie mistake. It is, always, best to mentally prepare for the worst. The magistrate remanded me for a further three days. Throughout my detention. I came to look forward to being brought to Dang Wangi by car—barefoot—to continue with the interrogation because it meant going out of my cell and enjoying the view of the journey (as well as using proper, private toilets).

Another of my lawyers, Melissa Sasidaran, asked me whether it was okay for her to take a photo of me walking barefoot and handcuffed in remand clothes. Some did not like the indignity of it, but I knew I did nothing wrong, and I wanted the public to know how we were being treated. The photo went viral along with my mother's message on Facebook:

'Stay strong my son we will continue to pray for you. It breaks my heart to see you shoeless in prison attire and being handcuffed. I will never forget what the government is doing to my son, he looks like a criminal even before being charged. May Allah keep you strong.'

Fortunately, I was released one day short of the original remand, spending a total of three days and two nights in lockup. It was a blip compared to many others, but eye-opening nonetheless. My comrades from KEADILAN, but also DAP, PAS, and the civil society all had their turns in the lockup. I dropped by the old Coliseum steak house in Kuala Lumpur with my wife and son after my release, before going to another vigil for the remaining detainees. During my arrest, Ilhan was told that I was helping the police with something. He was only four, too young to understand much of what was happening.

Collapse of PR

In early 2015, PAS Spiritual Leader Nik Aziz Nik Mat passed away. In June, the party held its annual meeting and party elections. I attended the PAS Youth annual meeting and could sense that the mood was different. The moderate, pro-PR faction that was supported by Nik Aziz was comprehensively defeated by the conservatives. Previously, the party's earlier shift to the centre had allowed it to attract strong non-Muslim support. In 2013, there were photos of Chinese girls clad in shorts and skimpy t-shirts waving PAS flags!

But as stated earlier, there was always a tension with the conservative wing that wanted to forge closer cooperation with UMNO, in spite of the fact that the latter was their traditional rival since its establishment. Probably, it was the charisma and strong will of Nik Aziz that had prevented this all this while. PAS decided to break ties with DAP, and DAP responded by declaring that PR was dead. This was confirmed by KEADILAN President Dr Wan Azizah Wan Ismail.

Things were complicated in Selangor due to the fact that the three parties were evenly balanced: DAP fifteen, PAS fifteen (of whom thirteen were conservatives and two pro-PR), KEADILAN thirteen, UMNO twelve, and one independent. Eventually, the status quo prevailed. All the three State EXCOs from PAS were conservatives. While Chief Minister Azmin Ali kept insisting that his administration was still a 'PR State Government', it was essentially a looser arrangement between KEADILAN, PAS, and DAP.

In July 2015, I was touring Australia, giving speeches to academics and the Malaysian diaspora. I did a video interview at the Australian National University in Canberra.

This was the very first question: 'Is PR dead?'

My answer: Yes, the coalition has ended. But we were working on a new movement founded on the PR spirit.

6. The Rise of PH

The victory of the conservative faction in PAS was not total. In PAS Kelana Jaya, the incumbent Division Chief and pro-PR leader Izham Hashim succeeded in defending his position in the 2015 party election. Having known each other closely since 2008, when my candidacy to the PAS grassroots was announced at his house, we frequently shared stories of what was happening behind the scenes. Izham and two-thirds of his committee members stood down to join a new movement formed by the moderate-minded PAS leaders. But many of the mosques, including in Kampung Lindungan, were still controlled by PAS.

Eventually, the ex-PAS moderates launched Parti Amanah Negara (AMANAH), which I attended. They took an inclusive approach, while portraying Islam as '*rahmatan-lil-alamin*' ('a mercy to the world'). They maintained their commitment to the Shariah, but there was more emphasis on the higher objectives of the Shariah or '*Maqasid Shariah*', rather than just specific punitive aspects favoured by the conservatives. Traditionally, these objectives were the preservation of religion, life, intellect, property, dignity, and progeny, guided by the twin objectives of justice and mercy.

A New Coalition

For KEADILAN, this was a massive change, as our cooperation with PAS started from our inception in 1999. Just as how the mosques in my constituency—one of the most important Malay-Muslim institutions—remained largely in the control of PAS, this scene was replicated across the country and was of greater significance in places with a larger Malay population and in the rural areas. While we have attracted majority urban and non-Malay support since 2008, the game changer would be the Malay voters, and how on earth were we to win this without PAS? Many within KEADILAN, and even civil society, were doubting our decision to break away from PAS.

In September 2015, KEADILAN President Wan Azizah decisively steered a discussion between opposition parties and civil society to form a new coalition—'*Pakatan Harapan*' ('The Pact of Hope'). Some felt that the prospect of winning federal power was so remote that our focus should be on retaining Selangor, and doing so could only happen by cooperating with PAS. But my faction felt that Selangor was not at risk and the focus should be on winning national power instead.

Within KEADILAN, debate over the direction we should take heated up. Two weeks after the launch of PH, almost half of the KEADILAN Central Leadership Council that were aligned to Deputy President Azmin Ali called for a meeting to review the formation of PH. They argued that the President was only mandated to discuss, but not to launch a new coalition. Wan Azizah had, in fact, ended the meeting asking for the Council to give her the mandate to do what was necessary to form an alliance with other opposition parties and this was endorsed by the Council. Wan Azizah showed her steel and resolve that people often underestimated.

Setiawangsa

In 2015, I sat down with Rafizi Ramli to discuss my next step in politics. I had been a Selangor State Assemblyman for two terms. On top of that, I had held many senior positions within the state government. I felt that it was the right time for me to run for the federal parliament in the next election, especially, now that I was the party's Youth Leader.

We discussed a few seats in the Klang Valley, but eventually settled on Setiawangsa. This was the last bastion of BN in Kuala Lumpur. Even in 2008, when all the other seats in Kuala Lumpur fell to the opposition, Setiawangsa remained safely in UMNO's hands. It had been carved out as seat with a small electorate of just over 70,000; out of that, there were over 17,000 military and police personnel that traditionally voted for the government. Historically, much of it came out from the Setapak Parliamentary seat, which was first won by PRM in 1959. DAP won it in the 1969 elections. But like much of Kuala Lumpur, it attracted many Malays (including Kelantanese) during industrialization and its demographics changed.

In 1999, KEADILAN (then PKN) fielded Vice President Marina Yusoff in the seat but she lost to Zulhasnan Rafique by over 5,000 votes. Five years later, Setiawangsa was taken out from Wangsa Maju. Zulhasnan was fielded in the new constituency and won with a majority of almost 20,000 against PAS. Zulhasnan defended the seat in 2008 against my boss from Anwar's office, Ibrahim Yaacob, who represented KEADILAN. This time, the BN majority shrunk to just over 8,000 votes. Ibrahim stood again in 2013 and lost by a mere 1,390.

However, after the delineation conducted in 2018, a predominantly Chinese locality was taken out of Setiawangsa, increasing the Malay voters to 62 per cent. Chinese voters made up 26 per cent and Indians 10 per cent. It was not an obvious seat for the opposition, but I felt that as Youth leader, I had a responsibility of going after the marginal seats to help PH win federal power.

Much of Setiawangsa was previously part of Hawthornden Estate rubber plantation owned by the tycoon Loke Yew (1845–1917). He was buried in a tomb on a hill in what is today Desa Tun Hussein Onn, a housing complex for military personnel located next to the Ministry of Defence headquarters (also in my constituency). Some of the old rubber trees remain in Bukit Dinding, a popular haunt in recent years for hiking and cycling. However, much of the hill is now privately owned since the turn of the century. This was also the site of the Battle of Bukit Dinding during the Selangor Civil War in 1870.

Today, the constituency has massive PPR public housing flats in Semarak, Kampung Baru Air Panas, Desa Rejang, and Sungai Bonus. While the majority of the PPR residents (who came from various squatter villages nearby) are Malay, there are considerable numbers of Chinese and Indian residents as well. There are also Perbadanan Kemajuan Negeri Selangor (PKNS) flats in Keramat and low-cost flats in Setapak. There are posh bungalows in Taman Tasik Titiwangsa and Bukit Setiawangsa, middle-class condominiums and terrace houses across Wangsa Maju, and gritty, poorly planned, old terrace houses in Rejang. There is even a new village built to resettle the Chinese community during the communist insurgency in Air Panas. Previously it was separated from the outside with a barbwire fence and had a market, central cooking area, community hall, and animal shed. Today, only the market survives. Nearby is a football field where Malaysian legends Santokh Singh and K. Rajagopal honed their skills.

The local Malay community is colourful. There is a sizeable Bawean community around the area, and many of them were known for their skills in working with horses in the old Turf Club nearby (which was replaced by the Petronas Twin Towers). More recently, there have been droves of migrants from Kelantan. Probably, the location of Setiawangsa along with Wangsa Maju and Gombak near the highway that leads to the East Coast made it an attractive prospect for recent arrivals from the state. Many military veterans, too, choose to continue staying on in Setiawangsa upon retirement.

In November 2015, I rented an office in Sri Rampai to be my campaign centre. I spent about RM11,000 every month—mostly from my salary, sometimes from donations—to run my Setiawangsa operations, including hiring full- and part-time staff as well as running events.

One of my earliest events was to have a dialogue with military personnel and veterans. To 'invite' them, I stood with my volunteers and party members distributing leaflets and Jalur Gemilang car flags outside the entrances to the Ministry of Defence Headquarters (MINDEF) and Desa Tun Hussein Onn. We were pushed further and further away by the military police when our activity was seen from the minister's office. The dialogue itself—attended by Rafizi as well as Retired Admiral Imran Abdul Hamid, the KEADILAN MP for Lumut and former Navy senior officer—was a good start, attracting the audience of a few hundred people. The major issues we covered concerned the governance of the armed forces pension fund.

We also opened booths for residents to register as voters or volunteers and check their voting status. To distribute leaflets, we would concentrate on the Setiawangsa LRT station, which was used by many residents to get to work. We also distributed leaflets in the Rejang as well as Air Panas markets.

1MDB scandal

Originally established in 2008 as the sovereign wealth fund for the oil-rich state of Terengganu, 1MDB was taken over by the federal government a year later. Questions over what the corporation was actually doing were first raised in parliament by Opposition Leader Anwar Ibrahim in 2010. 'I'm not jealous of Jho Low spending time with Paris Hilton, but the fact is that upon checking with the companies commission, 1MDB has no business address and no appointed auditor . . . What is the PM's interest in this?'

The 'Jho Low' Anwar was referring to a mysterious, young businessman close to Najib Razak's stepson, Riza Aziz. Photos of the stocky, boyish playboy—then only twenty-nine years old—

partying wildly with American socialite Paris Hilton had gone
viral. He would then buy jewellery for model Miranda Kerr,
paintings by Picasso for actor Leonardo DiCaprio and a Ferrari
for reality television personality Kim Kardashian. Low and Riza
also worked on a Hollywood movie production company, where
much of the money was alleged to come from 1MDB.

In 2012, I raised concerns over the overpriced purchase of two
ageing independent power producers by 1MDB for over RM11
billion. One of the power plants was owned by Genting Berhad
and was bought for RM2.3 billion, meaning that its price to book
ratio was six times higher than any other power utility companies
in the region. A few months after the sale, one of Genting's
subsidiaries made a donation of RM10 million to a foundation
chaired by Najib, to be used for his election campaign.

The investigative journalism site *Sarawak Report* had zoomed
in on the issue in detail. I had first met the Sarawak-born Claire
Rewcastle Brown in 2010, when I visited her home in London.
I did not realize that she was the sister-in-law of UK PM Gordon
Brown until I saw an old photo of her husband with a young
Gordon Brown in her living room.

After six years in operation, 1MDB managed to incur debts
reaching RM42 billion. In July 2015, *The Wall Street Journal*
revealed that RM2.6 billion had been channelled to Najib's
personal bank accounts. Not long after, Attorney General Abdul
Ghani Patail, who was leading the taskforce investigating claims
of misappropriation of 1MDB funds, was terminated abruptly,
ostensibly 'on health reasons'. In April 2016, Bank Negara
Governor Zeti Akhtar Aziz, who was on the taskforce, resigned.
Not long after that, another member of the taskforce, Chief
Commissioner of the MACC, Abu Kassim Mohamed also left
the taskforce.

In September, it was revealed that Najib was facing a
corruption inquiry by the United States Department of Justice.
In 2017, it was announced that the Department of Justice
was seeking a total of US$1.7 billion, making it the largest

action brought under the Kleptocracy Asset Recovery Initiative of the department.

Apandi Ali, the new Attorney General, declared in January 2016 that the investigation was closed and no wrongdoing was established. The money supposedly came from a Saudi royal as a donation to Najib. The PM claimed to have returned most of the money—except for US$61 million. International media revealed that Najib and Rosmah spent millions of ringgits on luxury items during their trips abroad.

Around the same time, in April 2015, the GST was first implemented in Malaysia. In many ways, GST was a more effective and efficient tax instrument. Malaysia's individual tax base had always been relatively small. Nevertheless, after decades of low wages, rising costs of living, and a weak social safety net, combined with the images of the lavish lifestyle of the PM, his family, and their cronies in light of the 1MDB scandal, it riled up many ordinary Malaysians.

Cooperating with Mahathir

During the Bersih 4 rally in August 2015, Dr Mahathir Mohamad dropped by, shocking many Malaysians. As mentioned in the earlier chapters, the Bersih rallies had been gathering steam over the years, a highlight for those calling for change, but more importantly, it was about pushing for concrete reforms. The rally was held for two days on the eve of Independence Day. Bersih had to make new arrangements for security without the participation of PAS, and KEADILAN Youth arranged for our security squad to be marshals for the rally.

The rally was still massive—estimates placed the crowd at over 100,000 people. Mahathir was responsible for much of the damage to the country's institutions that had led to the state of the country during *Reformasi* and also enabled the 1MDB scandal to take place. He had been critical of other public rallies, including earlier Bersih marches. A year before, Mahathir announced that he had withdrawn his support for Najib Razak. The same pattern of Mahathir fighting a Malaysian PM and withdrawing his backing from a leader he had previously supported continued. In the beginning, he claimed that Najib was giving in too much to the opposition. Najib had abolished the ISA and committed himself to repeal the Sedition Act.

At the end of the year, I took a strident stance against Mahathir during the KEADILAN Youth Congress:

> 'Dr Mahathir states that 'bad leaders are born from a democratic system that has been misused.' Therefore, we must realise that the PM we have today is actually born from a misused democratic system, including by Dr Mahathir himself.
>
> 'We can thank him for speaking out for freedom of speech, the supremacy of the rule of law and fight corruption as well as abuse of power today. But we will not forget who weakened our democracy . . .
>
> 'We will not forget who was the PM when the rakyat was oppressed while demanding for *Reformasi*.'

In the press conference afterwards, I said I was open to working with Mahathir to bring down Najib, but we would not forget the past. The fact that the former was campaigning for the opposition or attacking UMNO was nothing new. Time and time again, he would always return to the Grand Old Party of Malaysian politics. In February 2016, the former UMNO strongman left the Malay party again. The reason this time was 1MDB. He was embarrassed, he said, to be associated with a corrupt party. Now, the lines he took resembled those of PH.

A month later, the major leaders from KEADILAN, DAP, AMANAH, civil society, and former UMNO leaders joined Dr Mahathir in signing the People's Declaration. The declaration called for the removal of Najib as PM, abolishing unjust laws, and restoring independent institutions in the country.

In May 2016, the Sarawak State Election was held. This time around, I was again stationed in Nangka, Sibu. The Sarawak Chief Minister Adenan Satem ensured that BN emerged stronger with 72 out of 82 seats in the Sarawak State Assembly by exploiting the disunity and playing up the 'Sarawak for Sarawakians' sentiment. The DAP's share dropped from twelve to seven seats while KEADILAN retained its three.

By-elections in the traditional UMNO parliamentary seats of Kuala Kangsar and Sungai Besar respectively became the first test for PH and Mahathir supporters in the Peninsula. Some in KEADILAN, who still believed in the option of working together with PAS, attempted to reach an understanding with them, but Abdul Hadi Awang insisted that the party would not negotiate with PH. AMANAH was finally given the mandate to contest the two seats for PH.

Logos matter a lot in Malaysia. While canvassing during the bye-elections, Opposition Leader Dr Wan Azizah asked the crowd for their votes. And old man came to her and said he will vote for her as always—for the 'moon' (PAS)! AMANAH President Mohamad Sabu, who for a long time was among the most visible PAS icons, encountered similar incidents. Dr Mahathir campaigned for PH in the two by-elections. I remember the mood was awkward, campaigning against old friends and having old enemies campaigning for us. We were still colleagues after all in the EXCO. I remember breaking fast behind the MCKK campus after campaigning in Kuala Kangsar, and reflecting what lay ahead in the country's political fortunes.

BN won both seats comfortably. The only positive news was that in the rural seat of Sungai Besar, AMANAH pipped PAS to second place. But there still did not seem to be dividends for PH from cooperating with Mahathir or the national scandal engulfing Najib.

While this was going on, however, UMNO was facing its own leadership turmoil. In July 2015, UMNO Deputy President

Muhyiddin Yassin was sacked. In the same reshuffle, Vice President Shafie Apdal was dropped from the cabinet while Mukhriz Mahathir, Mahathir's son, was removed as Kedah Chief Minister in February 2016. They had all been critical of 1MDB. By June, Muhyiddin and Mukhriz were sacked from the party while Shafie left UMNO a month later. Not long after, Muhyiddin submitted the registration for a Malay-based party, Parti Pribumi Bersatu Malaysia (PPBM).

In September 2016, Mahathir visited Anwar at the Kuala Lumpur High Court. The latter was challenging a government security legislation, but obviously, everyone focused on the significance of not just two rivals, but the jailor and the jailed that sparked *Reformasi* in 1998 meeting up again. They shook hands briefly and Mahathir told the press that he had a 'long chat' with Anwar. I recalled when I was Anwar's staff about a decade previously, how pensive and reluctant he seemed when we talked about the scenario of meeting Mahathir. Personally, I would not be able to do it if I were Anwar, after what he and his family had to go through.

In 2017, Dr Mahathir surprised everyone by appearing at a gathering of those who had participated in *Reformasi* since 1998. This was a movement whose midwife was none other than Mahathir due to his disregard for the rule of law and using the state's apparatus to trample on the people. As the audience hissed and booed, he called on the need for everyone to focus on removing Najib. In March, PPBM joined PH as the fourth component party.

When I delivered my policy speech at the KEADILAN Youth Congress in 2017, I took a softer line on Mahathir than I did in 2015. PPBM Youth, along with DAP Youth and AMANAH Youth, attended the event as guests.

'Now we also accept PPBM as a new party to cooperate in PH. I know this acceptance has been greeted with mixed feelings by many sides. But I am confident the politics of change requires many compromises. History tells us that rotten regimes can only be brought down by the power of the people that are diverse. If in the past we say to Dr Mahathir Mohamad that no leader should be absolutely powerful, now we have the opportunity to show him how complex but principled negotiations can happen before we come to a common decision. We are not only talking about power, but most importantly about how to run this country better.'

Some said I was being arrogant. But I believed I owed it to the ordinary people and the party members who had suffered tremendously under Mahathirism during *Reformasi*.

The following day, Dr Mahathir and PPBM leaders attended the opening of the KEADILAN main Congress in Shah Alam. Again, one could sense the mixed feelings among the delegates and the observers who crowded the hall. Mahathir was on the stage when the party faithful and DAP and AMANAH leaders held up placards calling for Anwar to be made the Seventh PM. He reacted by grinning and taking photos of the audience with his smartphone. He did, however, sign the Free Anwar petition when he left the hall.

In May 2017, PAS decided to end the party's political cooperation with KEADILAN. The reason given was that KEADILAN was against amending the law to expand the powers of the Shariah courts. It was also alleged that KEADILAN had gone against the ethics of political cooperation by attacking the leadership of the Islamic party. However, when it came to PAS' involvement in the Selangor State Government, it would be up to the 'public and Islamic interest'. The WhatsApp group between Selangor State Government Assemblypersons became a bit awkward, to say the least. Occasionally, there would be some heated exchanges, but overall, it was cordial.

As a response, the KEADILAN Political Bureau meeting was held to discuss PAS' decision. Some had expressed a reluctance to let PAS go. Dr Wan Azizah Wan Ismail stated that KEADILAN must also protect its own dignity. I was among those who supported her. I argued that we should not stand for PAS' unfair insults and attacks when the public was watching. As it was, Selangor Menteri Besar and Deputy President Azmin Ali was overseas at the time. We agreed to discuss the matter of PAS' office holders in Selangor with him, but to take the moral high ground, KEADILAN's political appointees in Kelantan would have to step down.

Unfortunately, those who supported working with PAS continued to defy the decision on the pretext that they were doing so to complete projects for the public. I was informed in August 2017 by a majority of KEADILAN Kelantan Youth division leaders that they were disappointed that the State Youth Leader Dr Hafidz Rizal continued to support being part of the PAS-led State Government. I duly exercised my power in changing the leader after informing the Chairman of KEADILAN Kelantan and Dr Hafidz. They protested but grudgingly accepted that the power to appoint the State Youth Leader lay with me.

Things continued to move nationally. Parti Warisan Sabah (WARISAN) was established in October 2016 with Shafie Apdal as the president, while Darell Leiking, who had brought me to Sabah and became KEADILAN Vice President and Penampang MP, became the deputy president. Darell felt that the way forward for Sabah was to ride on the sentiment for local parties. Talks went on between WARISAN and KEADILAN as well as DAP. In a few PH Sabah events that I attended, KEADILAN invited WARISAN leaders, but other PH leaders took a strong line against all local parties—WARISAN included. In my speech, on the other hand, I distinguished between local parties that cooperate with PH and those simply out to split the votes and help BN win.

Finally, on the eve of the 2018 elections, WARISAN and PH announced an electoral pact in Sabah.

INVOKE

In 2016, former Barack Obama campaign staffer during the 2012 US Presidential election, Andrew Claster met up with Rafizi Ramli and Kelana Jaya MP Wong Chen. Claster shared ideas on predictive modelling and micro-targeting voters that became possible due to the wide adoption of social media. Getting these pitches was not something new for us, but we were always hampered by a lack of resources. There was also the question of credibility as well as transferability—even if it worked well in the US, could it apply to Malaysia?

But encouraged by Wong Chen, Rafizi warmed up to the idea. INVOKE was set up as a platform for political campaigning, independent of the party, and run by young Malaysians. In some ways, it was similar to the Momentum group that supported Jeremy Corbyn as Labour Party leader. Rafizi, eventually, spent the bulk of his savings, almost a million ringgit, to set it up. There were a few key donors, but most of the rest of the money came from small donations of ordinary Malaysians of all races who wanted change. INVOKE would eventually employ almost 100 staff members in its headquarters in Sungai Besi and in more than a dozen field offices across peninsular Malaysia.

This was complimented by their volunteers—reaching almost 10,000—who supported election candidates and party machinery on the ground. I met up with Johan Kasah, a party member and engineer from Setiawangsa, who joined in 2013, but did not receive much updates about what the party was doing. Another volunteer was Low Wah Meng, who was not from Setiawangsa but was inspired by Rafizi's focus on marginal seats. He was talkative and friendly, always smiling and would bring along his wife and seven-year-old child to our events in his old van. During the election, his daughter would sleep under one of the desks while the parents went through the election data in detail. He passed away shortly after the 2018 election due to a sudden illness.

INVOKE focused on the thirty marginal seats that PH needed to win. They conducted canvassing exercises to meet voters on the ground and establish phone banks. From time to time, I would join in the phone banks. An automated calling system was utilized for surveys. Candidates and field coordinators for INVOKE had access to a dashboard to assess our work on the ground. This would be combined with the latest polling data to compare with our opponents. I could see in Setiawangsa that throughout the campaign, we were always leading. INVOKE also helped to manage our social media accounts.

The door knocking and phone banks were challenging—it was almost like 2008 again as I had to introduce myself to the voters in Setiawangsa. Anyone who does marketing will tell you that this is not easy. We got many cold responses but we didn't let it get us down because, traditionally, Malaysians are very guarded in sharing anti-government political views with strangers. The number of volunteers peaked closer to the election, with Malaysians from all over the Klang Valley helping out. Even my neighbour all the way from Shah Alam came to volunteer. The focus shifted to not only marginal constituencies, but fence sitters in each constituency identified from polling and predictive modelling.

Candidates working with INVOKE also committed to declaring our assets. In total, sixty-four candidates declared their assets through INVOKE—including myself. After 2008, this practice was initiated by two PSM legislators. Rafizi then started doing it annually since 2015, followed by AMANAH MP Mujahid Yusof Rawa a year later. State EXCOs in Selangor and Penang had been doing it since 2008. Within PH, opinion was divided on this issue, but after the 2018 election victory, all PH MPs promised to declare their assets and this has since been adopted for all MPs.

Youth Leader

In October 2015, I visited Pos Tohoi, an Orang Asli settlement in Gua Musang, Kelantan. We had to use dirt roads to access the settlement. Seven primary school students there had disappeared in August, and after about fifty days, two of them were found alive but four turned up dead. One more remained missing. I met the parents and was brought to where the dead bodies were found. Too often, the Orang Asli community found themselves facing a system that was not sensitive to their needs and was still shaped by an outdated outlook on development. Sadly, in the Bumiputera and non-Bumiputera debate that dominates the headlines, the plight of the earliest communities in the country, the Orang Asli, frequently gets overlooked.

As Youth Leader, I helped out on the KEADILAN Internship Program initiated by Rafizi. I had taken in interns from the beginning of my career as a legislator, but this time, we wanted a structured party program that would expose university students to the multifaceted functions of a politician. They were given a small stipend (I don't believe in unpaid internships), expected to do policy reports, produce videos, and also organize real 'ceramahs' on the ground. They were brought to the parliament, and met with Anwar Ibrahim and the other leaders.

We did a nationwide tour to promote affordable higher education. Students had been relying on Perbadanan Tabung Pendidikan Tinggi Negara (PTPTN) loans for tuition fees, and for those from poorer families, pocket money as well. Established in 1997, a year after the passing of the legislation regulating private universities and colleges, PTPTN allowed private institutions to expand exponentially. Alongside credible institutions—some owned by major GLCs, some started by pursuing collaborations with overseas universities—were many more less credible colleges and universities. Many of their graduates who took up huge PTPTN loans were unable to obtain commensurate jobs.

Even today, graduate unemployment and underemployment is a serious problem in the country. This led to a shortfall in repayment of PTPTN loans that affected the sustainability of the fund. We argued that the present model could not survive and had to be reformed to ensure not only the fund's viability but also to see that the graduates can afford the repayment of the loans. My experience as part of the board of directors and as the chair of the board of governors of UNISEL exposed me to the intricacies of the finances of private higher education.

Meanwhile, tensions festered in PH after the entry of PPBM due to issues over the coalition's structure. Previously, the anti-BN coalitions had always functioned loosely, partially because successive governments refused to allow them to be formally registered. But PH also had a problem over who would actually lead it. Dr Mahathir Mohamad wrote to PPBM President Muhyiddin Yassin, instructing him to withdraw the party from PH before the former flew to London for the 2017 Aidilfitri holidays. In an attempt to salvage the coalition, Nurul Izzah Anwar, the KEADILAN Vice President flew to the UK, and stressed to him the need for compromise and engagement. She managed to persuade Mahathir to keep PPBM in PH.

Eventually, it was agreed for Anwar Ibrahim to be PH's de facto leader, Mahathir to be the chairman, and Dr Wan Azizah Wan Ismail to be the president. PH Youth was also asked to settle on a structure. I sat down with my counterparts: Wong Kah Woh (DAP), Sany Hamzan (AMANAH), and Syed Saddiq Abdul Rahman (PPBM), and I was chosen as the first PH Youth Leader.

On New Year's Eve, while others were partying to usher in 2017, the PH Youth worked with civil society organizations to stage a rally holding PM Najib Razak accountable for the government's failure to manage high petrol prices. We marched from Sogo Kuala Lumpur, the usual gathering spot for demonstrations, and tried to get to Dataran Merdeka, but were barred from crossing into the square.

In February, the PH Youth Convention was held, where we presented our offerings to young Malaysians. In my keynote speech, I emphasized on the need not to merely harp on Najib's scandals or merely portray ourselves as a better BN. Instead, I argued that we needed to focus on major economic, administrative, and social reforms. We focused on jobs and wages, cost of living and quality of life, housing, education, and recreation.

Then, I journeyed to all corners of the country to promote our policies, along with other young leaders. We focused on marginal seats including Kangar near the Thailand border, Kuala Terengganu and Kota Bharu on the East Coast of the peninsula, Pensiangan on the Sabah-Indonesia border, and Johor Bharu in the southern tip of the peninsula. My interns—one was just eighteen—joined me in the tours. I recalled my first election campaign, when I turned twenty and was stumping for the party in Kangar. The interns helped out in my events, managed my social media (they were much more adept at it than I was), and joined the INVOKE activities. Our events consisted of distributing leaflets, holding 'ceramah kelompoks', and organizing dialogues with the youth. The crowds were initially quite small, but grew gradually.

In Sarawak, I went to campaign for Roland Engan in Baram. He lost the constituency narrowly in 2013, riding on the anger of the residents unhappy at a proposed hydroelectric dam in the area that would have displaced 20,000 residents. I went to two longhouses—one an Orang Ulu longhouse while the other an Iban one. There was a strong awareness and desire for change. I was given the honour of wearing the Orang Ulu headdress—the symbol of a warrior—while delivering my speech at their longhouse. In both longhouses, I met residents who had been radicalized by encroachments on Native Customary Land. At the Iban longhouse, the *'tuai rumah'* even hosted our event. He is the chief of the longhouse and earned a government allowance. Originally, they would be the ones who stopped opposition events from taking place in the longhouses, but times had changed. In 2011, the first time I was involved in a campaign in Sarawak, some of them allowed opposition events to take place, but they would stay in their house or absent themselves.

In Johor Baharu, there was only a small crowd when I first campaigned there for Akmal Nasir. He was up against the formidable Shahrir Samad, who first won the seat in 1978. We began by distributing leaflets as champion football team Johor Darul Ta'zim was playing that night. Akmal had the task of overturning a BN majority of over 10,000 votes. I tried to be optimistic as I spoke to him, but I was not sure that I was very convincing. But when the second time I went to the constituency, closer to the election day, we attracted a bigger crowd.

Both KEADILAN Youth and PH Youth made music videos to engage young Malaysians. For '*Jiwa Merdeka*', the KEADILAN Youth campaign song, I had asked for it to be composed along the lines of Goo Dolls' 'Iris' (I know, I am that old). At the PH Youth level, there was the more upbeat '*Aku dan Kamu*'. I also appeared in the music video and it again confirmed that I certainly did not have a future in acting or music, should I lose the election!

Personally, I also started live Facebook shows that featured both young politicians and non-political figures: actors, NGO activists, and singers discussing the issues of the day. It was an effective way to reach non-political young Malaysians. 'Ceramahs' and straight out political shows don't often appeal to them, but I believed they were more open to those featuring non-political personalities. Some guests, however, were reluctant to appear in my show, as they would be associated with the opposition.

Ilhan Goes to School

Ilhan started standard one in 2018. Imaan and I decided to send him to the Taman Megah National School in Petaling Jaya. There was a growing trend among the middle classes to send their children to private or Islamic schools, but we felt that being educated with students from various backgrounds was best. At the same time, the Taman Megah School was among the most racially diverse in the Klang Valley. This was reminiscent of the schools Imaan and I attended three decades back, but became less common due to the flight of the middle class to private and vernacular schools.

The school is a testimony to what is possible in national schools across the country. We realized how active the parents were, although both of us were unable to be that committed, due to our jobs. The parents organized fund raising activities, helped to paint and clean classrooms in *gotong-royong* events, and have storytelling sessions in the hall before school starts to improve the students' command over English and Malay. Ilhan enjoyed the school; at first, he enrolled in robotics classes and then switched to drama class.

In order to make national schools the school of choice, the government must empower parents. Teachers from diverse backgrounds must be brought into the profession and there needs to be a strong directive against efforts to make schools less welcoming to minority students. Even in schools where students are entirely—or predominantly—of one race, the government should encourage programs with institutions where other races make up the majority to enable students to appreciate diversity. Teachers must be able to focus on teaching, not on administrative tasks.

In the aftermath of the 1969 racial riots, and as the country pursued a more inclusive development with the NEP, much of the positive legacy was due to a laser-like focus on education. Hostels were built in elite city schools to expose those from the rural areas (predominantly Bumiputeras) to the diverse city population. More residential schools were built to bring the benefits of what MCKK had achieved across the country. Now we need to pay attention to education all over again with a framework that is relevant for the 21st century, if we are to successfully overcome today's challenges.

Part Three

1. The 2018 General Election

PH held its convention in January 2018. There, it was announced that ninety-two-year-old Dr Mahathir Mohamad, the country's fourth PM, was the coalition's candidate to become the seventh PM of Malaysia. Anwar Ibrahim, who was in prison, was nominated as the eighth PM. PH's leaders pledged that upon victory, Anwar would be released, pardoned, and be allowed to play an active role in the administration, before taking over from Mahathir. Meanwhile, Mahathir's Deputy PM would be Anwar's wife, Dr Wan Azizah Wan Ismail. PH also concluded seat negotiations for the peninsula where PPBM—the newest coalition partner—would get the lion's share of the seats.

But the convention faced various dramas, the main one being a group of KEADILAN delegates loyal to Azmin Ali walking out of the convention upon the announcement that Mahathir would be our PM candidate. They demanded that Azmin should be PH's candidate for either the PM or the DPM role.

I chaired a PH Youth meeting not long before the convention. One matter that was raised was that we should give feedback on the PM candidate issue. A straw poll was conducted: Mahathir came first, while Azmin trailed far behind. However, members of the Azmin faction who were there took a photo of the poll to claim that Mahathir and Azmin were the PH Youth's top two candidates for PM.

Leading up to the convention, PPBM stated that if there was no announcement on the PM candidate during the event, they would prefer for it to be cancelled altogether. Even up to a week before the event, there were no posters, teaser videos, or even a press statement announcing the convention. Some members of the organizing committee were looking at postponing the event. To make matters worse, the PH Presidential Council postponed a meeting they were supposed to have on the various outstanding issues to 4 January 2018, three days before the convention. Like a kid throwing a tantrum, Azmin had also stated that he would 'politely decline from speaking at the Convention, but will be attending it.' The Presidential Council finally gave the go-ahead seventy-two hours before the event. Even then, negotiations over the candidates for PM and Deputy PM dragged on.

Initially, PPBM wanted eighty Parliamentary seats. KEADILAN had always had a tough time in seat negotiations because, as a multi-racial party, we had to negotiate with DAP for Chinese-majority seats, and with PAS previously and PPBM and AMANAH now for Malay seats. Two days before the convention, the focus fell on the seventeen marginal seats that were eyed by KEADILAN. In Kuala Lumpur, we were looking at Titiwangsa and Setiawangsa. PPBM wanted one seat in the capital city, and finally Rafizi Ramli, who had asked me to start work in Setiawangsa in 2015, managed to keep Setiawangsa.

The deal for the premiership was reached the night before the convention and was brought back to KEADILAN's Political Bureau. Azmin expressed his incredulity at this arrangement, saying that the process for Anwar's release and pardon will take time. Leveraging on his position as Selangor Chief Minister (who sits on the State Pardon Board), he claimed that the Malay rulers would not take well to something 'imposed' by the new government. A few, including me, responded that if Mahathir could accept this arrangement, it would seem funny if Anwar's own party was cynical about it. It was clear as broad daylight what Azmin's motives were.

A few days after the announcement, Rafizi mentioned that the seat allocation was clearly to avoid any single party from being dominant in government. While Dr Mahathir had previously pushed for his party to dominate PH on the pretext that it provided certainty for the Malays, we managed to convince him that the 'Big Brother model' of BN was irrelevant. The idea, we posited, was to allow all four PH parties to push for a more consensual Prime Ministerial government—as opposed to the strongman presidential-style that had been the model since Mahathir's first stint.

On 28 February, KEADILAN Youth launched a 100-day countdown for Anwar's release. Other than our own party leaders, PPBM President Muhyiddin Yassin was also in attendance. We put up a huge banner with a manual counter on the façade of the party's Petaling Jaya headquarters. It could be seen clearly from the Damansara toll plaza heading into the North Klang Valley Expressway.

Legal Ordeal

In January 2018, the Court of Appeal dismissed the government's appeal to increase my fine of RM1,500 under the Peaceful Assembly Act for the 2013 'Blackout 505' case. The federal and state constitutions disqualify a citizen who has been fined not less than RM2,000 from contesting in elections. It was a long and arduous legal journey for me. I was charged for not giving sufficient notice in 2013. First, my legal team challenged the constitutionality of the provision under the Act, losing in the High Court.

However, in a pioneering decision at the Court of Appeal in 2014, the three judges unanimously decided that the provision was unconstitutional. They allowed my appeal, set aside the charge, and acquitted and discharged me of the same. Justices Mohamad Ariff Yusoff (later Speaker of the Parliament), former Bar Council President Mah Weng Kwai, and former academician

Dr Hamid Sultan Abu Baker delivered individual judgments declaring that the fine for not abiding by the required ten-day notice of the Peaceful Assembly Act was inconsistent with the fundamental Freedom of Assembly as enshrined in the Federal Constitution. Essentially, the three judges agreed that the government cannot criminalize the basic freedom to assemble.

'That which is fundamentally lawful cannot be criminalized,' said Mohamad Ariff.

I was pleased and relieved. Unfortunately, it did not stop there. The government tried to charge me again in the lower courts. The judges rightly declared that they were bound by decision of the Court of Appeal. In the following year, in a second case involving KEADILAN Johor Executive Secretary R. Yuneswaran, the Court of Appeal departed from the decision in my case and upheld the constitutionality of the Section 9(5) of the Peaceful Assembly Act.

Three years after first being charged for 'Blackout 505', I was brought to the court again in 2016. I talked things over with my legal team and we decided that as the government seemed hell-bent on finding me guilty—and with the decision of the Yuneswaran case—I pled guilty. There were other such cases and we reached an agreement with the Deputy Public Prosecutor where we were told that the sentence would be below the RM2,000 threshold—allowing me to keep my Seri Setia seat and contest in the next election. I was fined RM1,500. The government appealed again, pushing for a more severe sentence. It was a nightmare that I could never seem to wake up from. The High Court maintained the sentence, but surprise, surprise, the government appealed again, to the Court of Appeal. Then came the January 2018 decision where the Court of Appeal saw no need to increase the fine.

Due to the repeated trials on 'Blackout 505', I decided to sue the Attorney General and the Malaysian Government. My legal team argued that the decision to charge me repeatedly, in spite of my 2014 acquittal in the Court of Appeal, proved that this was a case of malicious prosecution. At the Kuala Lumpur High Court in December 2017, Justice Ahmad Zaidi Ibrahim ruled that the decision to prosecute me was 'shocking and arbitrary'. The court awarded me RM230,000 in damages.

Build-up in Setiawangsa

'. . . in Nik Nazmi, political observers say Pakatan has a good candidate—winnable even.

'He is said to be quite well-known in the area, with his experience as Selangor EXCO member coming in handy.

'And in his capacity as KEADILAN Youth Leader, he has been seen saying the 'right things' on national issues—a valuable asset for parliamentarians.

'The big problem for Nik Nazmi, and Pakatan for that matter, is to get access to the military personnel. In the run-up to the 2013 polls, it was rumoured that military personnel were 'ordered' not to attend 'ceramahs' held by the then Pakatan Rakyat.'[41]

There was no double-decker bus or trailer for KEADILAN this time around, but INVOKE had a mid-sized truck that transformed to a stage. It came to Setiawangsa twice in 2018: in March and April. In his speech at Taman Setiawangsa, Rafizi said he was confident we would win, and while the other MPs might focus on being appointed to the cabinet, he had only one item on his wishlist: to accompany Najib Razak and his wife Rosmah Mansor to Sungai Buloh Prison. Throughout the campaign, every mention of the couple would energies the crowd. Wong Chen, Tony Pua, and local PPBM leaders joined us on the stage.

---

[41] Mohsin Abdullah, 'Run-Up to GE14: Zulhasnan eyes comeback in Setiawangsa', *The Edge*, 4 May 2018, https://www.theedgemarkets.com/article/runup-ge14-zulhasnan-eyes-comeback-setiawangsa, Accessed 10 September 2021.

On 4 April—the 19th anniversary of PKN—Dr Wan Azizah Wan Ismail came with Nurul Izzah Anwar to announce selected candidates from the KEADILAN Youth at an event in Setiawangsa. The event would also see the launch of the youth wing's campaign music video. We hired buskers, who had only practised the song for two or three days before the event. Busking was gaining popularity in Malaysia as the 'in thing'.

The day before the event, during a Political Bureau meeting, a few leaders were not pleased over the move to name youth candidates. One insisted that the names should only be announced as 'potential candidates'—a few days before dissolution of the parliament—but the rest of us fought back. Izzah managed to push through naming the four of us, but without naming the seats—much to my supporters' disappointment. In a press conference afterwards, Wan Azizah said that the seats we would contest had been decided, but would be publicly announced at a later date.

Finally, at the end of April, after almost three years of working the ground, I was officially announced as the KEADILAN and PH candidate for Setiawangsa. Even BN had issues with settling on a candidate for Setiawangsa. The incumbent MP, Ahmad Fauzi Zahari had only been in place since 2013. Zulhasnan Rafique was an MP from 1999 to 2018. Zulhasnan was still an important warlord, as UMNO Setiawangsa Division Leader. He was a former Royal Malaysian Air Force pilot—this meant something in an area with so many military voters. From 2004 to 2006, he was Federal Territories Deputy Minister, and in 2006, he was promoted as Federal Territories Minister, serving until 2009. Going into the 2018 election, he also happened to be the incumbent Malaysian Ambassador to the US.

In February 2018, at an event in Setiawangsa with Tengku Adnan Tengku Mansor, the Federal Territories Minister, Zulhasnan announced that he was ready to serve as MP if nominated for the 14th General Election. Although I was yet to be named as a candidate, Tengku Adnan attacked me anyway, claiming I had failed to serve Seri Setia. Coincidentally, his brother had been named by Najib Razak as my challenger for the 2013 elections, but was dropped due to pressure from the UMNO grassroots. Finally, on 22 April, Zulhasnan was announced as the BN candidate for Setiawangsa. He resigned as Ambassador to the United States the next day.

After I was named as the candidate, I maintained a tradition that I started since I first ran for elected office a decade before by releasing a video introducing me to the voters. In 2008, I used video CDs and YouTube. In 2018, I had, in addition to YouTube, graduated to Facebook and WhatsApp. Social media was now a huge part of campaigning and INVOKE assisted us with that. INVOKE's canvassing and phone bank efforts resulted in us being able to identify fence-sitters and supporters, which we targeted with crafted messages for them with the objective of getting them out to vote. With the limited resources and means at our disposal, this proved to be very effective and beneficial.

Central to my campaign was reforming the City Hall. A draft plan for Kuala Lumpur (to govern spatial planning in the capital) had been unveiled in 2008 and was supposed to be gazetted five years later, but up to the 2018 election, it remained ungazetted. Then, there is also the issue of democratic deficit in Kuala Lumpur as one of Malaysia's three federal territories. For instance, Canberra is part of the Australian Capital Territory with its own democratic self-government. The US capital city, Washington DC, now has its own elected mayor and council. Historically, Malaysian opposition parties did well in municipal elections and the non-Malays dominated as they were the majority in the urban areas. This was why municipal elections were abolished. Similarly, a desire to dilute the political strength of the non-Malay population in Selangor was why Kuala Lumpur was taken out from the state after the 1969 racial riots and made the first federal territory, governed directly by the federal government.

Yet, with migration into Kuala Lumpur and higher birth rates, Malays in 2015 form 40.3 per cent of the residents of the city, compared to 36.9 per cent Chinese. In 1970, Malays made up only 15.5 per cent of urban residents in peninsular Malaysia. In 2016, Bumiputeras made up 56 per cent of urban residents. Overall, 68 per cent of Bumiputeras reside in urban areas. Thus, many of the assumptions made about municipal elections are outdated. At the very least, there should be a revival of local council elections in Kuala Lumpur due to the democratic deficit it suffers, of having MPs but no State Assemblymen, meaning that the voters in the capital city get one ballot less.

I also continued to speak out about urban poverty. Much of the NEP were shaped by assumptions made in the 1960s and 1970s (and partly from the colonial legacy) that the Bumiputeras were primarily a rural community. Another assumption was that most of the Bumiputeras were poor, consequently the policies were designed to address rural poverty. But as the figures above show, the NEP and industrialization had led to massive migration to the cities and the towns, while urban areas expanded. As I had experienced in Seri Setia, in spite of the almost total replacement of squatters with low-cost houses and PPR estates, the issue of urban poverty was not resolved.

Yes, in the kampungs, jobs are harder to find and the pay is low. Yet, the residents have access to their extended family networks, livestock, and crops while the cost of living is lower. Some rural folk can live off inherited family land.

UNICEF published a study in early 2018, *Children Without.*[42] Seventeen low-cost housing estates were surveyed, of which four were PPRs in the Setiawangsa constituency, while one was Desa Mentari in my old Seri Setia constituency. 12 per cent of

---

[42] UNICEF Malaysia (2018) *Children without: a study of urban child poverty and deprivation in low-cost flats in Kuala Lumpur* https://www.unicef.org/malaysia/media/261/file/Children%20Without%20(ENG).pdf. Putrajaya: UNICEF Malaysia. Accessed 12 September 2021.

children in those areas consumed less than three meals a day, while malnutrition among the urban poor was higher than the national average. What makes these dire statistics even more deplorable is that the per capita income in Greater Kuala Lumpur is almost equal to many of the developed economies in Asia.

The Campaign

The PM called for the dissolution of the parliament on 7 April 2018. Election day would be 9 May 2018, a Wednesday (election days are not automatically public holidays in Malaysia). The government was accused of attempting to suppress voter turnout, which was assumed to be advantageous to BN. Yet, the uproar only convinced more Malaysians to turn up to vote and a movement to spoil votes, 'Undi Rosak' (partly as a backlash against PH for working with Mahathir), fizzled out. Companies responded by giving their workers the day off—some even paid for them to return to their 'kampungs' to vote. Finally, after the uproar, 9 May was declared a public holiday.

As usual on nomination day, my family, friends, and supporters gathered to walk to the nomination centre at the Titiwangsa Stadium. My father, a young eighty-eight years old, and mother, seventy-eight, continued the tradition of joining me since my electoral debut in 2008. I greeted my opponents Zulhasnan Rafique and Ubaid Akla from PAS.

When I met the press, I narrowed down the choice as between BN and PH, even though I said BN had a slight advantage in Setiawangsa. Ubaid responded that PAS were the 'real' underdogs in facing 'Manchester United and Manchester City', the two giants of English football. Perhaps he knew that I was a Liverpool fan. But the two Manchester clubs were not invincible, he said, and lose sometimes. At least, he recognized the reality: PAS had for years now been arguing that the only reason KEADILAN ever won anything was due to the strength of the Islamist party's grassroots and machinery. Now, he admitted that KEADILAN was one of the two 'giants' in the three-cornered fight, although I would have preferred that we be dubbed 'Liverpool'.

Having recently declared my assets, I challenged Zulhasnan to do the same, as well as debate me. In both instances, he refused. Other than the 1MDB affair that had embarrassingly put Malaysia on the world map for the wrong reasons, I zoomed in on scandals involving other Malaysian institutions that were of concern to the Malay community—the pilgrimage fund that was used by Muslims to save for hajj; the business and educational fund for Bumiputeras; and the Federal land resettlement scheme. Convincing the Malays of how much damage corruption had done to the fabric of the country was most effectively done by detailing the damage to institutions that were closely associated with the Bumiputera.

Almost a quarter of Setiawangsa voters in 2018 were military personnel. Najib's weak stand in relation to the US and China were not popular with the armed forces and the veterans. Of course, addressing the issue of China was tricky in a diverse constituency like Setiawangsa, particularly among the older working class voters, but my line was that we simply needed a balanced foreign policy. Ultimately, Chinese-Malaysians are Malaysians.

Another thing I kept hammering on was on City Hall reform, including the gazetting of a local plan for Kuala Lumpur and the democratic accountability for City Hall. But much of the campaign revolved around bread-and-butter issues. Many liberal democrats tend to focus on institutional reforms but forget about these basic issues of economic justice. Nevertheless, it has emerged central to global political campaigns after the Global Financial Crisis in 2008 and was the main thrust of 'Buku Harapan', PH's manifesto—reducing the cost of living as well as increasing wages and jobs. A major plank of our manifesto was to remove the GST. We were also pushing to standardize the minimum wage across the country and then gradually increasing it to RM1500. Part of the steps to help achieve this aim was by reducing the number of foreign workers, not out of xenophobia but also to prevent the exploitation of these migrants. Our foreign worker system was broken and politicized, with workers being treated as cash cows.

I crisscrossed the constituency. Unlike campaigning in the kampungs, which I did as PH and KEADILAN Youth Leader, most of the campaigning involved climbing stairs and going up and down elevators in flats and apartments; or waiting for commuters at the LRT stations during rush hour. There are a few major malls in Setiawangsa—Wangsa Walk, AEON Setiawangsa, and AEON Big Wangsa Maju. When it rained, we opted to go to the mall. But I also went to eateries and night markets, as well as places of worship and we had a few 'ceramah kelompoks' at night. While most of the Malays (many were civil servants, military or police personnel) only whispered words of encouragement, the Chinese and Indians were openly supportive. I was quietly confident.

I teased the Chinese middle-aged ladies saying, '*Ni hao*! Do remember, *leng luis* (pretty girls) vote for *leng chai* (handsome boy), okay?' They would respond by giggling among themselves and promising to vote for me.

On 5 May, early voting was held for military and police personnel. I visited the military polling centres, and the soldiers were friendlier compared to my first engagement in 2015, when I distributed the Malaysian flag and organized a dialogue with them. A few wanted to take photos with me, and even shared with me that they were voting for me. A senior military officer told me as I was walking out from one of the polling centres, 'PH is going to do well, because the rank-and-file are leaning towards you'.

Still, the disappointment I felt when PR failed to win federal power in 2013 meant that I was more measured. My confidence notwithstanding, I did not want to get excited too early. And not all were receptive. I bumped into a Malay couple in the Setiawangsa food court who said coldly that they would be voting 'for Islam' (i.e., PAS).

INVOKE released a video by Rafizi Ramli endorsing my candidacy close to Election Day. After sharing how he recruited me into the *Reformasi* movement, he said that I could have easily chosen to contest from a safe seat. 'But he has a strong spirit to help PH to win in Putrajaya. For him, it is not enough to be comfortable as an EXCO in Selangor, if PH does not win in Putrajaya. I am touched by his willingness and spirit to fight in Setiawangsa, although this puts his political career at risk. A young man like this is a true fighter, compared to his opponent who ran away to the United States when no longer an MP.'

The last part was a dig at my opponent, Zulhasnan, who was a former air force pilot.

The effort by Malaysians to raise funds to assist voters to get back to vote was simply incredible, energized by the government's move to do it on a Wednesday.

'We have a culture called '*gotong-royong*'—helping each other. Usually, it's for weddings and the whole village will come to help you. We're trying to bring that spirit here.'[43], Tengku Elida Bustaman, a friend who helped me since 2008, told *Huffington Post*.

Buses were chartered to transport voters across Malaysia. More than RM200,000 were raised for the initiative from 250 sponsors. Tengku Elida and Alzari Mahshar spent an hour every day at the cash machine to pass money to students and workers who wanted to go back to vote. Voters earning below RM1,000 a month qualified for this initiative. There was another initiative to allow voters to carpool or contribute funds to provide travel subsidies. In less than two weeks, 4,000 donors and 2,000 carpool drivers were gathered by the website. Many Sabahans, especially, registered with the initiative, as they needed flight tickets back to their state.

---

[43] Seiff, Abby, 'This Country's Election Shows The Complicated Role Twitter Plays In Democracy', *Huffington Post*, 5 May 2018, https://www.huffpost.com/entry/twitter-malaysia-elections_n_5aeafdd5e4b00f70f0efe0bf, Accessed 12 September 2021.

This was not confined to within the country. One Malaysian in a condominium in Singapore, upon hearing from his worker there that he did not feel that voting would make a difference, gathered some funds to help the man go back to his constituency in Penang. A friend of mine, who was a member of the Singapore Cricket Club, said that since many of the staff were Malaysians, the Malaysian members of the club pooled funds to allow the workers to return to vote *and* for the club to hire contract workers for the day.

There were also countless complaints by Malaysians overseas that they received their postal ballots late. Kristina Mariswamy, a Malaysian in Texas only got her ballot on 7 May, two days before voting day. She initially gave up on any hope of getting the ballot back on time. But someone suggested they gather at the Houston airport, which had a flight to Kuala Lumpur via Taipei. It happened that a Malaysian pilot was going home to vote and he happily took the ballots back with him to Kuala Lumpur, where a volunteer passed the ballots to another Malaysian flying back to Penang and then handed it to a voter who went to vote in Machang Bubok, Penang. Three other ballots from Houston were successfully delivered to constituencies in Kuala Lumpur, Selangor, and Negeri Sembilan. Some Malaysians in the UK received their ballots on 8 May, a day before voting! They held a protest—where else, but in Trafalgar Square, where I had protested against the ISA as a university student. Then, they pooled funds to buy flight tickets to get a few Malaysians to fly back to lodge their ballots!

I had two 'ceramahs' outside my constituency. On 1 May I went to Subang Jaya. The state seat was under the new Subang Parliamentary constituency, where KEADILAN's Wong Chen was standing, while the PH Youth candidate from DAP, Michelle Ng, replaced Hannah Yeoh in Subang Jaya. Three days later, I flew to Johor Bahru to help out KEADILAN Youth candidate Akmal

Nasir for the second time that year. Unlike the safe seat of Subang, Johor Bahru was an UMNO fortress that we had to win. I saw how the mood had changed from my previous visit. At the airport in Kuala Lumpur, I bumped into Nik Omar Nik Aziz, the son of the late PAS Spiritual Leader. During the PAS split, he chose to join the moderate AMANAH, while many of his family, including his brother Nik Abduh—who became a MP in 2013, remained in PAS as it became more conservative. Although I was not running in an easy seat, as the coalition and party's Youth Leader, I had a responsibility to help our candidates.

My one and only major 'ceramah' during the official campaign period in Setiawangsa was on the eve of election day, held in front of my campaign office and done together with the Wangsa Maju team where the candidate was KEADILAN's Dr Tan Yee Kew. It was only apt that Rafizi was the keynote speaker after making stops at Selayang and Segambut. Victory, he said, was ours and tomorrow would be the dawn of a new Malaysia—to a massive roar from the audience.

Ilhan was now seven, and played a more active role. He knew about my ordeal with the police (even if we couched it in terms that I was helping the police) and I told him how Anwar was imprisoned for trying to stand up for ordinary Malaysians. At times, when his mother was on call or needed to rest, Ilhan got used to joining me at my constituency events. A few times, he and Imaan joined me on the campaign trail and we ordered a special kid-sized campaign t-shirt for him. He would play with Low Wah Meng's daughter, who accompanied her parents throughout the campaign. Sometimes, he would fall asleep in the campaign MPV.

Election Day

My wife and I voted early in my old state constituency, Seri Setia—which is now part of the new federal constituency, Petaling

Jaya. I bumped into Hadzrin, my MCKK classmate who was also my seconder both times I contested from Seri Setia. The queue was long. We, then, went to Setiawangsa and had a breakfast of 'roti canai' and coffee. Typically, I went from one polling station to another. I, then, received a call that Daim Zainuddin, a former finance minister closely associated with Dr Mahathir, wanted to drop by and visit a polling centre with me. I brought him to Section 5 Wangsa Maju. He was frail and climbed up to the third floor (where the voting was going on) on a walking stick, where he smiled and greeted the voters with me.

After doing my rounds and freshening up (campaigning in the hot and humid Malaysian weather requires regular showers and wardrobe changes) I returned to my campaign centre. The team of young lawyers that volunteered for me dealt with issues faced by our polling and counting agents with EC officials. As the results of the early votes by military and police personnel trickled in, I sensed that change was possible. As expected, BN was ahead among early voters, but by a smaller margin than previously. When the regular votes came in, we saw that we would win Setiawangsa comfortably. The team doing the number crunching said that our lead had extended to over 10,000 votes, but I kept reminding them to check and check again. Winning, I knew, was possible. But with this majority?

Initially, I told one of my volunteers, Syazwan Rahimy, to work with my eighteen-year-old intern Ameerah to prepare two statements for each possibility: a win and a defeat. But by now, I could afford to tell them to just focus on the victory statement. My fourth sister, Nazifah, and her husband, Reza, brought my parents to my campaign centre. Another brother-in-law, Khuzaini, who was a counting agent, asked in the family WhatsApp group why we were not at the vote-tallying centre at Stadium Titiwangsa yet, as he was sure I had won.

I waited until 10.00 p.m. before going to the stadium, an hour after my team had asked me to, to make sure that our victory was certain. Eventually, I received 34,471 votes; BN 20,099, and PAS 6,282. My majority was 14,372. Turnout was 85.8 per cent. I obtained 56.8 per cent of the popular vote. A journalist who covered Setiawangsa during the election, Intan Farhana Zainul, put up a photo with me and the media team at Stadium Titiwangsa on Instagram with the caption: 'We stayed back until 2.00 a.m. in the morning after camped for more than eight hours with mosquitoes and no food outside the polling station. We had goosebumps when reading and reporting the unprecedented results, thinking 'is this really happening?'

UMNO strongholds Johor and Melaka fell to PH. Akmal Nasir overturned Shahrir Samad's 10,000 majority in Johor Bahru to win with a majority of almost 20,000. The opposition finally defeated BN in Negeri Sembilan after making steady inroads into the state since 2008. PH's grip in Penang and Selangor strengthened. In 2008 PR won 36 seats in the State Assembly, which increased to 44 five years later. This time, PH took 51 out 56 seats in Selangor. Setiawangsa completed the rout for BN in Kuala Lumpur, where even in Batu, where the KEADILAN candidate was disqualified, the twenty-two-year-old independent candidate P. Prabakaran, who was endorsed by KEADILAN, won, becoming the country's youngest-ever MP in history. WARISAN and PH did reasonably well in Sabah, resulting in a hung State Assembly. Sarawak, where the state BN was dominant, saw PH doing well not only in the Chinese states, but KEADILAN and the combined Opposition won six Dayak seats from BN.

Besides Sarawak, BN also retained control of Perlis and Pahang. Kelantan remained in PAS hands while Terengganu swung to PAS. INVOKE had predicted a PAS defeat in the two states but the anti-Najib vote swung to PAS as many felt that PH was not a genuine challenge to BN in the two states. There was also a sense for many voters sympathetic to PAS that AMANAH was a traitor to the Islamic party and the prominent role given to AMANAH in the East Coast affected our campaign. On the other hand, the local KEADILAN leadership at that time took too soft a line on PAS. PH did not win a single federal or state seat in the two states, yet having campaigned in the two states frequently before the election, I could not have predicted such a dismal result.

As in 2008, there was delay from the EC in releasing the official election results in the seats won by the Opposition. They had promised results to be out by 10.00 p.m., but it only began coming out at midnight. In the statement prepared by my team, I thanked the Setiawangsa voters for making a historic decision and allowing KEADILAN and PH to win this UMNO bastion. I promised to honour their mandate, that I would voice the issues affecting the constituency and fulfil my election promises. I ended by saying that the voters had delivered on what I repeated to my supporters, donors, and the voters in 'ceramahs': 'When we win Setiawangsa, we win Putrajaya.'

Although the PH secretariat had asked us to go to the Sheraton Hotel in Petaling Jaya, I realized that I had not had a proper dinner yet. We were already in the wee hours of 10 May. We stopped by a mamak shop and I felt I could satisfy an irregular guilty pleasure of mine (okay, more than that, to be honest): a bowl of instant Maggi curry noodles with egg and bird's eye chillies. I saw excited supporters waving flags on the roads. Overall, however, people were calm. PH leaders had instructed everyone to avoid any provocation as memories from 13 May 1969 were still fresh in the minds of the older generation.

Dr Mahathir Mohamad and the other PH leaders declared victory when the coalition passed the simple majority mark at 2.30 a.m. The King summoned Dr Wan Azizah Wan Ismail as President of KEADILAN, whose party logo was used by most of the PH candidates as the coalition had yet to be officially registered. She was offered the position of PM, but she remained faithful to the deal for Mahathir to become PM first. But she did express her wish for her husband, Anwar Ibrahim, to be released from prison and pardoned.

We were advised to spend the night in a hotel and were told to be careful until the PM's swearing in was over and done with; this was similar to what we did after the 2008 election in Selangor. I should have slept immediately, but there was just so much adrenaline coursing through me that I surfed the channels to see how the media reported on the election. The EC officially declared all the results by 5.00 a.m.—the longest election night in recent history. That morning, the dwindling print newspaper industry received a shot in the arm as Malaysians bought copies to commemorate the historic occasion. Unfortunately, they could not report the certified and official results due to the belated announcement by the EC.

My intern, Ameerah commemorated the win on Instagram: 'I've never felt more contented. I can't quite put my finger on what I was feeling yesterday but I know for sure that it all felt so surreal. This will go down in the books, and to know that I was part of it—is something different altogether.'

I contemplated the significance of this long-awaited victory. Change had finally come to Malaysia. Six decades of rule by Alliance and BN came to an end. Personally, for me, it was a journey of almost two decades, but compared to those who consistently challenged the system from the beginning, believing not in a Malaysia based on racial dominance or supremacy, but rather forged through genuine unity, mine was merely a blip. I was fortunate to come in at the right time to win all the elections I contested; others were only elected after several tries, and many were never successful at all. But I was no longer a greenhorn like I was in 2008. My optimism and excitement were tempered by caution in the face of the hard work we would have to do in meeting the great expectations of the voters as well as dealing with the unintended consequences of the victory.

My friend, Pritam Singh, the first recognized Opposition Leader in Singapore, wrote after the victory:

'Who would have imagined Nik Nazmi Nik Ahmad in government 15 years later? Many people rejoice over the results of the 14th General Election, but for many children and believers of the *Reformasi* generation, it was a hard slog with many disappointments, bouts of sadness and defeat, doubts, family disapprovals and abject frustration. It was a struggle. The road was a long one.'[44]

---

[44] The post can be found at https://www.facebook.com/permalink.php?story_fb id=1809577485731223&id=211352328887088.

2. The PH Government

Anwar Ibrahim was treated for a shoulder injury in a hospital in Kuala Lumpur in the run-up to the election. His only option for television was watching TV3 every night. The day after the election, TV3 played old cartoon episodes, not knowing how to cover the election results. When Dr Mahathir Mohamad announced the holders of the key cabinet positions, KEADILAN's wish for Anwar to be consulted was ignored. The party's leadership decided to skip the announcement.

Things had somewhat cooled down as Mahathir had arrived at the hospital to have a discussion with Anwar. Mahathir had left when KEADILAN's Political Bureau met Anwar for the first time in three years. We were informed that Anwar would be granted a full pardon soon. Dr Wan Azizah Wan Ismail appeared calm and contented. After two decades of reluctantly being thrust into the forefront of politics, she would soon be Malaysia's first female Deputy PM. It was the ultimate vindication for a softspoken woman leader who was often underestimated by friends and foes alike. In Malaysia, women have made enormous strides in education, to the point that there is a problem of male underrepresentation in universities. But much more has to be done in terms of participation in the workplace, as well as in leadership positions. Wan Azizah not only held her own as the first female Opposition Leader for many years, but also reached the second highest political position in the country.

Anwar was released on 16 May 2018. He left the hospital for the Istana Negara for an audience with the king. I recalled how Azmin scoffed at the prospect of our ability to obtain a quick pardon for Anwar, saying that this would appear like pressuring the king. But we did it. I dropped by Anwar's Bukit Segambut residence in the afternoon, and many supporters as well as local and international press were there.

KEADILAN Youth organized a rally in the evening to welcome Anwar's return. It was attended by more than 5,000 people and started with special prayers, as it was the start of Ramadan, before the inevitable speeches. In my speech, I remarked that it was a victory for those who had never lost faith in the *Reformasi* struggle. It was a victory for Malaysians who kept alive the fire of hope and justice in their hearts. Anwar spoke at the end. He mentioned that he had politely declined Dr Mahathir's offer for him to be in the cabinet. The people had decided, and space must be given to the PM and his ministers. Most crucially, he said, PH must not let power corrupt them and turn them into the new UMNO. 'But if there are weaknesses, we will advise; if they get carried away in luxury, we will criticize.'

PH Cabinet

The complete Mahathir 2.0 cabinet included a few firsts in Malaysia's history. As mentioned previously, Wan Azizah was the first female Deputy PM (she also held the position of Minister of Women, Family, and Community Development) while my PPBM counterpart Syed Saddiq Syed Abdul Rahman was the youngest cabinet minister in history at twenty-six. At 18 per cent, women representation in cabinet was still a long way from the targeted 30 per cent minimum, but it was still the highest in our history. DAP Secretary General Lim Guan Eng became the first Chinese-Malaysian Finance Minister since MCA's Tan Siew Sin, who retired in 1974.

Some of my friends and members of the public were perplexed that my name, as the PH Youth Leader who served various positions in the Selangor State Government, was overlooked for the cabinet. The fact was that Mahathir had suppressed KEADILAN's representation for reasons he knows best. KEADILAN was given a quarter of the ministerial roles, although almost 40 per cent of PH's Members of Parliament were from our party. Some of the other ministers Mahathir chose—particularly from the PPBM— were especially wanting in capability. Additionally, the PKR cadres that became ministers were predominantly from Azmin's faction: five out of seven ministers. This weakened Anwar Ibrahim's hand and sowed the seeds of discord from early on. There were also hidden hands involved—one KEADILAN MP received a call from Mahathir that she would be Deputy Minister. The next day, someone else in the PM's circle called her up to say that her name had been withdrawn. Despite all the hope and optimism many Malaysians were feeling, behind the scenes, things were more surreal than a *Yes Minister* or *Veep* episode!

I took things in my stride. Publicly, I stated that I would focus on being a vocal backbencher, speaking up for my constituents and holding the government to account. Frankly, I also did not envy the ministers, many of whom had their plates full with various legacy issues.

Parliamentary Duties

MPs elected in the 2018 polls were sworn in on 16 July 2018. I misplaced a new black 'baju Melayu' that would have fitted me for the ceremony (I had two older ones that, unfortunately, no longer fit my expanded girth; Malaysian politics is sometimes a high-carb business!) and wore a suit instead. These formalities are always nerve-wrecking, especially in getting the dress code right. The former Court of Appeal Judge in my Peaceful Assembly Act case, Mohamad Ariff Yusoff, was elected as the Speaker. BN and PAS, however, made a fuss about things and walked out during the ceremony in protest (although they participated in the swearing in ceremony).

The next day was the opening of parliament by King Sultan Muhammad V of Kelantan. After he entered the chamber and greeted the MPs, the King proclaimed, 'Sit down . . . and don't run away,' in reference to the antics the day before. Everyone laughed.

My maiden speech was debating the Royal Address. I touched on a long list of issues—urban poverty, City Hall accountability, environmental protection, Parliamentary reform, upholding the dignity of security personnel, the welfare and development of the artistic and creative community as well as the abolishment of obsolete authoritarian university and security laws, and Biro Tatanegara (BTN).[45] In a way, I was fortunate to have been seated in the middle block of the chamber. The Lower House seating is U-shaped. At the front row were senior backbenchers, including DAP stalwart Lim Kit Siang who first entered Parliament in 1969 and the Chief Ministers of Sabah, Perak, Kedah and Penang—who were all MPs as well. When Anwar Ibrahim entered Parliament in October 2018, he sat there as well. Although the order of participating in a debate is usually fixed beforehand with the Speaker through our party whip, being in the middle block enabled us to catch the eye of the Speaker easily when we wanted to put in an additional question or a point of order.

In October 2018, I was part of the Malaysian delegation to the Inter-Parliamentary Union (IPU) Assembly in Geneva. Two senators and four MPs from across the aisle were part of the delegation. I spoke in the debate on the role of free and fair trade in achieving sustainable development goals. Only through a rules-based, open, and multilateral trading system that is inclusive of the least developed countries can this be achieved, I said. I also joined the Forum for Young Parliamentarians and spoke about the challenges to increasing youth political participation in Malaysia

---

[45] On 13 August 2018, BTN was finally abolished.

as well as the ongoing efforts by the new regime to lower the voting age. I found it awkward to speak through interpreters and not being sure how the listeners in other languages processed my words.

Party Elections

From September to November 2018, fresh after the general election, KEADILAN held our party polls. While the party contests in 2010 and 2014 had attracted a lot of attention, this time the focus was even more intense as we were the biggest political party in parliament and were, for the first time, in power federally. For the first time, too, the party would be using electronic voting through tablets to conduct our one-member-one-vote election.

While Anwar Ibrahim won the presidency uncontested, taking over from Dr Wan Azizah who had held the position since 1999, all eyes were on the Deputy Presidency contest between Azmin Ali and Rafizi Ramli. I was thirty-six, and therefore, over the thirty-five years age limit for the youth wing and could not defend my position as Youth Leader. Instead, I offered myself for the Central Leadership Council and as Setiawangsa Division Chief.

Azmin upped the ante by declaring that he feared nothing facing a 'jobless' opponent as Rafizi was no longer an MP. That was truly below the belt, as his opponent was unable to contest in the general election due to having been unjustly convicted for his relentless efforts at exposing BN's scandals, which, along with his work at INVOKE, were crucial to PH's victory. Eventually, Azmin, the incumbent and a powerful minister, won with 71,635 of the votes compared to the 'jobless' Rafizi, who got 68,730 votes. Azmin's share of the vote was barely above 51 per cent. As for me, at the national level, I obtained 46,521 votes, which placed me at the 11th place in the Central Leadership Council. The top 20 candidates get voted in. But most of those who won at the national level were Azmin's allies.

There was a brief 'distraction' when the Port Dickson by-election was held in October and Anwar ran as the PH candidate for the seat. As the coalition and party Youth Leader, I ran a campaign to mobilize outstation voters to come back to vote as some quarters tried to paint the by-election as an unnecessary 'waste'. We were upfront about getting Anwar in Parliament, and this was part and parcel of democracy. He won with 72 per cent of the popular vote and a majority of 23,560—larger than the KEADILAN candidate had scored in the general election. Turnout was however 58.3 per cent, less than what we were hoping for.

Not long after my term as KEADILAN Youth Leader ended, I relinquished my position as the PH Youth leader. PPBM's Syed Saddiq was chosen by the other youth leaders as my successor.

Rising Racial and Religious Tensions

UMNO's first ever defeat at the federal level brought it closer to PAS. This collaboration, in turn, intensified the use of racial and religious rhetoric against the PH government. At the same time, our policy missteps and poor communication put us on the defensive. When Minister of Finance Lim Guan Eng presented the 2019 budget in November 2018, he announced a cut in incentives to smallholders and rubber tappers as well as fishermen, as well as slashes to fertilizer subsidies and paddy production incentives. While the beneficiaries were not all Bumiputeras (I know of one DAP MP who was critical of this move as the largely Chinese and Malay smallholders in his constituency were complaining about it), many were, and it allowed the opposition to accuse PH of being anti-Malay.

When Dr Mahathir addressed the UN General Assembly in 2018, he announced that Malaysia would ratify all the remaining core UN human rights instruments. This included the International Convention on the Elimination of All Forms of Racial Discrimination (ICERD) and the Rome Statute. With regards to ICERD, Malaysia and Brunei are the only majority Muslim countries that are not signatories to it. Other non-signatories include North Korea, Myanmar, and a handful of small countries. But the opposition at that time claimed that ratifying ICERD would impinge on the constitutional special position of the Malays and Bumiputeras in Sabah and Sarawak. Malaysia, ironically, was actually involved the drafting of ICERD at the UN General Assembly before its adoption in 1965.

Similarly, the proposed ratification of the Rome Statute of the International Criminal Court was objected to on the basis that it would affect the immunity of the king. The statute covered four crimes: genocide, crimes against humanity, war crimes, and the crime of aggression. In fact, the Najib Razak administration stated that it intended to ratify the statute. The Crown Prince of Johor expressed concern that it would affect the king as the Supreme Commander of Malaysia's Armed Forces, but the government explained that a constitutional monarch would not be at risk of prosecution if violations are committed by Malaysia's soldiers, as the monarch acts on the government's advice.

I fully supported these ratifications. Unfortunately, the government did not properly engage its stakeholders, and perhaps rushed things against the backdrop of the recent political change, with many Malays feeling anxious. In contrast, the campaigners who wanted Malaysia to ratify the Convention Against Torture engaged with a few staunchly right-wing Malay and Muslim groups to explain that even countries such as Saudi Arabia, Pakistan, and Iraq have all signed the convention.

In September 2019, UMNO and PAS formalized their cooperation that began casually in a few successful by-elections and by having pushed the PH government to reverse its commitment to ICERD and the Rome Statute. This was what we had feared. In 2018, PH won in many seats due to three-cornered contests between PH, BN, and PAS.

A month later, the 'Malay Dignity Congress'—a gathering of right-wing Malays who wanted to discuss how 'Malay rights' were allegedly under threat—was held. But most crucially, it was backed by Mahathir's PPBM, which was part of PH. It was a response to the UMNO-PAS unity. Attended by leaders of PPBM, UMNO,

PAS, and KEADILAN (Azmin's faction), the organizers began by insisting that the country belonged to the Malays and that the 'social contract' where citizenship was given to the non-Malays could be suspended if Malay privileges were challenged. Mahathir took his usual hectoring grandfather tone in urging the Malays to grab opportunities and not lobby for more aid.

Responding to the event, I said that much of the problems of the Malays were rooted in socio-economic inequality, but Malaysia has always tried to tackle it by putting on racial lenses as opposed to a class perspective. As such, Malays are encouraged to find scapegoats among the other races, instead of confronting their own elites who had benefited disproportionately from the benefits and privileges afforded to them. The fact that Mahathir was not ideologically committed to PH and was still stuck to his old ways of thinking was pretty clear by then. The governing coalition was merely a coalition of convenience.

Broken Promises

Then, from October 2018, UMNO MPs and leaders began crossing over to PPBM. The argument was that this was necessary to shore up Malay support for PH and to counter the UMNO-PAS cooperation. As these crossovers intensified in February 2019, I argued that instead of this, the ruling coalition should return to its roots:

'Why can't the various components of PH evolve so that we can, finally, access, engage and win the support of all Malaysians, including the rural Malays?

'Why do some of our leaders seem intent on taking short-cuts, rather than the path of hard (but ultimately rewarding) work? Have we totally abandoned the idea of bipartisanship?

'Why do some Harapan leaders assume that the Malay community will necessarily be impressed by taking in these defectors? Is the rural Malay community that monolithic? Is quantity really that more important in governance and politics rather than quality?'[46]

I kept stressing on the need to enable UMNO and the other parties to become an effective opposition, instead of trying to crush them through defections. There were rumours that UMNO would be dissolved due to various alleged irregularities. It all felt so very demeaning.

The fear was that young voters, that we were empowering through a historic constitutional amendment to lower the voting age to eighteen, would see the crossovers as a sign of the government belittling the democratic mandate. Don't be surprised, I said, if the high turnouts we enjoyed in the past few elections would plummet due to our misdoings. I joked that I sympathized with the parliamentary staff who had to keep changing the MPs' seats due to the multiple defections taking place, one after another.

The issue of the handover from Mahathir to Anwar also became contentious. A timeline was not literally spelt out in the deal between the PH parties. This was because, at that time, in January 2018, Anwar was still in prison and needed to not only be released but to be pardoned in order to run as an MP. Before and after the PH victory, Mahathir, ninety-three, kept repeating that he would honour his deal of handing the premiership over to Anwar in one or two years.

But a different tune was soon coming out of that side of the coalition. Mahathir started saying that it was best if he handed over after resolving the economic problems he inherited, with no deadline. Then, it was mentioned that the changeover should be after the APEC Summit in 2020. This would be Mahathir's second time hosting the summit, having done so in 1998 after the Asian

---

[46] Nik Nazmi Nik Ahmad. 'Pakatan Harapan must return to its roots' *Malaysiakini*, 15 February 2019, https://www.malaysiakini.com/news/464186 Accessed 23 September 2021.

Financial Crisis and the sacking of Anwar. US Vice President Al Gore attended it instead of President Bill Clinton, and insulted Mahathir by praising *Reformasi*. Some DAP leaders whispered to me that this was the most reasonable timeline for Mahathir to go—resigning after hosting a global summit.

This was problematic because Mahathir kept shifting the goalposts. The encouragement of crossovers from UMNO also seemed to be an attempt to strengthen Mahathir's hand at the expense of Anwar. Everyone I met—civil servants in Putrajaya, corporate leaders, my constituents—asked: will the handover actually happen? Most felt that this was a crucial election promise that must be fulfilled, but they did not see the plans for it. Businesses were nervous about investing. Anwar would also need to appoint his cabinet and implement his policies, as well as prepare for the next election that must be held latest by the third quarter of 2023.

Respite

In March 2019, Tanjong Malim MP and KEADILAN Vice President, Chang Lih Kang and I went to the UK on an invitation to give a few talks there. I brought Ilhan along, and having gone through 2018 with its exhausting general and party elections, took the opportunity to get some respite as well.

In London, we met with inter-faith leaders from the Christian, Muslim, Jewish, and Sikh communities. The most interesting conversation was with Rabbi Alexander Goldberg who happened to be the Jewish chaplain of the English national football team. He shared his experience visiting the International Islamic University of Malaysia.

We went to Cambridge, where we spoke about the challenges of New Malaysia at the Centre for Development Studies. We were privileged to have Azman Mokhtar—the former Managing Director at Malaysian sovereign wealth fund Khazanah Nasional, and whom I had helped briefly way back after my graduation

in a turnaround project for MCKK (he was another old boy)—
moderate the session. He was in Cambridge as a visiting fellow.
We also paid a courtesy visit to Abdal Hakim Murad, the British
Muslim scholar, and we were brought to the modern and eco-
friendly Cambridge Mosque which was not open to the public
yet to perform our prayers. We capped off our trip to Cambridge
with a formal dinner at Malaysia's founding PM's alma mater,
St Catharine's College. I was only informed that Ilhan, who was
eight, received a special dispensation to join the formal dinner upon
arriving in Cambridge, so we had to rush to a Gap store to find
a shirt, sweater, slacks, and formal shoes for him! Unfortunately,
he was too sleepy and was not impressed with the dinner—to
the point that he rolled his eyes when the main course of grilled
salmon was served, as he was expecting salmon sushi!

But we saved the best for the last. We stopped at Anfield to
catch the game against Spurs. Liverpool led through a Roberto
Firmino goal early in the game, and in the 70th minute, Spurs
equalized. But Spurs conceded an own goal in the 90th minute!

Divorce

In July 2019, after fourteen years of marriage, Imaan and I officially
divorced at the Kuala Lumpur Shariah Court. It was a difficult,
painful decision, which I do not want to get into here. Suffice to
say, a busy public life is a satisfying one, but it takes its toll on the
personal front. We were already separated for quite some time.
We reached a mutual agreement, especially for the benefit of Ilhan.
I prepared a brief statement as I knew the press would immediately
break the story when they found out about the court proceedings:

'We will now focus on our son's happiness and wellbeing and
we are committed to raising him together. I hope all quarters will
respect our privacy for the time being. No other statement will be
issued on this matter.'

I, then, asked everyone for some privacy. The court photographer
and journalists were snapping photos when we arrived at the court.

3. Things Fall Apart

On 23 February 2020, several political parties had separate meetings: PPBM, the UMNO-PAS coalition, and Gabungan Parti Sarawak (GPS) MPs. The GPS were Sarawak parties that used to be part of BN, but split to become a local-based coalition after the 2018 election. Separately, Azmin Ali's faction met at the Sheraton Hotel Petaling Jaya—the same hotel PH had used to assemble after our victory in 2018. Rumours spread of a 'Stop Anwar Coalition' being formed. This was the start of the 'Sheraton Move' political crisis: parts of PPBM and KEADILAN collaborated with the then opposition to bring the government down. Azmin along with Muhyiddin Yassin, PPBM's president, and the leaders of UMNO, PAS, GPS, and WARISAN went to seek an audience with the king in the evening. They then gathered at the Sheraton.

I went to Anwar's residence in Bukit Segambut along with a few other party leaders while the press gathered outside. I was captured in video busy with my phone as I smiled in response to the questions from the journalists. Later, Anwar gathered with supporters at his residence for a prayer session, and afterwards on Facebook Live, claimed that former PPBM friends and a small group from KEADILAN were engaged in treachery.

Things had moved fast in the two days before that, during a PH Presidential Council meeting. Mahathir's supporters—including Azmin and PPBM's Syed Saddiq—insisted that setting a timeline for a transition would make Mahathir a 'lame duck' PM. It did not seem to matter that no one in the world believed that Mahathir would ever be a 'lame duck'; and even if it were to be true, was that not the expectation with the proposed handover to Anwar anyway? But it was clear by the crossovers of UMNO MPs into PPBM as well as the courting of PAS that Mahathir had other plans. Anwar ended the meeting that evening by attempting to cool things down, saying that the PM should have the space to decide when to step down.

On 24 February, Anwar, Dr Wan Azizah, and the other PH leaders went to see Mahathir at his home where he claimed he was not involved in the latest plot. Muhyiddin declared that PPBM had withdrawn from PH. After KEADILAN sacked Azmin Ali and his ally Zuraida Kamaruddin for taking part in the 'Sheraton Move', nine more MPs from the party announced their withdrawals as well. Mahathir sent a letter of resignation to the king, bringing the PH government to an end.

But Mahathir—who was interim PM—then made another stunning announcement: he wanted to form a unity government, bringing all MPs under his premiership. But he also wanted the freedom to appoint ministers bypassing the political parties. Superficially, it seemed attractive—but anyone could see this was how authoritarianism and dictatorships began (or in this case, return). I appeared in a heated TV panel with former Bar Council President and former Bersih chair Ambiga Sreenavasan, who tried to defend the unity government route as a solution to the failure of political parties to get out of this impasse. I remember re-watching the video and seeing myself rolling my eyes when I heard her arguments; I could not help it.

It was now up to the king to identify a successor to Mahathir. The MPs were summoned to the palace according to party, to then individually meet the king. My KEADILAN colleagues and I were summoned on 26 February. It was a Wednesday, and I wore my MCKK tie along with my suit (and 'songkok'—as protocol dictates when meeting the king). When it was my turn, he saw my tie and asked, 'Ah, you are from MCKK?' His father was an old boy. I, then, dutifully filled in a form stating that my choice was Anwar for PM, along with the other KEADILAN, DAP, and AMANAH MPs. But after all the meetings were over, this effort, too, failed to produce a candidate with a majority in the Dewan Rakyat.

Two days later, the king, after consulting the Conference of Rulers invited party leaders to the palace to present their choice from PM as a means to break the deadlock. KEADILAN was camped in the Eastin Hotel, Petaling Jaya as we frantically reached out to some MPs from other parties that we knew well to get the temperature from their side. Anwar was persuaded by the other PH parties to make a last attempt by nominating Mahathir as PM again. It was finally announced on 29 February that after meeting the party leaders, the king believed that Muhyiddin was likely to command majority support of MPs and would be appointed PM.

The Pandemic

Imaan, my ex-wife and our son, Ilhan, had moved to Penang as she was posted in the government hospital there. I would see him twice a month, usually alternating between visiting him in Penang or him visiting me in Kuala Lumpur. On 14 March 2020, he came over at the start of his school holiday. He was supposed to stay for a week. He would end up staying for more than two months.

The WHO had reported the spread of a novel coronavirus in Wuhan, China in the second week of January 2020. Malaysia reported the country's first cases on 25 January—from three Chinese tourists. At the end of February, a major event among the Tablighi Jamaat group in Kuala Lumpur attended by 12,500 participants, including more than 1,000 foreign visitors, caused a surge in infection. On 16 March, two days after Ilhan was in Kuala Lumpur, the new PM, Muhyiddin Yassin announced a national lockdown of the country known as the Movement Control Order (MCO) that was to last for two weeks. It was later extended three times, only ending in early May.

Ilhan was supposed to be in Penang for his birthday on 24 March, but I managed to organize a small celebration with me (and face paint) at my place in Petaling Jaya. We followed exercise routines on YouTube. I shaved off his hair (and he, mine) with no foreseeable visits to the barber. And when I was with him, we went through my old DVD collection as well as movies on Netflix to occupy our time, while I signed him up to online coding, science, and mathematics classes.

But I had to attend to my constituency as well. I used whatever government allocation I had left (I was now an opposition MP, so this was significantly reduced) and did a crowdfunding exercise to provide basic food items to poor families in my constituency—everything from rice to sanitary pads. During one of my visits, I met a sixty-year-old Malay man living in one of the PPRs in my constituency. He had been working in one of the old, prestigious hotels in Kuala Lumpur since the 1980s and before the pandemic brought home about RM3,000 a month. His 750-square feet apartment was pretty much bare and housed three generations of his family—including his children and grandchildren. The living room was where the younger family members slept. By then, he was only paid his basic salary—a meagre RM1,300— and he considered himself lucky as many hotels had closed down and their workers were made redundant. '*Alhamdulillah* (thank God) the hotel union is strong. It's difficult for the hotel to lay people off,' he told me.

He had tried to sell cakes on a small scale since the MCO. This made him about RM20 a day. One of his daughters was abandoned by her husband and she worked in a nearby pharmacy. Another child was studying early childhood education at a college. But it was hard keeping his sons in education after they finished secondary school, he told me. Chicken—usually the most common source of protein—had become expensive. Fish was rare as well due to the price. When the electricity meter reader came over, an argument broke out about how high the bill was—but he managed to keep the power on by paying the outstanding amount in instalments.

Another story involved another elderly man who came to my office. He was almost seventy and is a stroke survivor. To support his family, he took a loan to purchase a taxi, just before the MCO. Every day, he had to pay RM26 for his taxi. Before the pandemic, he would work for about 12 hours—from 8.00 a.m. to 8.00 p.m.— and collect about RM60. But the combination of his age, health, competition from ride-sharing apps as well as the MCO, made just getting by increasingly difficult. One of his children received an offer to study at a public college. but even though it was heavily subsidized, the basic registration cost was still prohibitive. Another child was studying in a college in Kuala Lumpur, but with classes being moved online. She was complaining that it was difficult to keep up with the poor quality handphone she had, and was asking for a laptop. Another child had a diploma, but has been unable to find a job in his line of study, and was working a job that did not require higher education—basically he was underemployed.

There were so many, too many, heart-rendering stories like this. We tried to do what we could for them. At the same time, we provided a grocery delivery service for the elderly and disabled so that they could stay home safely. The Setiawangsa Community Centre was used to house the homeless and I visited the medical officers as well as City Hall staff members who were taking care of them.

I shared with Ilhan many of these stories, reminding him of how fortunate we are. The whole country was under lockdown, and the mental toll was immense on everyone, particularly for school-going children, rich and poor alike. Yet, some had it easier than others.

Ilhan celebrated Aidilfitri with me. A few days later, I obtained police permit to drive him back to Penang. On a different note,

Liverpool, which had won the Champions League in the previous season and the FIFA World Club Cup in December 2019, was leading the Premier League by 25 points when the league was suspended in March 2020. Liverpool had never won a Premier League title and there were talks that the season might just be forfeited. Fortunately, it continued in June, without any spectators. By the end of the month, Liverpool finally won its first Premier League title. Miracles do happen!

Sabah State Election

There was a clear tension in PH after the collapse of the Federal Government. Everyone was pointing fingers at each other, while there is a sense not being able to move on to focus on the next election. Upon reflection, I believed the fact that I was a backbencher helped: even the most seasoned opposition leaders who spent time in detention quickly got used to the trappings of being a minister. Some strident critics of the government went native the moment they were surrounded by the civil service. For me, I suffered from having access to the grassroots government machinery in my constituency as well as the allocation. Painful, but nothing compared to the fall from grace of members of government.

At the same time, PH states collapsed like dominoes due to defections to Muhyiddin's new Perikatan Nasional (PN) coalition that brought together PPBM infused with UMNO and KEADILAN crossovers, BN, PAS, and GPS. This began with Johor on 28 February 2020, Malacca 9 March, Perak 13 March, and Kedah on 17 May. PPBM seemed intent on taking a shortcut to growing via crossovers rather than organically, aware that as a party, its only strength was holding on to power, and not being able to challenge the established Malay parties, UMNO and PAS. In Sabah, two state assemblypersons supporting the WARISAN-led state government defected in June. On 29 July, former UMNO Sabah Chief Minister Musa Aman declared that he had sufficient numbers to form a new state government. On the following day, however, incumbent Chief Minister and WARISAN President Shafie Apdal advised the Governor to dissolve the State Assembly, paving the way for a state election.

Muhyiddin announced a new coalition called Gabungan Rakyat Sabah (GRS)—an alliance of BN, PN, and a local party—Parti Bersatu Sabah. However, the component parties of the fledgling coalition wound up facing off against each other in seventeen seats. WARISAN, UPKO, and PH, on the other hand, managed to sort out our seat negotiations.

As usual, party leaders were assigned to help out with the state election. The difference this time was that it was against the backdrop of a pandemic. I flew out on AirAsia to Kota Kinabalu. The airports were seeing a revival (which turned out to be brief) due to the end of the MCO and the opening of state borders. A state election added to that boost in traffic and activity (and money pouring into the state, with at least some of it trickling down to the ordinary folk). I spent some time in Murut territory, in Sook, Pensiangan. The community inhabit the interior northeast of Borneo—mostly in Sabah, but also in Sarawak, as well crossing the international borders into Brunei and Kalimantan, Indonesia. Centuries ago, they provided military protection to the Sultan of Brunei and they were the last tribe in Sabah to give up headhunting. Most are now Christians.

My former KEADILAN Youth Vice Leader Raymond Ahuar was contesting. He was only thirty-five then, but this would be his third contest—having tried to contest Pensiangan and another state seat since 2013 under the party banner. During my first trip a few years back, I was introduced to a tradition where the honorary guest would be asked to shoot a blowpipe. I remember failing spectacularly the first time, but had learned to do it decently, since then. In one campaign event, even Sabahan band Atmosfera, known for their hit 'Original Sabahan', made an appearance. On the way back, I stopped by to speak at a 'ceramah' in Inanam, where KEADILAN nominated an engineer from the Dusun community, Peto Galim.

Voting took place on 26 September 2020. WARISAN obtained the most seats, twenty-three, an increase of two seats compared to 2018. But the total number of seats won by WARISAN-PH-UPKO was thirty-two, out of a total of seventy-three seats that were up for grabs. In spite of the intra-coalition fighting among GRS, the new coalition obtained thirty-eight seats and they formed the new Sabah state government.

But most crucially, the State Election led to a third wave in COVID-19 outbreaks. I returned before election day but was already worried about getting infected and did a test. Fortunately, I tested negative. New daily local transmission was zero for a few days in July, but after Sabah, new daily cases began to reach three, then four, and eventually five digits. Understandably, I got dirty looks when people found out I had come back from Sabah!

Emergency

On 25 October 2020, the king rejected PM Muhyiddin Yassin's request to declare a state of emergency, which the latter had asked for to supposedly help the government deal with the pandemic. But it was so obvious that he was hoping to head off pressure from both PH (Anwar, during the Sabah elections, had claimed he had support of enough MPs to replace Muhyiddin) and UMNO, which had grown resentful of having to play second fiddle. There were too many questions about the legitimacy of his government that could not be answered, even though he managed to get the 2021 Budget passed in the parliament.

But as cases continued to rise and with no sign of political stability on the horizon, the PM advised the king to declare an emergency again on my 39th birthday, 12 January 2021, and this time, the king acceded to his request. This had followed a few withdrawals of support from UMNO MPs that put Muhyiddin's majority in question. The number of new COVID-19 cases had reached over 3,000 on that day. Parliament and elections were suspended, and the government was able to legislate and spend without going through the legislature. Meanwhile, states kept moving back and forth through the various stages of MCO without the pandemic seeming to improve.

As the daily new COVID-19 cases increased again in April, the hashtag 'Kerajaan Gagal' or 'failed government' trended on social media. While the parliament and schools remained closed, many factories were categorized as 'essential services' and allowed to operate. Previously, we had taken various precautions to allow the parliament to continue. The devastation brought by the pandemic and the ensuing closure of economic activities, as well as the initial slow vaccination process angered the public. When I was invited to a forum at the end of May discussing 'Kerajaan Gagal' with a representative from PPBM, I pointed out how new COVID-19 cases reached over 7,000, more than double the number when the Emergency that was supposed to deal with the pandemic was declared. While on a partisan basis witnessing the failure of Muhyiddin's administration may appear beneficial, but as someone with elderly parents and a school-going son in the country, there was no *schadenfreude* from the government's weaknesses.

In June 2021, the stricter Enhanced Movement Control Order (EMCO) was declared in a massive public housing estate in Setiawangsa, Desa Rejang for two weeks. This meant soldiers set up barbwire around the neighbourhood and residents were barred from going out. One of the biggest PPRs in my constituency consists of almost 2,800 households and 11,000 people.

I managed to work with the local welfare officer to coordinate basic groceries and sanitary items being sent in, raising money from corporate and individual sponsorship, including my MCKK batchmates. I received frantic messages and calls over the first few days as people panicked over the lack of groceries. A one-day notice was given to allow households to prepare, but it was the middle of the month and not everyone had cash to spare on the day to stock up for the EMCO. Eventually, a few more PPRs fell under the EMCO, but the experience of dealing with Desa Rejang helped us to be better prepared. By July 2021, most of Selangor and Kuala Lumpur had been placed under EMCOs.

There was a collapse of trust between the people and the government. Between January to July 2021, the cases of suicide increased 143 per cent compared to the same period in 2020. Concerned Malaysians encouraged those who needed help, and were unable to get it from the authorities, to put up white flags, which were ridiculed by some of the government politicians. People were especially angry at cases where ordinary Malaysians were fined heavily for not following regulations (often, just to get some income to sustain themselves) while the elites either got away scot-free or punished only with slaps on the wrist. In a move led by young Malaysians, a concerted campaign to hoist black flags were initiated to show the people's displeasure against the government that coincided with the widespread use of the failed government hashtag.

Parliament finally reconvened for a special sitting on 26 July 2021. It was not a regular session with question time or legislative debate, rather the ministers would be briefing the MPs on the country's recovery plan for the pandemic and we would only be allowed to discuss it. But on that very first day, the law minister dropped a bombshell in Parliament. The State of Emergency had been annulled on 21 July.

More fundamentally, the revocation of an Emergency can only be done by the king via a published notice in the Federal Gazette or if Parliament itself votes to annul it. The government could not give a satisfactory answer as the Opposition demanded them to explain what was going on. The basis that the Emergency was declared to combat COVID-19 was proven to be false—new cases by the time it was revoked were almost three times the number in January, rising to almost five times by the time the parliament convened.

On 29 July, I was walking from my office in the parliament towards the chambers when I saw on the closed-circuit TV Anwar reading out a statement that was just released by the Palace: the king was 'deeply disappointed' (and it carried a graver tone using the Malay royal language) with the conduct of the law minister and the Attorney General for not allowing the revocation of Emergency to be debated in Parliament. The king also stated that the 26 July statement by the law minister 'was inaccurate and misled the MPs'.

The government and its enablers always boasted of their supposed close ties to the institution of the monarchy—which had now issued a stern rebuke to them, for announcing that the Emergency was over without the king or the parliament having actually consented to it as the constitution demanded. Confusion reigned and debates broke out amongst legal scholars. It felt like the country was undergoing another constitutional crisis, thanks to yet another screw-up by a government that claimed it had 'saved' Malaysia from PH's alleged folly.

Parliament was adjourned a few times that day, as news spread of ministers gathering at the PM's residence, trying to find a way out from the political imbroglio. Finally, it was announced that parliament was adjourned until the next Monday, supposedly because a few cases of COVID-19 were detected among MPs and parliamentary staff! It would have been comical if it did not involve the constitutional integrity of the country.

Another PM

After the unprecedented constitutional crisis, UMNO announced its withdrawal of support for Muhyiddin in early August. But the Grand Old Party suffered just like KEADILAN under Mahathir 2.0. Its members who were in the government seemed more comfortable with their colleagues in office than those in their own parties. As a result, Muhyiddin had largely retained the support of the UMNO Ministers and only fifteen UMNO MPs (out of a total of thirty-eight MPs) actually wanted him out. But that was still enough, given how narrow his majority in the Dewan Rakyat was. On 13 August, Muhyiddin made a desperate, last-ditch attempt to save his collapsing government by offering to implement reforms in exchange for the opposition's support. But this confidence-and-supply agreement was only negotiated by Muhyiddin with a few representatives from one party in the opposition, and was immediately rejected by the PH leadership and most of the other opposition parties.

Two days later, Muhyiddin resigned as PM. Elections were ruled out due to the critical state of COVID-19. In fact, Sarawak, which was supposed to have its state elections in 2021, was still under an Emergency, which allow their polls to be delayed. The king met the party leaders from all sides and then the MPs were asked to send a written declaration of support for the MP of their choice to become premier. This time around, Deputy PM and UMNO Vice President, Ismail Sabri Yaakob obtained 114 votes, while PH Chair and KEADILAN President Anwar Ibrahim obtained 105 votes.

Ismail Sabri ended up reconstituting more or less the same government as Muhyiddin had, except with a new PM. UMNO, wounded as it is, was back in the driving seat and KEADILAN and PH remained in the opposition.

Married Again

I tied the knot with Noor Farah Rahim on 8 January 2021. I kept it under wraps, and the public only found out when I posted a photo of us at the solemnization ceremony on social media, declaring it was conducted under the 'new normal' of COVID-19. Since both of us had been married before, it was a simple ceremony involving mostly Farah's family and friends. Ilhan was there, along with Farah's children Aisyah, Maryam, and Sarah.

In a sign of the times, I got to know Farah through Instagram. A Kuala Lumpur girl through and through, she grew up in Keramat, not far from my constituency and attended Bukit Bintang Girls School, like three of my sisters. We had an awkward first date at a Korean restaurant, but soon began to hit it off and I decided it was best to settle down again. Ilhan, thankfully, was comfortable with her and her girls.

The timing was fortunate. Four days later, the Emergency was declared, followed by another round of MCOs the day after, which in the Klang Valley lasted until March 2021. We initially wanted to have a reception for my family and friends (and the list can be quite long for a Malaysian politician), but eventually, with the rising COVID-19 cases and uncertainty over the procedures to be followed (and nervous guests), we decided to cancel it altogether.

A Midway Epilogue

I have had the privilege of living a truly Malaysian life. I was born in Kuala Lumpur and spent my first twelve years in Petaling Jaya. My classmates were students of all races in a Catholic mission school. But I spoke Kelantanese at home, and then found myself in an all-Malay environment in MCKK. In the UK, I was active with Malaysian and Singaporean societies as well as Islamic and centre-left student organizations. I came to appreciate that pushing for change in Malaysia would not succeed without my people—the Malay majority—being convinced that it was necessary. Ultimately, however, I am convinced that the fate of any individual in the country depends on us dealing with the various challenges that confront us as *Malaysians*.

I read about the Malay Left's attempt to liberally define the Malay identity to encompass all citizens in the 1940s; on the right, UMNO founding President Onn Jaafar failed in his attempt to open his party to all Malayans; as well as the struggle for multi-racial parties in the 1960s and 1970s. As mentioned, one of the earliest books to have impacted me was Malcolm X's autobiography. The searing *American History X* also made me think deeply about the issues of race. At university, I was captivated by John Rawls' magnum opus, *The Theory of Justice*. Thus, whether it was my family's strong religious outlook, the interest in history cultivated by my father, or the influence of popular culture on my generation—it all led me to form a view that challenged the narrative of Malay Supremacy.

When you are stuck in your own bubble, it is tempting to conclude that other segments of society are unable to change. In 1999, 'the Other' in Malaysian popular discourse were the Chinese and the Indians. From 2008–2013, it was the Malays as well as Sabahans and Sarawakians. In 2018, it was the rural Malays. Today, if you are privileged, living in the Klang Valley, it is easy to dismiss people living in the low-cost flats or the kampungs as being racist or irrational. Sometimes, however, such attitudes, tellingly, reveals one's own racism and irrationality. It is easy to generalize or simply give up when confronting Malaysia's political situation, especially when the naysayers do not get out of their own bubbles.

The fact remains that any genuine national campaign to democratize our country must be as broad-based as possible. That also means forging alliances and sometimes having to compromise on ideological projects for the sake of greater progress that remain committed to a set of basic core principles. It's painful and difficult—but it's the most sustainable way to do it, especially in a diverse country like Malaysia. I hope this is something young Malaysians who are interested in entering public service remember: it helps with the staying power you need.

People always ask me—should one go into politics young, like I did, or wait after one builds a career and is professionally stable? There is no certain answer to this question. I believe that those who have pursued a professional career would certainly bring an extra edge in making laws, policies, or governing that can be missing from a career politician. On the other hand, we must always have the voice of the young represented, passionately and earnestly pushing the boundaries of what is possible—the path that I have pursued.

Ultimately, it is a mix of will and circumstance. What is absolutely crucial is that one does it for the right reasons, aware of the challenges of public service. Public service can be an acquired taste—not all who succeed in other fields can do well in politics. I do believe deeply, however, that it is a rewarding privilege to make a difference in society.

Nevertheless, and I speak with some experience here as someone who had written extensively on politics from a young age, there is also the challenge of taking the leap from being an armchair critic to actually dealing with *realpolitik* on the ground. Whether it was organizing a voluntary tuition project in low-cost flats or helping the vulnerable during the COVID-19 lockdown, bringing the different segments of Malaysian society together in governing requires patience, commitment, and even guile. This might put off the most inflexible. But idealism needs to be translated into action on the ground. Today, I am inspired by what Malaysians in their teens and twenties are doing, not only in galvanizing protests against the government, but also in creating a system of support for those in need. Whether in pushing for the lowering of the voting age, the rights of contract doctors, fighting climate change, or the resignation of Muhyiddin Yassin—young Malaysians have been at the forefront. And I am sure that time and time again, successive generations of the youth will heed the call to serve.

Having spent more than a decade in frontline politics, I have experienced, in equal measure, the ups and downs of political life, of how public opinion can be fickle. I would have my constituents, MCKK friends, or family members sending me news articles on WhatsApp or pulling me aside during festivities and asking why my party was doing this or that, and giving their advice on how it *should* be done. The more emotionally invested people are, the more disappointed they will be when things turn out differently. It is also easy for Malaysia's diverse public, who are extremely demanding of their politicians (and rightfully so), to be riled up by what they watch, listen, and read in their social or cultural milieus without realizing what is happening elsewhere. When I speak up against the NEP, I earn the wrath of many Malays, and get praise from most non-Malays. When I speak up about the plight of the Rohingya in Myanmar or Uyghur in China, some of the same Chinese-Malaysians that praised me before will criticize me for supporting 'terrorists' or stirring up trouble with China. This is not something new, but in our era of the 24-hour news cycle and social media permeating everything, it is amplified.

Politicians are far from blameless. We both feed into and contribute to building up of expectations; and often our actions lead to the subsequent disappointment. Buying your own hype can be dangerous: it can either lead to disillusionment and despair; or forgetting the original idealism that called you to serve in the first place. Ultimately, the ability to take a step back and reflect, to look at yourself and the circumstances around you objectively, is something all politicians need. As has been said before, politics is a marathon, not a sprint. It is physically, mentally, and spiritually draining. And it affects your loved ones.

The struggle for democracy and social justice continues, not just in Asia or the Muslim world, but even in the West. Donald Trump was elected President for a term, and the coalition that brought him to power is still strong, as are the nativist, atavistic politics of resentment that fuelled them. Within the EU, authoritarian leaders are waging battles against liberal democratic norms by playing up anti-Semitism and Islamophobia. In the Muslim world, the delicate balance struck by Recep Tayyip Erdogan between liberal democracy and Islamism in his early days has been unwound after his long dominance and confrontational battles with Turkey's secular elite as well as its traditional Western allies. Tunisia, which was the only country that enjoyed a democratic transition following the Arab Spring, suspended its parliament in 2021. In India, Narendra Modi has destroyed Mahatma Gandhi's and Jawaharlal Nehru's vision of a multi-confessional nation.

Countries in Southeast Asia, too, have gone through different—often fraught—transitions in the last couple of decades.

Many were one-party states. Singapore, which separated from Malaysia in 1963, has developed impressively, but inequitably. However, a new generation of leaders from the opposition like Pritam Singh have been pushing for a fairer and far more open society. The world's most populous Muslim country, Indonesia, was strongly backed by the West during the authoritarian Suharto era. Yet, the Asian Financial Crisis brought him down and after a period of instability, it is now poised to become a force to be reckoned with. Importantly, the country's democracy has now taken root, thanks in no small part to its fiercely independent media and civil society. The Philippines has and continues to be dominated by traditional political and business elites. After the People Power Revolution brought down Ferdinand Marcos, populists appealing to the country's underclass such as Joseph Estrada and Rodrigo Duterte have been able to get elected—it remains to be seen whether the current incarnation of its republic will continue in the face of the latter's impact. Thailand, the only country to not be colonized by the West in the region, has been plagued by numerous military coups, as has Myanmar.

This allows us some context about what is happening and what needs to be done to forge ahead in Malaysia. Economically, the country has made significant progress from Malaya's independence in 1957 and the formation of Malaysia six years later. Our political system was much more open back then but pretty much kept the colonial economy intact. Then the 1969 racial riots took place, and the government took an activist, developmentalist approach to eradicate poverty and reduce the socio-economic gaps between the ethnicities.

But UMNO became more dominant. During the era of Mahathir 1.0, after I was born, this dominance led to the destruction of many institutions. Ironically for Mahathir, who spoke of a truly united Malaysian nation, 'Bangsa Malaysia'—the most formidable movement that led to a truly multi-racial politics was the *Reformasi* that came about when he sacked Anwar Ibrahim in 1998. But in plot twists that seemed more appropriate for a M. Night Shyamalan or Christopher Nolan movie—Mahathir and Anwar combined in 2018 to finally bring down UMNO and BN for the first time, and the PH government fell apart less than two years later due to the former's enabling efforts to sabotage the promised transition.

Today, our politics is a mess. We are still nervously trying to recover from the global COVID-19 pandemic. My children—like the rest—suffered from the halt of in-school learning. And the destruction wrought on the economy has left ordinary Malaysians on the edge of despair. The optimism of 2018 has given way to pessimism and cynicism. The reality is there is no perfect moment—each snapshot of history belies the difficult decisions and the subsequent unintended consequences. Nevertheless, two things ought to be apparent to anyone.

The first is that genuine multi-racial politics is the only way forward for our country. There simply is no other way for Malaysia to survive and achieve its goals, including, yes, the long-cherished quest for the socio-economic upliftment of the Bumiputeras. Only this time, the suffering of the pandemic has shown us that policy and aid cannot be done in isolation, according to race or creed. We must stand together or be destroyed one by one.

Secondly, an active, engaged, and emphatic citizenry will also be essential. Malaysians, as noted, are extremely discriminating and hard on their politicians. This, however, also needs to be tempered with an appreciation of how differently our fellow Malaysians may often view politics, governance, faith, ethnicity, and social issues. It does not necessarily mean that social progress must be indefinitely delayed or never pursued: but rather, it must be done in tandem with the creation of a more just economic order while building confidence as well as integration between the different communities. That is the only way to burst our bubbles—whether rural or urban, Bumiputera or non-Bumiputera, Muslim or non-Muslim, Peninsula or East Malaysian—to defeat the divisive politics that have held us back.

This will, perhaps, be the work of generations, which is why the marathon analogy may be apt. Certainly, we will need to constantly and consciously reflect on our journey, even while seeking to continuously move forward, especially when we stumble or the obstacles facing us seems insurmountable.

For my part, as I write these words, just a few months short of my fortieth birthday, I will continue to work hard, serve the people, and engage Malaysians from all walks of life for the sake of—as from the words of our national anthem –*Tanah Tumpahnya Darahku*—'the land where my blood is spilled.'

Glossary

Hari Raya Aidilfitri	Malay for Eid al-Fitr or festival of breaking of fast, one of the two Muslim festivities. In most states in Malaysia, Aidilfitri is the bigger festivity.
Bangsa Malaysia	Malaysian Nation
Bumiputera	Malays as well as Sabah and Sarawak natives in Malaysia
Ceramah	Talks, usually political or religious; if used in a political context, tends to suggest a big event
Ceramah kelompok	A smaller political talk
Hari Raya	The two days of festivity or Eid celebrated by Muslims annually
Islam Hadhari	Civilizational Islam introduced by the fifth Malaysian PM Abdullah Ahmad Badawi; in theory, a moderate form of Islam that he argued would combine moderation and modernity in an Islamic framework
Jalur Gemilang	Lit. Stripes of Glory; the national flag
Kampung	Village
Klang Valley	The conurbation consisting of Kuala Lumpur and its environs

Malaysia Boleh	Lit. Malaysia Can. The slogan was popularized by the government during the boom years in the early 1990s during the 1992 Thomas Cup and Olympic Games in Barcelona.
Pesantren	Madrasah, traditional religious school in Javanese
Pondok	Madrasah in Malay
Reformasi	The reform movements that began in Indonesia and then Malaysia in 1998
Rock Kapak	Malay rock genre that began in the 1980s with heavy influences of hard rock and glam metal
Songkok	Malay headgear similar to a fez
State EXCO	State Executive Council, the executive authority in state governments in Peninsular Malaysia
Tok Guru	Lit. Respected Teacher. Used for eminent Sheikhs or Ulamas in the Malay world
Surau	In Sumatra and Peninsula Malaysia, a smaller mosque, usually built by the community as opposed by the state religious authority
Teh tarik	Lit. pulled tea; a type of hot milk tea made by 'pulling' the beverage to cool it down and create a frothy top